For years now, Justin Brierley h[...]s
on his *Unbelievable?* program, [...]
thinker. He's heard every argur[...]re
warnings about the "crisis of m[...]
somehow, this wide-ranging and stimulating book [...] [...]eful
note. It represents apologetics at its best, a fearless engagement with
the most daunting issues of our time.

> **PHILIP YANCEY,** author of *What's So Amazing about Grace?* and
> *Where the Light Fell*

Smart, inspiring, and ripped with incredible stories!

> **BEAR GRYLLS,** survivalist and host of the former television adventure
> series *Man vs. Wild*

Belief in God is back. Despite the claims of New Atheists,
a surprising number of leading thinkers are taking the Christian
faith seriously. Brierley tells the fascinating story of how the big
questions have shifted from the existence of God to whether or not
life can have meaning without God. *The Surprising Rebirth of Belief
in God* needs to be read and discussed by people of all faiths.

> **SEAN McDOWELL, PhD,** professor at Biola University, popular YouTuber,
> and author or editor of over twenty books, including *A Rebel's Manifesto*

In this eminently readable book, Justin Brierley gives us a ringside
view of his personal engagement with the big issues over the past
fifteen years with a wide variety of thought leaders. He chronicles how
New Atheism, with its attempted critique of religion in the name of
science, rose to dominate the debate only to find its increasingly shrill
voice running out of steam until the movement itself disintegrated
into a thousand warring fragments. Brierley shows how the culture has
shifted to more human concerns about morality, value, meaning, and,
above all, personal identity. He showcases this shift by describing his
"big conversations" with the perceptive thinking of public intellectuals
like Canadian psychologist Jordan Peterson, cultural commentator
and journalist Douglas Murray, and historian Tom Holland, among
others, who hold that the loss of the shared narrative Christianity once

gave us is one of the main causes of cultural fragmentation and loss of identity. That leads to a discussion of the important—yet frequently underappreciated—contribution of the Judeo-Christian worldview to moral values and civil institutions most of us count dear, such as human rights and dignity, medical care and education, that form the bedrock of civilised society.

Brierley has engaged all of these people and many more in his flagship radio show, *Unbelievable?* His description of the cut and thrust of these fascinating "big conversations" gives readers a unique insight, not only into important issues, but on the leading people involved in discussing them. He highlights how leading thinkers are currently reading the Bible and coming to accept its authenticity—which is leading to a surprising rebirth of belief in God.

Brierley has done us a huge service in bringing a wealth of material together and breathing life into it, just as he does regularly in his *Unbelievable?* programme This is a first-rate book: get it, read it, and give it to others.

JOHN LENNOX, PhD, Emeritus Professor of Mathematics, University of Oxford, and Emeritus Fellow in Mathematics and Philosophy of Science, Green Templeton College, Oxford

We have all seen the statistics about the decline of Christian identity in the West. But the story of Christianity is far from over. There are few better guides to religious trends than Justin Brierley, who has a lifetime of experience interviewing secular and Christian intellectuals. In this exciting and timely book, he reveals why religion hasn't gone away and what the church can do to bring the greatest story ever told to a new generation. Read it and be encouraged!

ANDY STANLEY, founder and senior pastor, North Point Ministries

Against the predictions of many, Justin Brierley sees the early stirrings of Christian revival in the UK today. His is a voice worth listening to, with a unique perspective as someone who has spoken to many of the prominent figures who either espouse or oppose the role of religious faith. This book recounts those conversations, considers the big faith issues of contemporary life, and suggests some fascinating and plausible ways forward.

RT REVD DR. GRAHAM TOMLIN, PhD, director of the Centre for Cultural Witness

One of the most fascinating books of the year. Has the "Sea of Faith" gone out, never to return? In this brilliantly written book, Justin Brierley takes a look at the growing numbers of public intellectuals— from historians to scientists to writers to journalists—who have begun to rediscover Christianity. Given the failure of secularism to answer our deepest-felt questions about meaning, value, purpose, and identity, it is perhaps no surprise that the so-called New Atheism failed and that rumours of Christianity's death were premature and exaggerated. Dive into *The Surprising Rebirth of Belief in God* and discover the personalities, stories, and arguments that have led some to suggest that the tide of faith is on the turn.

ANDY BANNISTER, PhD, director of the Solas Centre for Public Christianity

The claim that Christianity is making a comeback in Britain might seem so counterintuitive as to verge on the lunatic, but Justin Brierley, in making this argument, speaks with the authority of a man who has had a ringside seat for the past decade watching the great debates on religion, and reports on them with learning, subtlety, and grace.

TOM HOLLAND, author of *Dominion* and cohost of *The Rest Is History* podcast

Is there a supernatural realm? Does God exist? According to atheists, the answer is a firm no. Our world, our bodies, and our minds are comprised of atoms merely arranged in a sophisticated way. But under this premise, many accepted values and traits become much harder to explain. Why do we believe in inherent human dignity and worth? Why do we pursue significance in life? Why do we have a sense of self and an inner thought life? Justin Brierley, in his compellingly and skilfully written book, shows that a host of public intellectuals who recognise the shortcomings of a purely materialistic outlook have begun speaking openly about the need for a more nuanced, spiritual, and holistic perspective. Drawing from fifteen years of radio interviews and debates, Brierley tells story after story of people changing their minds about God, life, and the universe, along with the reasons why. It's a riveting read. If you are disenchanted with the status quo—or even if you aren't—I highly recommend this book. It could be the most important book you read this year.

SHARON DIRCKX, PhD, speaker and author of *Am I Just My Brain?*

In this characteristically well-researched and readable book, Justin charts the rise of interest in God in the public discourse with an engaging blend of analysis and personal anecdote. *The Surprising Rebirth of Belief in God* is a must-read, and it is a book to share with friends.

AMY ORR-EWING, PhD, Honorary Lecturer at the School of Divinity, University of Aberdeen

In the West, the tide of Christian faith may be at a low ebb, but our "post-Christian" landscape remains utterly shaped by the "Sea of Faith." And we should never forget that tides also come in. This refreshing and encouraging book introduces us to thinkers rejecting the assumptions of our secular age and discovering an ancient wisdom that was there all along. Justin Brierley is lighting a path back to belief, and I hope that many will follow.

GLEN SCRIVENER, director of Speak Life and author of *The Air We Breathe*

Atheism is about as satisfying as reading recipes to starving people. Justin Brierley brilliantly shows how the hunger for meaning and truth is leading intelligent people back to Christianity or to Christ for the first time. This engaging and well-reasoned book will not only encourage you, it will also equip you to show spiritually starved people where the real food is. Highly recommended!

FRANK TUREK, author, speaker, and president of Cross Examined

The Surprising Rebirth of Belief in God

THE SURPRISING REBIRTH OF BELIEF IN GOD

WHY NEW ATHEISM GREW OLD AND SECULAR THINKERS ARE CONSIDERING CHRISTIANITY AGAIN

—

JUSTIN BRIERLEY

TYNDALE
elevate
ask. seek. find.

Visit Tyndale online at tyndale.com.

Tyndale and Tyndale's quill logo are registered trademarks of Tyndale House Ministries.
Tyndale Elevate and the Tyndale Elevate logo are trademarks of Tyndale House Ministries.
Tyndale Elevate is a nonfiction imprint of Tyndale House Publishers, Carol Stream, Illinois.

The Surprising Rebirth of Belief in God: Why New Atheism Grew Old and Secular Thinkers Are Considering Christianity Again

Cover design by Faceout Studio, Jeff Miller

Edited by Jonathan Schindler

For information about special discounts for bulk purchases, please contact Tyndale House Publishers at csresponse@tyndale.com, or call 1-855-277-9400.

Library of Congress Cataloging-in-Publication Data

A catalog record for this book is available from the Library of Congress.

ISBN 978-1-4964-6677-8

Printed in the United States of America

29	28	27	26	25	24
7	6	5	4	3	2

To Lucy.

There's no one I'd rather share this adventure with.

Contents

Foreword

THE BOOK YOU ARE HOLDING in your hands uses, as its central metaphor, Matthew Arnold's poem "Dover Beach" and the "long withdrawing roar" of the "Sea of Faith." That was Arnold's perception of the nineteenth-century phenomenon in which many Europeans simply stopped believing the Christian message. Some years ago I wrote an Emmaus Road–style parable that invoked the same poem, but this time moving in the opposite direction.

I imagined two serious-minded unbelievers walking home together, puzzling out how to make sense of the world towards the end of the twentieth century. Modernity's Enlightenment dream of progress had run out of steam: postmodernity's questioning of values, power, and identity had blown the whistle on the secular world they had come to take for granted.

As this pair walked along the road to Dover Beach, they discussed how this had come to be. Why had they been let down by the stories by which they once lived? How should they now inhabit a world where their dreams had gone sour, a culture where they didn't even know who "they" were anymore?

Into this conversation came Jesus, incognito. "Foolish ones," he replied, "how slow of heart you are to believe all that the creator God has said." And as they walked together, he showed them, beginning with Moses, then the prophets and apostles of the New Testament as well, how, through the story of Scripture and its culmination in the life, death, and resurrection of one person, God had acted in the world to create a new humanity. This person's identity transcended all other identities. His story redefined all other stories.

My version of the parable saw Jesus and the two travelers finally arriving at Dover Beach. On the shore stood a vast and hungry crowd. Modernism had caused the "Sea of Faith" to retreat, but the tide was now rolling back in. Yet, having scattered their bread upon the water, all that the incoming tide of postmodernity brought them was bricks and centipedes, proving G. K. Chesterton's dictum that when people stop believing in God, they do not believe in nothing; they believe in *anything*. That, I suggested, was the dilemma facing the serious secularist in the last decades of the last century.

Happily, Justin Brierley is more hopeful now than I was then about what the returning "Sea of Faith" might bring in its wake. In this book he describes how, despite the decline in church membership, attitudes towards Christianity among serious thinkers in many fields seem to be changing. Having interviewed many of the key players over many years, Justin offers a sharply drawn, enticing picture of the way public discussion of Christian faith has swung round to the point where the once-fashionable atheism has itself begun to look suspiciously threadbare.

In recent years, Justin and I have regularly conversed about these issues on the podcasts he hosts, and I have been a glad participant in some of the conversations with public thinkers that are referred to in these chapters. I am encouraged that so many of these thinkers seem disenchanted with secularism's empty promises and that, for many, the residual memory of Christianity still holds a wistful appeal. Interestingly, those of their number who find themselves attracted to the church are rarely looking for a spiritualized version of the current moral zeitgeist. What's attractive about the faith is precisely its countercultural stance—the "weirdness" of believing and living as if Jesus really has risen from the dead and is calling those who follow him to live a different story to the world around them.

G. K. Chesterton also said, "Christianity has died many times and risen again; for it had a God who knew the way out of the grave." What if the Christian story is poised to come rushing back into public consciousness in our day? Could it once again nourish the hearts and minds of people who have been starved of meaning and purpose for so long?

Like Justin, I hope so. Perhaps we are indeed seeing the early signs of such a returning tide.

My parable ended with the two travelers wearily opening a small picnic basket, totally inadequate for the task of feeding so many hungry people standing on the shore. Gently Jesus takes the basket from them and, in what seems like moments, everybody on the beach is fed. Then the eyes of everyone are opened, and they realize who he is. He then vanishes from their sight.

Whatever the returning tide looks like, the task of Christians in a postmodern world is to be the reembodiment of Jesus. We are tasked with bringing food to the hungry on the shores of the "Sea of Faith." We are to tell the story of the Creator and his world, and his victory over evil, to any serious-minded unbelievers who will listen.

Do such people exist? This book should persuade you that they do: that people who presently do not believe in the Christian worldview, or in its central figure and his victory over evil and death, are indeed ready to listen again. This is, after all, a real story. It is centered upon a real figure, a real hero. And it still has the power to change the world.

Rt Revd Prof. N. T. Wright
Senior Research Fellow, Wycliffe Hall,
University of Oxford

Introduction

The Sea of Faith
Was once, too, at the full, and round earth's shore
Lay like the folds of a bright girdle furled.
But now I only hear
Its melancholy, long, withdrawing roar.
MATTHEW ARNOLD, "DOVER BEACH"

WHEN THE VICTORIAN POET Matthew Arnold published his famous poem "Dover Beach" in 1867, it served as a eulogy for the certainties of a bygone era, especially religion.

One hundred years earlier the Enlightenment had swept through Europe, and its philosophers and scientists had announced the death of the age of superstition and the birth of the age of reason. The industrial revolution was creating social upheaval as engineering geniuses like George Stephenson and Isambard Kingdom Brunel constructed a technological future. Natural history museums in the style of Gothic churches were being constructed as new cathedrals to the modern sciences. Charles Darwin had recently published his theory of naturalistic evolution in *On the Origin of Species*, and Karl Marx was about to publish his materialist manifesto *Das Kapital*.

The advance of science, secularism, and technology was the backdrop to Arnold's haunting poem and its famous line about the "melancholy, long, withdrawing roar" of the "Sea of Faith." The receding tide of religious belief that Arnold witnessed in his day has only continued at an ever-increasing pace in the Western world. In the 1800s, the church and its Christian teachings still dominated society. One hundred and fifty years later we are undeniably living in a post-Christian world where the picture looks very different.

In my own country of Great Britain, churchgoing has declined steeply in the past several decades. The beginning of the twenty-first century saw a sharp turn against religious belief in popular culture with the rise of New Atheism, with over half the population now identifying as nonreligious in a recent survey.[1] A similar picture is emerging even in the churchgoing strongholds of the United States, as younger generations increasingly choose to label themselves as "nones" when it comes to religious affiliation.

As a Christian who believes in the supernatural claims of the Bible about the life, death, and resurrection of Jesus, I find myself in the minority in the twenty-first-century Western world. Some believers have responded by circling the few remaining wagons and hoping things might change; others seem to have given up on church altogether. However, in my personal and professional life I have been keen to engage the secular culture around me rather than ignore or bemoan it. Hosting the long-standing radio discussion show and podcast *Unbelievable?*, which has brought many Christians and non-Christians together for weekly dialogue, has allowed me to chair hundreds of debates between the most influential voices on both sides of the conversation on faith.

My ringside seat has had the unanticipated but welcome effect of fortifying rather than weakening my faith. I've come to see the intellectual strength of the Christian story as it has been tested by atheists, agnostics, and people of other faiths who have appeared on the show (a journey you can read about in my first book, *Unbelievable?:*

Why, after Ten Years of Talking with Atheists, I'm Still a Christian).
My vantage point has also meant being able to follow how the most
prominent questions and debates have evolved in the years I've been
hosting these discussions.

Notably, in the past several years the conversations have changed
in tone and substance quite dramatically. The bombastic debates
between militant atheists and Christian apologists have been far
less frequent. In their place have come increasing numbers of secular guests who are far more open to the cultural and social value
of Christianity, even if they are not believers themselves. Some of
these thinkers and personalities are concerned by the turn in society
towards a cancel culture of identity-based politics and often find
themselves more in step with their Christian interlocutors on these
issues than with some of their secular brethren.

Most significantly, as the influence of New Atheism has waned,
a variety of secular thinkers have been stepping forward to ask new
questions about the value of religion and where the West is heading
in the absence of the Christian story. Many of them have developed
large platforms and have a huge influence on a younger generation
searching for meaning. Many even seem to harbor a wistful desire for
Christianity to be true. As their influence has grown, it has led me to
wonder whether, even in the midst of our highly secular culture, we
are witnessing a sea change in people's openness to faith.

It was the journalist and author Douglas Murray who brought
this home most powerfully during a conversation I hosted between
him and New Testament historian N. T. Wright. Murray, an agnostic who describes himself as a "Christian atheist," remarked that a
number of highly intelligent friends and acquaintances of his had
converted to Christianity in recent years.[2] Perhaps they were an
exception to the rule, or maybe something else was going on. Were
people becoming more open to the Christian message? Were we
seeing a new opportunity for the church to speak (as Murray put it)
into a "more receptive crowd"?

He went on to reference that well-worn line from Matthew Arnold's poem and said something which, although blindingly obvious at one level, had never struck me before: "The interesting thing about the Sea of Faith is there's no reason why it can't come back in. The sea doesn't only withdraw. You know, it's the point of tides."

In this book I will make a bold proposition—that Matthew Arnold's long, withdrawing Sea of Faith is beginning to reach its farthest limit and that we may yet see the tide of faith come rushing back in again within our lifetime.

The reason I feel confident enough to make this argument is that faith has never really gone away. As I will argue in the rest of this book, people need a story to live by, but the stories we have been telling ourselves in the last several decades have been growing increasingly thin and superficial. Meanwhile, a plethora of thinkers have been reevaluating the Christian story and showing how it continues to undergird our most fundamental moral and cultural instincts. We may have forgotten the story, but it might be time to rediscover it afresh.

I believe we are seeing the firstfruits of the returning tide in the lives and stories of a number of public intellectuals who are finding themselves surprised by the continuing resonance of the Christian story. This includes people like the psychologist Jordan Peterson, the aforementioned journalist Douglas Murray, and the popular historian Tom Holland. You will find my exchanges with them and various other secular thinkers within these pages, along with the conversations I've shared with many other men and women who have crossed the line to Christian faith as adult converts. These include celebrated writers such as Francis Spufford and Paul Kingsnorth. The latter's faith journey was driven by his love of nature but took detours via atheism, Buddhism, and Wicca before arriving at Christianity. There are academics such as classicist James Orr, who first discovered Jesus by reading the Gospel accounts about him in their original Greek, or the equally surprising story of famed actor David Suchet, who encountered Christ by reading the letters of Paul as if they had been written personally for him. And you'll read the stories of everyday secular people such as Peter, Tamara, and Robbie, who had either rejected Christianity or never considered it to begin with. Yet they found themselves drawn towards a story that made sense of their deepest longings and desires. In sharing these stories I hope to show why Christianity can still make surprisingly good sense to twenty-first-century people and how the church can ready itself for those who may yet choose to walk through its doors again. But before we consider where I believe the conversation is heading, in the first chapter I will review how we got to this point, with the rise and subsequent fall of New Atheism.

Anybody who lives by the sea can tell you that tides go out and tides come in, but inexperienced holidaymakers can still be caught out by how quickly the water returns. If you are a person of faith, I hope that this book serves as an encouragement that the story is not over for Christianity. If you don't consider yourself a believer, first, thank you for getting this far, and I hope that as you read further, you may discover why Christianity has made sense to so many in the past and continues to do so today. You may even be tempted to dip a toe in yourself. Come on in! The water's lovely.

CHAPTER 1

THE RISE AND FALL OF NEW ATHEISM

I STILL REMEMBER THE FIRST TIME I saw a red London bus sail past me on Vauxhall Bridge Road, emblazoned with the words "There's probably no God. Now stop worrying and enjoy your life." There was something rather thrilling about it.

The 2009 bus poster campaign was the brainchild of comedian Ariane Sherine, who had become annoyed by religious adverts in public places that paraded Bible verses about heaven and hell. Sherine wrote an article in *The Guardian* newspaper suggesting that atheists needed their own advertising campaign, and with the help of the British Humanist Association, a fund was established to raise money for the project.

The cause quickly attracted public interest. Once the celebrity power of atheist Richard Dawkins was thrown behind it, over £150,000 was raised, allowing many more buses to carry the advert than the handful originally envisioned.

But why the word *probably*? The word seemed to leave room for doubt in a campaign aimed at settling the God question and backed by people who seemed very confident about the nonexistence of any deity. Richard Dawkins said he had wanted to opt for something stronger—"There's almost certainly no God." However, when I asked Sherine about it, she told me that the note of uncertainty was included for "scientific" reasons. Since it is logically impossible to disprove the existence of God, it was better to leave a window of possibility open. The softer wording may also have been calculated to ensure the message didn't fall foul of official advertising rules.

The Atheist Bus Campaign came at the zenith of the New Atheist movement and was the closest thing it had (in the UK at least) to an official advertising campaign. Like the movement that spawned it, it was a bold, unapologetic, in-your-face affair.

However, at one level, the campaign hardly seemed necessary. Encouraging people to ignore God in twenty-first-century Britain is a bit like asking a teenager to consider having a lie-in on a Saturday morning. It hardly needs saying. According to the most recent data, over half of the people in the UK claim no religion,[1] and only a fraction of the population attend church.[2] Even when regular churchgoing was part of the fabric of society, talking about faith in public was generally considered very bad form.

Yet the great irony of the Atheist Bus Campaign was that, by attempting to make people forget about God, it did precisely the opposite.

Oscar Wilde wrote, "There is only one thing in the world worse than being talked about, and that is not being talked about."[3] Hence, my thrill of excitement at seeing a bus emblazoned with the anti-God slogan. Apparently God was being talked about after all.

For several months buses circulated in London, bearing posters that forced the question of religion into the eyeline of any passersby, whether they liked it or not. Perhaps that's why some Christians, including Paul Woolley, then director of Christian think tank Theos, donated money to the bus campaign, saying it was "a great way to get people thinking about God."[4]

Furthermore, it confirmed a growing sense that modern atheism was starting to look suspiciously . . . religious. As Margaret Atwood shrewdly observed, "Once you're paying money to put slogans on things, well it's either a product you're selling, a political party or religion."[5]

If God does exist, then he must have a sense of humor.

At first sight, the high-water mark of New Atheism also marked a particularly low ebb for the tide of faith in the West. Religion was being cast not merely as old-fashioned and irrelevant—it was also seen as dangerous and irrational. Yet tides have a habit of going out and coming in. The popularity of the New Atheist movement would end up dissipating as quickly as it began. However, the rise and fall of this particular movement is worth spelling out in some detail. The way it dissolved so rapidly has opened many eyes to how insubstantial the answers were that it offered. In its wake, a fresh tide has begun to gather again—a new conversation on God, religion, and the deepest questions we can ask about what it means to be human. So . . . let us begin.

THE RISE OF NEW ATHEISM

"New Atheism" is a term that was first coined in the mid-2000s. It soon stuck as a useful label for the emerging cadre of celebrity scientists, journalists, and public intellectuals who were increasingly vocal about their opposition to religion and their commitment to reason and science.

At its helm were the so-called "four horsemen": philosopher Daniel C. Dennett, neuroscientist Sam Harris, journalist Christopher Hitchens, and biologist Richard Dawkins. Each had published his own bestselling book attacking religion.

Dennett's *Breaking the Spell* sought to give an evolutionary explanation for religion. *Letter to a Christian Nation*, written by Harris, was an extended essay on the evils of Christianity in the United States. Hitchens's *God Is Not Great* was a characteristically blistering polemic on the evils of religion generally. And the most popular of all, *The God Delusion* by Richard Dawkins, was accompanied by a TV series and a book tour that saw the author speak to thousands of enthusiastic fans across the world.

Atheism had been a common enough feature of twentieth-century culture, whether it was Bertrand Russell's scholarly skepticism or the existential angst of continental philosophers like Camus and Sartre. But their influence usually remained siloed in academia and didn't tend to trouble the general public. So what caused this particular manifestation of atheism to become so prominent in the early twenty-first century?

A variety of factors coalesced in the rise of New Atheism. The 9/11 attacks in the United States reminded the world that religion was capable of causing people to commit terrible atrocities. The leading voices of the movement have all cited the rise of religious extremism as a motivating force in their own vocal response.

At the same time, a culture war had also developed between the religious right and secular society, especially around science. The 2005 Kitzmiller v. Dover trial saw intelligent design pitted against evolutionary theory in the classroom. Many secularists saw it as an attempt to sneak God into schools and, in response, came out swinging for science and Charles Darwin.

Indeed, science was at the forefront of New Atheism. It was no accident that three of the four horsemen were academics before they found fame as celebrity atheists. (Hitchens was the only one who lacked a PhD.) From the outset, their movement cast religious faith as the enemy of science, reason, and progress. In fact, it was tantamount to mental illness. Dawkins pithily summarized this perspective, writing, "Faith is the great cop-out, the great excuse to evade the need to think and evaluate evidence. Faith is belief in spite of, even perhaps because of, the lack of evidence."[6]

Added to all of this was the rise of the Internet. Now any lone atheist in a small town in the Bible Belt could find a community to be part of. Blogs, chat rooms, and early forms of social media allowed like-minded skeptics to find common cause and organize together in ways that had never been possible before.

Within a few short years a variety of atheist and skeptic organizations were meeting, not just online but in person. Skepticon, the Global Atheist Convention, The Amazing Meeting (hosted by magician and paranormal debunker James Randi), and a variety of other public initiatives large and small proliferated in the "freethinker" community.

If the 2009 Atheist Bus Campaign represented the apex of the movement in the UK, then the United States's high-water mark was arguably the Reason Rally in 2012.

According to some estimates, between twenty to thirty thousand people gathered on the National Mall in Washington, DC, for a day that was described as "Woodstock for atheists."[7] The lineup included musicians, activists, and entertainers such as Eddie Izzard, Tim Minchin, Bill Maher, and Penn Jillette. Naturally, popular scientists like Lawrence Krauss and Richard Dawkins were a central feature too, given the ostensible purpose of the rally to champion reason and science.

However, Dawkins went somewhat further than just extolling the virtues of reason in his mainstage address. When talking about the religious beliefs of individuals, he encouraged the cheering crowd to "Mock them! Ridicule them! In public!" Dawkins brought his speech to a rousing close with these words: "Religion makes specific claims about the universe which need to be substantiated and need to be challenged and, if necessary, need to be ridiculed with contempt."[8]

This was not merely an invitation to critical thinking and intellectual inquiry. This was fighting talk.

"RIDICULE THEM"

Many of those spearheading New Atheism hardly needed encouragement on this front. Admittedly, the bouffant-haired-televangelist forms of fundamentalist Christianity had been ripe for scorn already (often deservedly). But this time, the target was religious belief in general. In the eyes of the New Atheists, religion had been afforded an undeserved respect for too long, often enshrined in outdated blasphemy laws and cultural Kowtowing. Now it was their job to dismantle the reverence with irreverence. Mockery and ridicule soon became the modus operandi of the movement.

Apart from the flood of online atheist memes disparaging faith, some leading public figures began to gain a reputation for deriding religion too. TV personality Bill Maher created a documentary titled *Religulous*, aimed at exposing the absurdities of various forms of religious belief, especially Christianity. Christopher Hitchens, whose unmatched rhetorical skills were frequently employed to devastating effect, enjoyed likening God to a "celestial dictator, a kind of divine North Korea"[9] in public talks and debates. British comedian Ricky Gervais, creator of *The Office*, became increasingly vocal in his mockery of religion on Twitter and dedicated a whole stand-up routine to making fun of the Bible.

While mockery was a given, outright offensiveness was not beyond the pale either.

PZ Myers, an evolutionary biologist and popular blogger, caused controversy when he obtained a Communion wafer from a Catholic church and made a show of publicly desecrating it to prove that no thunderbolts would rain down on him for his blasphemy. The picture he posted of the wafer pierced by a rusty nail and lying in a trash can was hardly the stuff of satanic ritualism, but it offended a good number of Catholics.

Of course, these personalities and their theatrical denunciations of religion were never representative of the vast majority of nonbelievers. But the actions of a few can taint the reputation of many. As these figures took center stage, so the public perception of atheism began to take on new associations. Whereas the word *atheist* might be defined by the dictionary as "a person who does not believe in God," in the mind of the public it increasingly came to mean something more like "a person who thinks the idea of God is stupid, along with the people who believe in it."

If a public intellectual like Richard Dawkins described Christians as "faith-heads" and their beliefs as "fairy tales" often enough, it was bound to breed a certain sense of superiority. Atheists were cast as the ones with science, facts, and reason on their side. Religious people were still bogged down in superstitious thinking based on ancient fables compiled by "Bronze Age desert tribesmen."[10] Atheism was gradually turning into *anti*-theism.

However, as the levels of condescension reached a crescendo, New Atheism itself was about to come under scrutiny.

NEW ATHEISM FALTERS

Early on in the movement, the term "brights" had been proposed as an alternative moniker for the New Atheist cause. It was intended as a way of replacing a negative-sounding term (atheism is, after all, a denial of something) with a positive-sounding one. The idea of atheists who valued science, reason, and skepticism renaming themselves "brights" was championed by at least two of the four horsemen, Dawkins and Dennett. Christopher Hitchens dissented, however, writing, "My own annoyance at Professor Dawkins and Daniel Dennett, for their cringe-making proposal that atheists should conceitedly nominate themselves to be called 'brights,' is a part of a continuous argument."[11]

It was perhaps a relatively small spat in the scheme of things, but even Hitchens could see that the atheism he championed was in danger of appearing presumptuous and arrogant.

Meanwhile, other notable atheist voices also started to air their concerns over the direction their movement was heading in.

On my own *Unbelievable?* show, bestselling novelist Philip Pullman, whose His Dark Materials trilogy takes aim at organized religion, told me he was very unhappy about the Atheist Bus Campaign. Given his role as a distinguished patron of the British Humanists, the sponsoring group for the campaign, his assessment was withering: "I thought that slogan ['There's probably no God. Now stop worrying and enjoy your life'] was demeaning and stupid beyond words and I wish I'd had some say in it because I'd have said . . . 'Don't do it! Say something else for goodness' sake; this is an absurd thing to say.'"[12]

Prof. Michael Ruse, a well-known philosopher of science, was aggravated enough to pen several articles stating that the New Atheists' bombastic approach to religion was "a disservice to scholarship" and that Dawkins's book *The God Delusion* made Ruse "ashamed to be an atheist."[13] He even penned several endorsements for Christian books that responded to the movement.

Another notable critic came in the form of atheist philosopher Daniel Came, whose open letter to Richard Dawkins was published in *The Daily Telegraph* in 2011. Came, who was an Oxford University lecturer at the time, criticized the biologist for taking aim at easy targets in religious circles while running away from Christianity's most serious intellectual advocates.

Dawkins had declined several invitations to debate philosopher William Lane Craig, a notable Christian thinker. Came's letter stated that Dawkins's refusal to debate Craig was "apt to be interpreted as cowardice on your part," going on to say (with just a hint of sarcasm), "I notice that, by contrast, you are happy to discuss theological matters with television and radio presenters and other intellectual heavyweights like Pastor Ted Haggard of the National Association of Evangelicals and Pastor Keenan Roberts of the Colorado Hell House."[14]

That same year, I was involved in organizing a speaking tour for the aforementioned William Lane Craig. As part of it, our small team had arranged several public debates with notable atheists. The icing on the cake (we hoped) might be a debate with Dawkins himself.

An invitation was sent, and a date was set for an event on Dawkins's home turf, Oxford University.

Daniel Came offered his help, hoping that his letter and further admonishments might cause Dawkins to seriously consider the invitation. There was even a tongue-in-cheek bus campaign of our own in the city that mimicked the atheist bus slogan, reading, "There's probably no Dawkins . . . but come along to the Sheldonian Theatre and find out."

Dawkins, as expected, did not put in an appearance. However, Came and a panel of fellow agnostic and atheist academics stood in to represent the loyal opposition at the auditorium packed with Oxford students. The organizers included one theatrical flourish. An empty chair was left onstage, a reminder to the audience of Dawkins's no-show and an invitation to the biologist to take up the challenge, if he so desired.

But that empty chair has increasingly stood for something else in my mind: the emptiness of the New Atheist project as a meaningful movement. It had declared belief in God a delusion, but what had it erected in its place? As the architects of the movement were about to discover, without proper foundations, even the most glittering of edifices will crumble under its own weight.

NEW ATHEISM UNRAVELS

The cracks in New Atheism began to show most visibly in 2011 in a controversy at the World Atheist Convention that came to be dubbed "Elevatorgate."

Rebecca Watson, the founder of the website Skepchick, had been speaking on a panel alongside Richard Dawkins and other guests on the subject of the sexualization of women in the online atheist movement and her own experience of the same.

That evening some of the panelists and attendees gathered for drinks at the hotel bar. When Watson made her way back to her room in the early hours, she was followed into the elevator by a man from the group whom she didn't know, who asked her if she would like to come back to his room for coffee. Watson says the uninvited proposition made her very uncomfortable.

"I was a single woman, in a foreign country, at 4:00 a.m., in a hotel elevator with you—just you . . . don't invite me back to your hotel room right after I have finished talking about how it creeps me out and makes me uncomfortable when men sexualize me in that manner."[15]

However, the incident itself wasn't the main problem—men who make inappropriate advances exist in all sorts of circles. It was the fallout from the episode that began to divide the atheist community. When Watson related her experience in a video on her YouTube channel, many fellow skeptics came out in support of her. But her reaction was also seized upon by many other atheists as an example of an overly censorious and politically correct culture that they didn't want infecting their oasis of freethinking. No harm was intended by the man, they claimed. What was all the fuss about?

The argument spilled over into the blogs and online forums of other notable atheists such as PZ Myers, who took Watson's side, arguing that their movement needed a more feminist outlook and denouncing atheists who were downplaying the incident. Then Richard Dawkins himself chimed in.

As the unofficial leader of the movement and someone present at the conference, you might expect him to have tried to extinguish the flames of the growing controversy. Not a bit of it. He chose instead to pour on gasoline by firing off a heavily sarcastic imaginary letter titled "Dear Muslima":

> Stop whining, will you. Yes, yes, I know you had your genitals mutilated with a razor blade, and . . . yawn . . . don't tell me yet again, I know you aren't allowed to drive a car, and you can't leave the house without a male relative, and

your husband is allowed to beat you, and you'll be stoned to death if you commit adultery. But stop whining, will you. Think of the suffering your poor American sisters have to put up with.[16]

He went on to poke further fun at Watson's experience in the elevator as trivial compared to the suffering of women in repressive religious cultures.

Up to this point Dawkins had enjoyed a relatively harmonious relationship with most sides of the atheist community, but now he was inundated with accusations of misogyny, sexism, and male privilege. Naturally, others leapt to his defense, claiming his was the voice of common sense and reason. It would turn out to be the first of numerous controversies stoked by Dawkins that divided the atheist community, but the charge of sexism was where it all began.

In recent years, the Harvey Weinstein scandal and the subsequent rise of the Me Too movement have made the world aware of the sexism and power dynamics that lurk behind the entertainment industry and arts. But years earlier, "Elevatorgate" had prompted a not-dissimilar movement to expose sexist behavior within atheist ranks. And it wasn't just run-of-the-mill conference delegates being accused of inappropriate behavior. The conduct of some of the best-known names on the atheist speaking circuit was also being called into question.

David Silverman was president of the American Atheists organization and the chief organizer of the 2012 Reason Rally. However, he was fired from his position after complaints of financial and sexual misconduct, with the website BuzzFeed publishing a string of allegations against him from various women. Other notable names in the atheist movement, such as Michael Shermer and Richard Carrier, have also had claims of inappropriate behavior at atheist conferences leveled at them and have subsequently been disinvited from public engagements. All three men have vigorously denied the allegations.

Perhaps the most widely publicized case has been that of physicist Lawrence Krauss. Krauss found recognition early in his career following the publication of the bestselling book *The Physics of Star Trek*. He went on to become a professor of astrophysics at Arizona State University in 2008, as well as holding numerous high-profile positions on scientific advisory boards. But it was his larger-than-life stage personality and scathing treatment of opponents that led to his huge popularity as a speaker at major skeptical gatherings and debates.

However, in 2018 allegations of improper advances toward female students while he was in previous teaching positions and a complaint about groping a woman at an Australian conference were published (again by BuzzFeed). Arizona State University investigated the latter allegation and concluded that Krauss had violated their sexual harassment policy, leading to his position as director of the university's Origins project not being renewed. Krauss has consistently denied the allegations, remaining on administrative leave from ASU before leaving his position at the end of the academic year.

As part of the viral BuzzFeed article that detailed the allegations, Rebecca Watson remarked, "Skeptics and atheists like to think they are above human foibles like celebrity worship. . . . In a way, that makes them particularly susceptible to being abused by their heroes. I think we see that over and over again."[17]

NEW ATHEISM SPLITS

Accusations of sexism weren't the only controversies brewing within atheist circles, however. Dawkins himself was continuously embroiled in a string of self-made squabbles and gaffes. Twitter is the Achilles' heel of many celebrities and has oft proved to be the same for Dawkins. Over the years, he has courted multifarious controversies—from tweets advising a woman to have an abortion if she ever became pregnant with a baby with Down syndrome, to downplaying the evils of date rape and "mild" pedophilia.

These episodes developed into a predictable cycle: the tweetstorm of criticism following each statement would be met with defensive tweets from Dawkins, recriminations about being taken out of context, and culminate in a lengthy blog post attempting to nuance his original 140-character statement. After the hubbub died down, the whole process repeated itself a few months later following another incendiary tweet.

However, some of his online activity has had offline consequences. In 2016, after retweeting a video parodying feminism and Islam, he was subsequently disinvited from a science and skepticism conference in New York where he had been booked as the star speaker. Other cancellations followed, including a book event hosted by a California radio station and an invitation to speak at the Historical Society of Trinity College Dublin. The organizer announced that the society would "not be moving ahead with his address as we value our members' comfort above all else."[18]

None of this is limited to the world of New Atheism, of course. Cancel culture has been increasingly under debate in recent years, as various individuals from the worlds of arts, entertainment, and academia have been disinvited from public events after airing unpopular views on hot-button issues. But the fallout from the controversies that have circled Dawkins and other leading atheists has revealed the deep rifts at the core of atheist communities, which were simply waiting to be uncovered.

The perceived sexism and privilege within atheist celebrity culture became too much for many. Skeptical conferences, once the lifeblood of the movement, had gotten a reputation for chauvinism. Feminist skeptics were recommending that people stay away from them, demanding more representation of women and an acknowledgment of the imbalance of power that existed within their community. On the opposite side, others believed their movement was being hijacked by an ideologically driven agenda that had nothing to do with the "freethinking" culture they valued in skeptical circles.

Those advocating for a more progressive, social justice–oriented version of skepticism began to draw up plans for "Atheism +." The plus sign indicated that those who stood under their banner were committed not only to reason and science but also to gender equality, anti-racism, LGBT rights, and a host of other causes. Those who championed this new brand of atheism-with-moral-requirements were painfully aware that the movement had thus far been primarily represented by a phalanx of old, white, straight men (just think of the four horsemen) and was therefore in desperate need of an overhaul at the leadership level.

However, the reality was that the New Atheist movement was largely dominated by white males—not only on the platform but also among the rank and file who occupied the online forums and physical chairs of their conferences. Rather like beard grooming, model railways, and Warhammer, atheism as an organized movement remains a largely male-dominated pastime. Many of those who had enjoyed the movement's honeymoon in the 2000s rounded on "Atheism +." This unwelcome new variant added a potentially endless sequence of causes to their manifesto, along with a lot of awkward questions about patriarchy and privilege. Atheism, they said, was simply a statement about what one did not believe in—namely, God. Yes, science and reason were welcome to the party too. But they balked at the idea of having to sign up for a list of additional ideological commitments. Atheism was starting to look more like a moralistic form of religion than they had ever anticipated.

Even a left-leaning skeptic like Sam Harris, someone happy to self-describe as a feminist, feared that the ideological doctrines of the "progressive left" were eroding the fact-based, science-driven culture of the skeptical movement. After receiving a volley of sexism accusations from atheist bloggers, he penned an article titled "I'm Not the Sexist Pig You're Looking For."[19] In it he defended the scientific arguments for the general differences in temperament and psychology between the sexes and why it could easily account for the fact that

84 percent of his Twitter following were men and the atheist movement was largely male-dominated.

Harris has likewise been accused of other prejudices such as Islamophobia but has refused to tone down his critique of the religion. Perhaps most controversially, Harris has been willing to give a platform to voices such as Charles Murray, a researcher who argues in his book *The Bell Curve* that there are genetically based disparities in IQ between different racial groups. Murray's work has (inevitably) been co-opted by racists to argue for white superiority, and many of his scientific peers have argued that the research is fundamentally flawed.

For Harris, however, the issue was about being able to openly discuss these ideas, regardless of whether society approves of them. Rational debate cannot be sacrificed for political correctness, he argued. It's why Harris is frustrated by the increasing amount of energy expended by his peers on "safe spaces, trigger warnings, and microaggressions"[20] that have marked the emergence of "woke" culture.

NEW ATHEISM IMPLODES

In recent years another major front to emerge in the culture war is the issue of transgender rights. The dramatic rise in the number of young people pursuing gender reassignment medication and surgery has been well-documented. Controversies abound over whether transgender women who have the physiology of a postpubescent man should compete against other women in sports. And then there's the thorny issue of changing rooms and female-only spaces.

Even beloved cultural icons like J. K. Rowling, author of the Harry Potter series, have been swept into the maelstrom of controversy. Since beginning to openly argue that transgender activism is eroding the gender rights that feminists fought for, she has become a social pariah in many progressive circles and heralded as a champion of free speech and feminism in others.

Transgender rights has proved to be yet another divisive issue within the atheist movement. In 2021, Twitter comments by Dawkins questioning the self-identification of transgender men and women led the American Humanist Association to strip him of his 1996 Humanist of the Year award. They said that Dawkins had made statements "that use the guise of scientific discourse to demean marginalized groups, an approach antithetical to humanist values."[21]

In 2019 *The Atheist Experience*, a long-standing, popular call-in show based in Austin, Texas, underwent a major split. The host Matt Dillahunty says that he and the Atheist Community of Austin who run the show are completely trans-affirming. "I was being called a transphobe while sitting with two trans women, a young trans boy, and two gay men, planning out our Pride festival event."[22]

However, the controversy was sparked when UK-based atheist YouTuber Stephen Woodford appeared as a special guest on the show. Woodford had gained prominence for his Rationality Rules channel, in which he seeks to debunk various apologetic arguments for religion. He also uses his platform to respond to various hot-button issues and had posted a video arguing that transgender athletes had an unfair advantage when competing in female sports.

However, following Woodford's appearance, a deluge of criticism came in from those who believed a "transphobe" was being featured on the show. Despite having been warmly welcomed onto the show (and the trans issue never raised), Woodford flew back to England only to find he had been officially denounced by the Atheist Community of Austin, who had issued an apology for the "pain and anguish" caused by his appearance.[23]

Despite the official apology, the backlash led to a number of staff and volunteers quitting the organization. Woodford himself subsequently revised his views on transgender athletes, admitting he had made some factual mistakes but denying accusations of transphobia. Dillahunty has since stepped down as host of *The Atheist Experience* and resigned from the Atheist Community of Austin due to ongoing disagreements.[24]

Similar fallouts and debates around gender, trans rights, LGBT issues, and race have increasingly marked popular culture. These rifts in ideology have tended to be inflamed by the "callout" culture of platforms such as Twitter, Facebook, and YouTube and the clickbait appeal of celebrity controversy. However, the phenomenon began early for the New Atheist community, which had already been driven by a sprawling network of blogs and websites before social media came to rule the roost. The "Elevatorgate" scandal of 2011 seems to have marked the pivotal moment when the New Atheist movement officially began to tear itself apart from the inside.

Up to that point, New Atheism had been largely united in agreeing that religion was bad and science was good. But it turns out that life is more complicated than that. Once the community discovered they held radically differing views about how life should be lived once religion has been abandoned, things quickly spiraled downwards.

Where the energy of the movement had once been dedicated to critiquing religious superstition and unscientific ways of thinking, now atheists seemed to spend most of their time attacking one another. The vitriol and anger of the exchanges between former friends in the skeptical community dwarfed anything that had preceded it between atheists and their religious opponents.

Popular atheist blogger PZ Myers, who stood firmly with the progressive "Atheism +" faction, fell out dramatically with Sam Harris and just about every other leading atheist voice in the community. He would later pen an article titled "The Train Wreck That Was the New Atheism," bemoaning the right-wing trajectory of the movement and asking, "Who put Dennett, Harris, Dawkins, and Hitchens in charge?" He concluded that his period as a standard bearer for the movement was "the deepest regret of my life."[25]

The once well-attended atheist conferences and speaking events were also feeling the strain as the infighting continued.

A low point was the 2017 MythCon, organized by the freethought group Mythicist Milwaukee.[26] Despite intense criticism, they had invited firebrand anti-feminist YouTuber Carl Benjamin (aka Sargon of Akkad) to be a contributor. Among other things, Benjamin had caused outrage the previous year after sending a tweet to British MP Jess Phillips, stating, "I wouldn't even rape you."

His onstage debate on feminism and social justice with atheist podcaster Thomas Smith culminated in chaotic scenes. Many in the audience were vocally behind Benjamin, while Smith denounced his debate opponent as "awful" and those cheering him on as "deplorables" and "sycophants." Smith eventually walked off stage, declaring, "This conference is an embarrassment." When heated arguments continued after the debate, security reportedly stepped in to eject some attendees from the premises.

Latterly, even before the COVID-19 pandemic paused in-person gatherings, numerous skeptical atheist conferences have been canceled altogether. Some have ended due to a decline in interest from those who once frequented them, but the endless political wranglings have also taken their toll.

The blogger "Atheism and the City" summed it up well in an article reflecting on the cancellation of The Atheist Conference 2018 following irresolvable disagreements about the proposed speaker lineup:

> The atheist community has splintered into a million shards in recent years. There are the atheist feminists and the atheist anti-feminists, the social justice warrior atheists and the anti-social justice warrior atheists. The pro-PC atheists and the anti-PC atheists. There are pro-Trump atheists and anti-pro-Trump atheists. Atheists are split over gamergate, elevatorgate, whether we should organize, or whether we should even call ourselves atheists at all. The divisions go on and on.[27]

THE FALL OF NEW ATHEISM

Today, New Atheism is a largely spent force, relegated to corners of the Internet where teenage bloggers continue to churn out antagonistic Bible memes in online echo chambers. It has faded from public view as a serious cultural phenomenon. The publishing boom in anti-God literature fizzled out almost as quickly as it began, and the atheist speaking circuit is a shadow of its former self.

The implosion of the atheist community into warring factions was accompanied by a waning of sympathy among the general public. What at first sounded like a principled stand against religious dogmatism and privilege had begun to sound like a form of dogmatism itself. The cause began to wear very thin.

For religious people, the scornful and condescending tone of the New Atheists had been a turnoff from the outset. As evangelistic strategies go, painting your potential convert as an ignoramus tends to be a poor one. And to the nonreligious who actually had religious friends, it was obvious that their friends' lives and faith were more nuanced than the caricature of faith presented by their detractors.

Moreover, in building a community of like-minded skeptics, New Atheism had inadvertently stumbled into the mold of a religious cult itself. This was, after all, much more than merely "disbelief in God."

There were the high priests (the four horsemen) and the sacred texts they had written. Science was their object of worship, and naturalism—the belief that all that exists can be explained by matter in motion and the blind forces of nature—was their creed. They gathered regularly to celebrate their beliefs, to praise the wonder of science, and to hear their leaders preach against those who believed another gospel. Atheists who questioned the strict materialist orthodoxy, or even lost their faith altogether, were heretics and rounded on with unswerving zeal.

However, religions are prone to schisms whenever they grow to a certain size and, as its implosion shows, New Atheism proved to be no exception.

In my own personal interactions, I was increasingly encountering nonbelievers who were keen to distance themselves from the movement. The phrase "I'm an atheist, but not of the Richard Dawkins sort" was invoked surprisingly frequently. There was a sense that the shrill religious fundamentalism opposed by New Atheism had simply been replaced by a shrill fundamentalism of another kind.

Part of the problem was that the atheist movement had primarily rallied around what it was *against*—religion. Consequently, it had struck a negative tone ever since its inception. Aware of this, some atheists have made attempts to create nonreligious communities that are aimed instead at celebrating what they are *for* and fostering an environment for genuine relationships to flourish.

One of the most prominent has been the Sunday Assembly, a regular church-like gathering on Sunday mornings in London that lacks any reference to God or spirituality. They make a point of avoiding any of the typical anti-religious sentiments that might be stock-in-trade for an atheist gathering. On the contrary, the stand-up comedians Sanderson Jones and Pippa Evans, who founded the weekly gatherings in 2013, were fully aware that they were borrowing from the Christian tradition. Uplifting pop songs stood in for hymns, an inspirational talk on the wonder of the universe might replace the sermon, and a meditation on love might be the equivalent of a prayer time. Perhaps most importantly, it brought people together in a regular weekly community. In all these ways, the Sunday Assembly has explicitly modeled itself on a typical church service (indeed, many labeled it "the atheist church"), but its only creeds are the values listed on its website: "Live Better, Help Often, Wonder More."[28]

Whether these cuddlier forms of nonreligious community actually catch on in the long term remains to be seen. The Sunday Assembly has seen its own splits and fallouts in the global franchise. Again, the religious parallels hardly need to be spelled out. However, the fact that such atheist gatherings exist demonstrates that people need more than facts about science and reason to sustain them. They need community, meaning, and a sense of purpose.

Many people had turned to New Atheism for its promise of a brighter, more rational, and more scientific future. They believed it held the key to human flourishing. Just as the secular anthem "Imagine" had envisaged a world without religion, heaven, or hell, it was only reasonable to suppose that the song's utopian "brotherhood of man" would naturally follow. Yet despite John Lennon claiming it was "easy if you try," it turned out to be quite complicated.

What could a movement that was built on tearing down God erect in his place? Science was the obvious alternative—surely that was an objective truth to which all people could aspire? But science turned out to be a poor substitute for a savior.

Science can tell you how the universe arose but not why it is there. Science can tell you what you consist of but not what you are worth. Science can generate solutions to poverty but not the compassion to implement them. Science can make you money but not purchase a meaningful existence.

"Science Works, B—s," declared one popular atheist meme. Yes, it does—for certain things, but not for everything. Most especially it won't inform us about what things we should value. In that sense, science is neutral. We can use it to create a cure for cancer or to create an atomic bomb. Science won't tell us which of those options is the right thing to do. That's a value judgment that must ultimately be derived from somewhere beyond science.

The question of which particular values we should celebrate and support was the issue that came to tear apart the New Atheist world, as proved by the rancorous infighting of its factions over feminism, race, gender, and LGBT issues. It turned out science and reason alone could not provide the answer to such vexed issues. In that sense, New

Atheism was shown to be a very thin worldview, not one that could provide a reason for living.

Certainly there were other options open to atheists who wanted to subscribe to a nonreligious ethical framework.

The "Atheism +" movement was one such attempt to flesh out a bare atheist worldview with a list of additional beliefs about rights and values. Likewise, gatherings such as the Sunday Assembly have tried to put a set of shared values at the heart of their own secular services. "Humanism" is another broad ethical system that many atheists choose to align themselves with today, where valuing the inherent equality and dignity of all humans is paramount. But, as I shall argue in subsequent chapters of this book, such value systems owe far more to the Christian societies they emerged from than the professed atheism of those who currently sit under their banners.

THANK GOD FOR RICHARD DAWKINS

Where did all this leave religion?

At the height of its influence, New Atheism looked like a serious threat to religious belief in the West. How could the average church minister shepherding their flock hope to compete with the intellectual prowess of the New Atheist authors and their books? How could the average Christian parent hope to compete with the avalanche of online atheist material that vied for the attention of their teenage children?

By some accounts, you might be forgiven for thinking there was a mass exodus from the church as the four horsemen and their growing army of skeptics came tearing through the culture. Atheist websites were filled with accounts of ex-Christians who had seen the light and abandoned the superstitions they had once gullibly accepted. Indeed, many of the most prominent skeptic organizations were started by ex-believers, now evangelizing as enthusiastically for atheism as they once had for Christianity.

It wasn't limited to Christianity, either. Ex-Muslim sites also became a feature of the movement, albeit with far greater potential risks for those who went public with their apostasy stories. Nevertheless, the attrition rates of atheism among Christians seemed to far outweigh their Muslim counterparts.

Perhaps churches in the West only had themselves to blame. The great Protestant revival movements of the eighteenth and nineteenth centuries led by Whitefield, Wesley, Edwards, and Booth that had swept the UK and United States were long gone. The Reformation that had renewed the spiritual fervor of mainland Europe was even further back in the rearview mirror. By the mid-twentieth century the living faith of a previous generation had calcified into the dead religion of the next, as cultural forms of nominal Christianity prevailed over personal transformation.

Meanwhile, Christianity's long-standing Catholic intellectual tradition born of Augustine and Aquinas had also begun to wither on the vine. Despite the best efforts of popular writers such as C. S. Lewis and G. K. Chesterton to reengage a lay audience with rational arguments for faith, churches were less inclined towards rigorous catechism of their members, who drifted instead towards more sentimental expressions of Christianity.

From the 1960s onwards, new church movements sought to counter what they perceived as the dead formalism of the mainline denominations and experimented with a new freedom in music, preaching, and spiritual experience. Both the post–Vatican II era of Catholicism and the "new wine" of the burgeoning charismatic movement and seeker-sensitive churches were arguably a necessary antidote to the dry stuffiness of a previous generation. But it also marked a significant transition towards a more experiential, emotional form of Christian engagement, often at the expense of an intellectually rigorous engagement with Scripture and the world.

By the time New Atheism swung into view in the 2000s, there were precious few churches prepared to equip their members for the onslaught of skepticism it brought. They might have been able to offer uplifting worship songs and an inspiring sermon series on "living your best life now," but few were in a position to offer a philosophical defense of God's existence or to defend the historicity of the Bible. There were notable exceptions, of course, but by and large the Western church was caught on the back foot.

How many people have permanently exited the church after falling under the sway of New Atheism is almost impossible to judge. Anecdotally, there's no doubt that many individuals have lost their faith as a direct result of Dawkins and Co. For some this may have come after a significant period of wrestling with questions. Often it was because they felt the lack of answers from their own church communities.

However, I would venture to suggest that New Atheism mainly reaped its de-conversions among those whose faith was already primed to be lost—those whose religious beliefs owed more to their cultural milieu and the extrinsic activity of churchgoing than to any deeply held personal convictions. To that degree, the church was already due to be winnowed of those whose faith was planted in such shallow soil. In the great scheme of things, Dawkins and his fellow horsemen were only handmaidens to the larger social forces of secularization and religious disaffiliation that have meant faith has not been transmitted to recent generations in the way it once was.

But I thank God for Richard Dawkins. Our harshest critics are often the ones who help us to grow the most. Just as those London buses bearing the words "There's probably no God" had the unintended consequence of putting religion back in the spotlight, so New Atheism has revitalized the intellectual tradition of the Christian church in the West.

New Atheism arrived with a whole bunch of awkward questions about science, history, and religious belief—questions the church had not had to think about for a long time. But now, with the four horsemen at their heels, the church was forced to put down its tambourines and guitars and pick up its history and philosophy books again.

In short, New Atheism gave the Christian church a kick up the backside that it desperately needed. Arguably, the last two decades have seen the greatest revival of Christian intellectual confidence in living memory as the church has risen to the challenge.

Apologetics ministries have flourished across the world as they've sought to make a defense (*apología* in the Greek) against the rising tide of secular critics. Organizations such as Reasonable Faith, founded by the aforementioned philosopher and formidable debater William Lane Craig, and Word on Fire, founded by Catholic "bishop of social media" Robert Barron, have equipped a new generation of Christians with rational arguments for the reliability of Scripture and the Christian worldview.

In the process, a flood of apologetics books, courses, and resources have been made available to churches, along with an ever-growing number of videos, blogs, and podcasts from apologists large and small. This includes a young, tech-savvy generation of YouTubers and podcasters who are taking the fight directly to their online atheist counterparts.

An increase has even been noted in the number of Christians entering academic institutions to take up studies in philosophy of religion, inspired by leading thinkers such as Alvin Plantinga.

This return to an intellectual, analytical form of Christianity can have its own pitfalls, just as much as the subjective, experiential sort that has dominated in recent years. As always, a balance between the mind and the heart is the best approach. But the swing back of the pendulum was sorely overdue and remains so in parts of the church that continue to self-insulate from the realities of our skeptical age.

While the rise in Christian apologetics has boosted the confidence of those already in the pews and perhaps stemmed the decline, it has also contributed to a significant number of people entering the church for the first time. As far back as the 1950s, C. S. Lewis had cause to remark that "nearly everyone I know who has embraced Christianity in adult life has been influenced by what seemed to him to be at least probable arguments for Theism."[29]

That anecdotal observation seems to be backed up by recent research. Dr. Jana Harmon earned her PhD in 2019 with a study on adult conversion of atheist skeptics to Christianity, which demonstrated the strong degree to which they are influenced by apologetic arguments.[30] Other factors are also significant, not least having their preconceptions of Christianity challenged by meeting intelligent and gracious Christians. However, once the barriers are lowered, the New Atheist objections have often been met and overcome by cogent Christian arguments in response.

A significant number of people can even trace their own conversion to Dawkins himself. Peter Byrom, who became a confirmed atheist while reading *The God Delusion* as a student, says that it was also the pathway towards his subsequent conversion:

> Looking through the Dawkins and Hitchens work . . . was when I started discovering Christian apologetics. I had seen some Christians who were terrible at defending their faith. . . . but I gradually discover[ed] lots of other, much more robust, academically credible apologists. . . . It made me realize that I've run out of arguments and objections. There is really good solid stuff here. I had to face up to the fact that all I was left with was not wanting it to be true.[31]

My own radio show and podcast *Unbelievable?* was born into this new and dynamic world of Christian apologetics. For over fifteen years I have hosted conversations that have frequently circled the key objections of the New Atheists, and the leading voices in that movement have frequently locked horns with their Christian peers on the show. Meanwhile, my role as host has also given me a front-row seat to the waxing and waning of New Atheism over the past two decades and the revival of Christian apologetics in its wake.

But in recent years, I have noticed an unmistakable sea change in the kinds of conversations that secular culture is now having around

Christianity, science, and faith. The excitement of the clashes between the titans of atheism and Christianity that once packed out debating chambers has faded with New Atheism itself. Nowadays, the most well-attended events are for an altogether different kind of conversation between a new breed of secular thinkers who are reconsidering the value of Christianity and asking big questions around meaning, purpose, and identity. This change in the tone and content of the conversation may be evidence that the receding tide of the "Sea of Faith" has reached its furthest limit. Thinking people are being given permission to take the idea of God seriously again. And I believe that the tide is turning.

The church was caught on the back foot by New Atheism and only latterly began to find its stride again. The danger is that, as this cultural conversation moves forward, the church will once again be left answering yesterday's objections, rather than engaging with those who are asking a different set of questions altogether.

The rest of this book will aim to show exactly what those questions are, who is asking them, and why this new cultural moment is an unparalleled opportunity for the Christian church to share its vision of reality to a world that may be ready to hear it once again.

CHAPTER 2

THE NEW CONVERSATION ON GOD

IT WAS JANUARY 2018, and it all seemed to be going smoothly. Could I book Jordan Peterson for an interview about his new book? "Yes," said the publicist. "He'll be in the UK soon, and his diary is fairly free."

However, as the date approached, my allotted time began to be whittled down. The publicist couldn't quite believe how much interest there seemed to be in the relatively unknown Canadian psychology professor and his new book *12 Rules for Life: An Antidote to Chaos*. Numerous media outlets were vying for his time, and two hastily booked lectures at a thousand-seat London venue sold out within hours. The events were packed out—not by crusty academics but by young male professionals.

I still managed to bag an hour with the increasingly in-demand author in the form of a recording for my discussion show *The Big Conversation* opposite atheist psychologist Susan Blackmore.

However, one of the next appointments in Peterson's diary turned out to be an interview with Channel 4 News presenter Cathy Newman, whose inquisitorial style often leaves politicians flustered. But when she challenged Peterson over his views on the gender pay gap, the psychologist's cool dismantling of her arguments meant the interview soon went viral, and Peterson was launched into the celebrity stratosphere.

The interview spawned a multitude of blogs, opinion pieces, and other interviews interrogating his newfound fame and the ideas he brings with him. His series of debates with Sam Harris in Vancouver and London filled two major arenas four times over. A two-year speaking tour saw him address hundreds of thousands in sold-out auditoriums across the globe. His podcasts and YouTube videos reached millions.

Then, suddenly, he disappeared from the public eye. The combination of a grueling schedule, his wife Tammy's shock cancer diagnosis, and an unwitting addiction to anti-anxiety medication left him a shadow of his former self. Gradually, over the course of a year of "absolute hell,"[1] with the help of his daughter, Mikhaila, he was able to detox from the medication and build his strength back again.

Despite the lengthy hiatus, the Jordan Peterson phenomenon did not go away. With a sequel to *12 Rules* now published, there are still millions of people, especially young men, who are following his podcasts, videos, and lectures. He remains an often controversial figure who divides opinion, yet his influence continues to endure. The *New York Times* has described him as "the most influential public intellectual in the Western world right now."[2]

But how did Jordan B. Peterson become the rock star of public intellectuals? And why are so many young men following him? His story and influence provide important perspective for understanding the changing dynamics of the conversation on faith.

THE JORDAN PETERSON PHENOMENON

Peterson first entered public consciousness in 2016. A psychology lecturer at the University of Toronto, he was popular with his students but relatively unknown beyond the confines of academia. However, when Canada proposed and later enshrined new laws which potentially criminalized anyone who refused to address transgender persons by their preferred pronouns, Peterson objected in the strongest terms.

The professor said it wasn't about being anti-transgender rights. His concern was about the state criminalizing the use of language—the first step towards, in Peterson's eyes, an Orwellian-style tyranny.

His public protest (delivered via YouTube) landed him in trouble with university authorities and campus protest groups. Videos circulated of Peterson being shouted down by angry students who accused him of being a stooge of the alt-right.

Yet Peterson has always disavowed any association with the fascism of the alt-right. He says he's defending the classic liberal values of academic liberty and freedom of speech but sees the growing popularity of identity politics among groups defining themselves by sexuality, gender, and race as a form of "cultural Marxism."[3]

But Peterson isn't the only public intellectual taking aim at the progressive left and drawing a crowd in the process. Since New Atheism got stuck in its rut, he has become the standard bearer for a new conversation among a collective of thinkers sometimes loosely labeled the "Intellectual Dark Web" (IDW). It consists of a band of secular journalists, psychologists, academics, historians, and scientists who share Peterson's concerns about the direction of academia and culture and who aren't afraid to declare that the emperor has no clothes.

Ostensibly there's plenty of overlap between the IDW and the New Atheist tribe that preceded them. Sam Harris is included in their number, and they look very similar in terms of gender and skin color—primarily male and pale.

But there's a big difference in the questions they are asking and the solutions they are proposing. Whereas New Atheism held religion up as a problem that the world needed to be rid of, the IDW is asking whether we can live without God at all. In the case of Peterson, the answer will include the qualifier "What do you mean by God?"[4]

The psychologist's own beliefs about the divine have been notoriously difficult to pin down, but they are a million miles from the anti-religion of his atheistic peers. However, Peterson is just one among a number of secular thinkers reconsidering the value of atheism and religion, including some who were once as dogmatically anti-religious as they come.

A CONVERT OF SORTS

If I had ever needed hard evidence that New Atheism was in full-blown retreat, it was confirmed in an email I received a few years ago from Peter Boghossian. I couldn't quite believe what I was reading.

Until his departure in 2021, Boghossian was an assistant professor of philosophy at Portland State University, and for a time he had been one of the most vociferous atheist voices in the blogosphere. His book *A Manual for Creating Atheists* is exactly what the title suggests—a set of strategies to help atheists persuade people to abandon their religious delusions. Boghossian was known as a champion of "street epistemology," a sort of reverse street evangelism in which skeptics would talk flustered religious people out of their faith through a series of questions. When Boghossian joined me on my show to debate his book, he even went so far as to suggest that faith beliefs should be officially categorized as mental disorders.

Yet just a few years later, his tone had changed dramatically. I had contacted him about the possibility of a public dialogue on Christianity and atheism. His response stunned me. He graciously turned down the invitation, telling me that he was finished with attacking God and faith and that I might be surprised at his new attitude towards Christianity. Ironically, he now frequently found himself on the side of Christians against his fellow secularists.

What had effected this remarkable change? Apparently, Boghossian had decided that Christianity was not the enemy of evidence-based thinking he had once imagined it to be. Instead, something far more pernicious was already rampant in culture and threatening to derail rational thinking from within the academy. He had turned his full attention to this new threat. I was told that all would become clear a few months hence.

And so it did. It emerged that Boghossian, along with coconspirators James Lindsay and Helen Pluckrose, was at the center of an audacious academic hoax. They had become troubled by the rise of so-called "grievance studies"—university courses and papers which placed critical theories about racial, gender, and sexual oppression at the center of every academic discipline.

This, they said, was going hand in hand with a woke cancel culture on campus that shamed into silence anyone who differed from the new, politically correct orthodoxy. Academic freedom was being suffocated by rapidly developing ideologies which, once published, became dogma.

Seeking to expose the perceived vacuous foundations for these academic arguments, Boghossian and his team submitted a series of bogus papers to various peer-reviewed academic journals. Before the ruse was exposed, they managed to see papers published on outlandish theories from dogs engaging in "rape culture" to why heterosexual men like to eat at Hooters. They even managed to dress up segments from Hitler's *Mein Kampf* with suitable-sounding academic language in a paper on intersectional feminism. The hoax was widely debated in mainstream media. The *New York Times* reported that the bogus scholarship had unleashed a "cascade of mockery" from like-minded critics.[5]

Boghossian, Lindsay, and Pluckrose describe themselves as left-wing academics, yet they concluded that the progressive liberal values they cherished were under threat by a culture "in which only certain conclusions are allowed" and which "put social grievances ahead of objective truth."[6] This was the pernicious trend that had replaced religious faith as enemy number one in the eyes of Boghossian. In fact, he and those leading the pushback have become unlikely bed-fellows with many Christians and people of faith who are similarly concerned by the dogmatism of identity politics and the curtailing of free speech.

Admittedly, Peter Boghossian has hardly had a Damascene conversion to Christianity. But he has undergone a remarkable change in his attitude towards the questions that matter and which battles to fight. The firebrand atheist is gone, replaced by someone deeply troubled by the direction that a post-Christian culture is traveling in. He, along with many of his peers, has begun to real-ize that the chickens are coming home to roost in the postmodern West.

THE STORY WE RECEIVED

Like Boghossian, other notable atheists such as Sam Harris seem to have lost interest altogether in haranguing Christians. They may even be realizing that the loss of Christianity's cultural dominance might be a significant part of the problem.

To understand this shift from dogmatic New Atheism to a renewed appreciation of what we may be losing in our post-Christian West, a brief history lesson is in order.

Despite the encroachment of secularism from the Enlightenment onwards, until the middle of the twentieth century, Christianity had remained the dominant cultural force in the West and had shaped the psychology of generations of people and their societies. For nearly two millennia, Christendom had given people a story to live their lives by. Regardless of whether the story itself was literally true (which we'll return to later), and even if those living within it were only dimly aware of the details, it had nevertheless provided a narrative about reality with a clear beginning, present, and future.

It could be summarized in five acts:

- *Creation:* In the beginning God created everything "good."
- *Fall:* But things went badly wrong as people went their own way. Our rebellion put humans in conflict with God, each other, and the world around us.
- *Israel:* Beginning with Abraham, God chose a particular people through whom to demonstrate his character and redemption plan.
- *Redemption:* God's rescue project for his creation involved coming in person. Jesus, the promised savior of Israel, lived the life that you and I failed to live, and in his death, he mysteriously bore the consequence of all our failures, bringing salvation to the whole world.
- *New Creation:* Now each person is invited to step into a future that is defined by the hope of his resurrection and a new world to come.

At a simple level, that story involves several key assumptions: Each human life is here by design rather than by accident. Every life, whether male or female, is created in the image of God and therefore has value. Evil and suffering are facts of our present existence but will one day be vanquished when justice is done in the world. And every person, whatever their profession, background, or station in life, is called to work towards creating a world shaped by the teachings and character of Jesus.

Doubtless, the Christian story was often abused by Christendom's gatekeepers or used as an "opium of the masses," as Karl Marx described it. For many centuries the threat of hell was wielded by those in authority to keep people in their place, just as much as the love of God taught them to remember their value. Likewise, for long periods Christianity's defining principles of justice and human value were often deployed with massive inconsistency (the "equal" value of men, women, and people of color being one obvious example).

And yet, for all its faults, the grand story of Creation, Fall, Israel, Redemption, and New Creation helped to frame people's day-to-day existence for centuries.

The idea that each individual life was intended by God gave meaning to each person's existence. That their troubles and afflictions had been the lot of Christ himself gave people the fortitude to bear their own suffering and to see it in the context of a greater, God-given purpose. Indeed, being part of a story that was cosmic in scale meant the humblest denizen of earth could yet be imbued with a sense of ultimate purpose. As the seventeenth-century poet George Herbert wrote, "A servant with this clause / makes drudgery divine."[7]

It's difficult to exaggerate the psychological difference that such a view made to the culture that fostered it. Much of the West was built on the back of a Christian vision of life and work that collectively drove society forwards. This vision was grounded in the idea that each person knew they had an identity as a servant of God and was called to model their life, work, hopes, and dreams in the pattern God had created and on the life exemplified in Jesus Christ. The narrative of Christianity gave people a story to be part of.

But as that story has faded in our communal consciousness, a shared existential question has come to replace it: What story are we now supposed to live by?

Psychologist John Vervaeke says, "With the Enlightenment and the move to a secular world, we lost a religious worldview that homed us and gave us access to wisdom."[8] As this phenomenon reached its zenith in the twentieth century, it was Vervaeke who coined an apt phrase for it—"the meaning crisis."

HOW THE STORY CHANGED

As well as giving us a story to live by, there is another concept which the Christian worldview gifted the modern world: objective truth. It placed this idea at the center of culture. Good and evil, truth and falsehood, beauty, virtue, and purpose were real things that formed part of the fabric of reality. These were concrete facts about existence, not mere opinions. Such pivotal concepts are what the modern age of science, reason, and moral progress was founded on.

However, the dramatic social shifts following the First and Second World Wars and the flowering of the sixties counterculture gave rise to a postmodern age. The certainties of the past were called into question. We no longer held to outmoded concepts like "good" and "evil." Morality was relative—just another evolutionary process adapting creatures to different times and cultures. In an age when all the old orthodoxies began to be questioned, the concept of truth became person-dependent. "You have your truth; I have mine" went the adage. What we each felt about something became as important as the actual facts about it. "All you need is love," sang the Beatles. And love was, above all, a feeling.

In tandem with this sidelining of objective truth, the Christian vision of reality has been increasingly in retreat for the past sixty years. In many parts of the West, churchgoing is regarded as a quaint relic of the past, along with the morality that accompanied it. The "nones" (those who claim no religious affiliation) have been the youngest and fastest-growing demographic in society for some time and have embodied the spirit of our age—progressive, tech-savvy, and convinced that there is no preestablished script for life.

Across the board, the tried and tested narratives that informed our past are now viewed with suspicion. Rebelling against tradition is a given in most popular art and music. (In fact, it has become such a hackneyed trope of rock music that a deeply religious artist now cuts a more rebellious figure than one who gives the finger to the establishment.)

All around we can see the signs of a postmodern age in which the certainties of the past are being questioned and turned on their heads: The irony of a piece of Banksy street art that juxtaposes beauty and violence, or his widely publicized painting that automatically shredded itself the moment after being purchased at auction. The rise of atonal forms of music and poetry that refuse to play by the typical rules of melody and structure. Even Hollywood resists the once familiar good vs. evil tropes of fairy stories like *Sleeping Beauty*. Now, in Disney films like *Maleficent*, the tale is inverted to tell the story from the perspective of the villain.

In fact, Disney has partly been responsible for this social shift. Walt famously declared, "If you can dream it, you can do it," and we have embraced that message en masse. For decades our music, films, books, and art have told us that we need to throw off the shackles of conventional morality and identity and just "follow our dreams."

This loss of a common story that binds us all together is part of the wider phenomenon of the rise of the self in society versus the communal identity that often used to define people. Our current time in history is unique. We live in an era of options, when we have fifty different choices for how our coffee is served in Starbucks and can have music delivered to us according to our individual preferences via Spotify. Likewise, we are the first generation at liberty to invent our own meaning, define our own identity, and create our own story. As that most succinct Gen Z slogan puts it: "You do you."

This postmodern trend, in which we broker our own identity rather than have it handed down to us, has gathered pace in recent years, thanks especially to the advent of social media.

The LGBT movement in particular, which fought long and hard for the rights and recognition of gay and lesbian people in past decades, has since spawned an array of additional sexual and gender identities that people choose to adopt. While critics may roll their eyes at the LGBTQIA+ "alphabet soup" this sometimes results in, those who embrace these identities nevertheless usually regard them as sacrosanct. Meanwhile, other forms of identity such as gender, race, class, and disability have become ever-more distinctive markers of who we are and of our place in society.

Many on the progressive left of culture have come to categorize these identities in terms of the privilege or oppression that often accrues with being Black, white, male, female, straight, gay, trans, etc. Critics often use phrases like "identity politics," "intersectionality," or "wokeness" as pejorative labels for this new cultural phenomenon. But such phrases do at least capture the claim that it is the overlap (or intersection) of these identities that describes just how oppressed or privileged any individual is in relation to others in society. To be "woke" is to be aware of such inequalities and willing to fight their cause. The progressive left's calls for justice are usually radical and nonnegotiable, requiring the dismantling of oppressive systems of patriarchy, racism, or heteronormativity.

While these overarching systems of oppression are viewed as objectively evil, the concept of truth has often become deeply subjective in the process. An individual's lived experience may effectively trump the views of someone who does not share the markers of their identity. Slogans like "my body, my choice" in the abortion debate, "love is love" in the same-sex marriage debate, or "transwomen are women" in the transgender debate reveal that personal experience is now key.

In turn, the conservative right wing of culture tends to react with an equal measure of scorn at the new lexicon of terms and identities, along with anger at the cancellation of those who critique the chosen ideologies. Yet many conservatives are just as prone to discarding the concept of objective truth when it suits them too.

In the United States it has been demonstrated by the almost cult-like devotion to Donald Trump that has gripped so many on the right, along with a willingness to blindly swallow all manner of alternative facts, conspiracy theories, and claims about "stolen elections." The meaning crisis has corroded the core values that many conservatives stood for—truth, integrity, and respect for the rule of law. The Christian identity that once grounded these values has often been replaced by a cynical political power grab in which the ends supposedly justify the means. Meanwhile, those on the right who question the ethical direction of conservative politics are vilified as quislings and "RINOs" (Republicans in name only). Facts, nuance, and reality are discarded in the process.

Social media and clickbait culture have only served to intensify these culture wars as those who shout the loudest gain the most exposure. But the politicization of identity at both ends of the left and right has left many in the "exhausted middle," either afraid to speak out or unable to make their voices heard.

The changing contours of the political landscape have also meant that the traditional battle lines between conservatives on the right and liberals on the left are now far more diffuse. It means liberal academics like Boghossian, old-school feminists like Germaine Greer, authors like J. K. Rowling, and comedians like Monty Python star John Cleese have often found themselves in unlikely alliances with more moderate conservative and religious voices in their concerns over politically correct culture and free speech.

MEANING CRISIS

So we find ourselves in the modern twenty-first century. The Christian narrative of the past that once gave people a sense of common purpose and their place in the created order has been overthrown or forgotten. Now a "be whoever you want to be" culture is in ascendancy as people search for a "true" inner identity—their "authentic self." This phenomenon is known as "expressive individualism," a term coined by sociologist Robert Bellah and popularized by Catholic philosopher Charles Taylor, who describes our modern era as "the Age of Authenticity."[9]

Graham Tomlin, the bishop of Kensington and author of the

book *Why Being Yourself Is a Bad Idea*, writes, "In the West, we have largely lost our belief in God or any sense of a given cosmic order. As a result, there is no longer any overarching 'sacred structure' that holds the world together. So we are left on our own as individuals in a world without any predetermined order that tells us who we are in that world, or that gives us a sense of security and 'fit' within a wider scheme of things."[10]

I believe that this loss of shared identity is part of the reason for the modern mental health crisis. This is the great irony of our age. We live in a more materially prosperous time than any other. Life expectancy is at an all-time high, and we have constant and ubiquitous access to the kind of technology that our ancestors would have considered nothing short of magical. Yet statistics tell us that we are more unhappy than we ever have been, and that's especially true of young people.

The prevalence of mental health problems has skyrocketed in recent years with nearly one-third of young women in the UK reporting anxiety and depression.[11] According to official statistics, in 2017, "the rate of US adolescents and young adults dying of suicide . . . reached its highest level in nearly two decades," with "47 percent more suicides among people aged 15 to 19 than in the year 2000." Suicide was the "second-leading cause of death for people in that age group," second only to road deaths.[12]

Multiple studies have linked the rise in anxiety and depression to the rise of social media and smartphone addiction. Social media is engineered to be addictive. That's why advertising revenues are so lucrative to the tech giants who own the platforms. But the constant distraction, scrolling, and clickbait material are breeding an inability to concentrate or even sleep properly. The never-ending stream of flawless selfies and Instagram influencers, along with a lack of face-to-face engagement, have contributed to this modern mental health crisis.[13]

Social media has gone hand in hand with the pursuit of the self.

Indeed, the selfie has become more than a mere self-portrait on a smartphone. It is part of the increasingly intolerable pressure upon young people to create and maintain a personal brand that can compete with their peers.

Again, Tomlin writes, "An increasing number of studies, especially during the enforced isolation of the pandemic, tell us that happiness and wellbeing are found not in isolated individuality but in social connection. It is through strong relationships with family, friends and community that we truly flourish. . . . In other words, focusing upon my own unique individuality is the wrong place to look."[14]

All of this helps to explain why young people are experiencing a crisis of meaning. A UK survey revealed the scale of the problem. Nine in ten young Brits aged 16 to 29 responded that their life lacks purpose or meaning.[15] What explains this massive change for the worse?

I would argue that it's not just that our brains are being rewired by technology. It's deeper than that. The stories we have been told for the last half century about discovering our "true selves" have reached a crescendo in the age of social media, yet most of us are not mentally or spiritually equipped to navigate this brave new world.

INNATELY RELIGIOUS

New Atheism sought to tear down the last vestiges of the Christian narrative that once gave shape to people's lives. But what has been erected in its place? The hopes of secularism have fallen flat. The rapid advance of science and technology has turned out to be incapable of delivering on its promise of a flourishing, connected, and happier future. Indeed, the reverse is true. Technology and social media have only contributed to the meaning crisis.

Yet we are innately meaning-seeking creatures. Indeed, I would argue that we are innately *religious*. And if one set of religious beliefs is taken away, it will only be replaced by another set of quasi-religious beliefs. Indeed, while churchgoing has been in steady decline in the West, the consequent rise of the "nones" does not necessarily mean people are becoming more atheistic.

In the UK, this was brought home by the death of Queen Elizabeth II. The loss of such an institutional icon (and a woman of deep Christian faith) seemed to cause a latent spirituality to surface in the general public. People paid their respects at cathedrals and parish churches in great numbers. Hundreds of thousands queued for long hours to see her lying in state. As they faced the coffin, many searched for an appropriate sign of reverence—a solemn bow, hands held in the position of prayer, or a whispered "thank you." In an age when most people have forgotten the ceremonies of religious tradition, many still grasped for ways to mark the meaningfulness and mystery of this moment.

To a large extent, the signs and sacraments of traditional religion have been replaced in our culture by a heightened interest in amorphous forms of new age spirituality, primarily focused on mindfulness and meditation. These are often practiced by those who describe themselves as "spiritual but not religious." At the same time, priests who offer rites of exorcism in the Catholic church say they have seen a significant spike in requests in recent years,[16] a phenomenon they say is linked to the increasing numbers of people who are dabbling in the occult.

Meanwhile, social media has become a breeding ground for QAnon and other conspiracy claims—from political pedophile rings in pizza parlor basements to Bill Gates taking over the world through microchips in COVID-19 vaccines. Likewise, flat-earthers and pseudoscientific medical practices still have a surprising amount of currency in our supposedly more rational age. Perhaps most worryingly, religious extremism continues to find fertile soil in the minds of the disaffected young men and women who are preyed upon by Islamic extremists, turning even apparently "normal" people into ISIS fighters and suicide bombers.

Whether the objects of faith appear mild or extreme, a willingness to believe in something beyond the confines of science and reason seems to be built into our species. In a 2005 commencement speech, the bestselling author David Foster Wallace said, "In the day-to-day trenches of adult life, there is actually no such thing as atheism. There is no such thing as not worshiping. Everybody worships. The only choice we get is what to worship."[17] Tragically, Wallace, who struggled with depression, took his own life three years later.

Whether we think of ourselves as religious or not, it seems there is always some ultimate reality to which we give our allegiance. "You're gonna have to serve somebody," sang Bob Dylan. And it's true.

When it comes to new forms of quasi-religious belief, the emergence of multiple new forms of sexual and gender categories is a case in point. They are often defended with religious fervor by those who champion them. Like any fundamentalist movement, there are ingroups, out-groups, heretics, holy texts, and witch hunts. But at the center of it is a belief in an internal identity that cannot be questioned.

Writing in response to the rise of rapid-onset gender dysphoria among young people, biblical scholar N. T. Wright likened it to the religious gnosticism (from the Greek for "secret knowledge") of the early centuries:

> The confusion about gender identity is a modern, and now internet-fueled, form of the ancient philosophy of Gnosticism. The Gnostic, one who "knows," has discovered the secret of "who I really am," behind the deceptive outward appearance. . . . This involves denying the goodness, or even the ultimate reality, of the natural world. Nature, however, tends to strike back, with the likely victims in this case being vulnerable and impressionable youngsters who, as confused adults, will pay the price for their elders' fashionable fantasies.[18]

Whether it be gender or the multiplicity of other political or social causes that describe the identity of individuals today, there exists a plethora of ways we can choose to define our lives, our purposes, and indeed our very selves. However, like the child who has only ever had to choose between vanilla, chocolate, or strawberry and now stands transfixed in an ice cream parlor with a hundred different flavors on offer, overwhelming choice has given rise to a sort of paralysis.

In a world which no longer provides any road map to follow and where the choices for self-actualization are potentially endless, we may frequently find ourselves driving down dead-end streets or simply immobilized by the myriad options on offer.

In that sense, the meaning crisis identified earlier is also an identity crisis. Who am I supposed to emulate when traditional role models are outmoded? To which causes must I signal my allegiance to earn the approval of my peers? And when identity is a free-floating concept, how do I decide on my own?

It turns out that losing the Christian narrative that once formed our decisions, purpose, and identity comes at a cost. And I believe we are only just beginning to see the effects it may have across the world.

SCRATCHING THE ITCH

Perhaps this crisis of meaning explains why Jordan Peterson has drawn such a following. Battling political correctness may have earned Peterson an audience, but his continuing connection with them still needs explanation. Perhaps the greatest mystery of all is his admiration for the power of religion and his fascination with the Bible.

Any reader expecting a secular approach to psychology in Peterson's bestselling book *12 Rules for Life* would have been surprised by his constant references to the Bible and Christian beliefs in the search for meaning and purpose. Equally, they might not expect a set of public lectures on the psychological significance of biblical stories to draw a sell-out crowd, but when Peterson books a theater for that purpose, it's standing room only.

Evidently the psychologist has exposed an existential spiritual itch among millennials and Gen Z and is scratching it for all it's worth. A generation of young men searching for significance and unsure of their identity have latched on to him as a surrogate father figure to help them find their way in life. Jaded by the unfulfilled promises of Dawkins, Hitchens, and the New Atheist intellectuals, they believe that perhaps it is Peterson who has the words of life.

Peterson's life lessons are couched in the language of biology, psychology, and theology, yet are also disarmingly simple. For instance, he may draw on the emotional significance of the Genesis account of Cain and Abel (a story so deep he describes it as having "no bottom"[19]), but the instructions dispensed are still "clean up your room, bucko" and "put the things you can control in order."[20]

Such advice may not seem radically new, but it has galvanized his followers. It's not unusual for the psychologist to be greeted on the street by men who say, "You've changed my life." Even once-ardent atheists have reported a new respect for religion. Multiple threads about Peterson on Reddit with titles such as "Atheist here, on the edge of conversion to Christianity!"[21] bear witness to the effect his writings and talks on faith are having.

No wonder so many Christian leaders have taken notice of Peterson and his overtures towards Christian faith. Young males are precisely the demographic most absent in churches, and Peterson's ability to draw them with a message that often resonates with the story of Christianity has led to endless blogs about the "Peterson phenomenon" as well as feverish speculation about his own personal beliefs.

JOURNALISTS, PUNDITS, AND PERSONALITIES

While Peterson may be the most prominent public thinker to be reexamining the value of Christianity in the modern world, he is certainly not alone.

After interviewing him, I became increasingly aware of numerous other high-profile secular public voices who seemed to be saying similar things about where society may drift in the absence of a prevailing Judeo-Christian worldview.

Take, for instance, Douglas Murray, the associate editor of *The Spectator*, whose bestselling book *The Madness of Crowds* is a stinging critique of the fragmentation of culture into warring interest groups based around identities of gender, sexuality, and race. Murray is an agnostic, gay journalist who lost his public-school faith by his mid-twenties and became friends with Christopher Hitchens and his co-horsemen during the heyday of New Atheism.

However, when I asked Murray for his thoughts on their legacy, his response was devastatingly critical: "New Atheism made claims that were self-confessedly wrong. The claim, for instance, that morality was obvious, was obviously wrong. The claim that the basic ethics that we might share are self-evident, is self-evidently not the case. You don't have to be an ethicist to know that, you just need to travel."[22]

Murray went on to describe how, in the absence of the shared narrative and identity that Christianity gave us, Western culture is in danger of unraveling in the face of the endless competing narratives and identities that look increasingly fundamentalist in nature. His book warns of the religious pharisaism of the new wave of identity politics and its heresy hunters who leave no room for grace or forgiveness.

Meanwhile, Murray finds himself haunted by the faith he once held, saying, "I'm now in the self-confessedly conflicted and complex situation of being, among other things, an uncomfortable agnostic who recognizes the values and the virtues that the Christian faith has brought."[23]

YouTube host Dave Rubin told a remarkably similar story when I sat down with him. As the face of the million-plus subscriber channel *The Rubin Report*, he's well known for having undergone a political transformation, from being a comedian on the progressive left in his younger years to becoming a right-leaning conservative pundit.

However, our conversation revealed that a spiritual journey had also been underway in recent years.

Having once been enamored with the promises of New Atheism, he told me why he now no longer describes himself as an atheist and was starting to reconnect with his Jewish roots and even explore the claims of Christianity. It turned out that Jordan Peterson, who had become something of a mentor to Rubin, was part of the reason. "I just don't like the word atheist—it doesn't fit what I believe," he said. "I think Jordan has gone a long way toward articulating the type of thing that I believe in."[24]

Like Murray, Rubin is also increasingly concerned by the aggression of activists in the secular sphere. Whereas he once might have considered evangelical Christians the intolerant ones, he now feels the opposite is true: "I don't think it's a coincidence that generally believers right now, are more tolerant. Who are the most intolerant people in society right now? It's the people that are constantly telling you how tolerant they are. That's the irony—it's the people that tell you you're a bunch of racists and bigots and homophobes."[25]

Another Jewish media personality, Bari Weiss, came to wide prominence in 2020 when she resigned her position as an op-ed writer and editor at the *New York Times* in protest at the curtailment of free thought within her profession. Weiss describes herself as liberal and center-left, but like many of those already mentioned, she found herself increasingly out of step with her progressive peers at the paper. In a widely shared resignation letter, she identified her concerns about the politically correct orthodoxies now being aggressively policed among journalists: "I was always taught that journalists were charged with writing the first rough draft of history. Now, history itself is one more ephemeral thing molded to fit the needs of a predetermined narrative."[26]

Weiss, who has written extensively on the reemergence of anti-Semitism (she describes being called a "Nazi and a racist" by colleagues who disagreed with her politics[27]), is another example of a secular thinker who has begun to reembrace a traditional religious identity in the wake of the rise of the quasi-religious "woke" identities she is concerned by.

In an interview, she said that a "reckoning" of New Atheism was taking place, as it had prepared the ground for the meaning crisis:

> When I look at the qualities of the people who have the strength and the fortitude to not go along with the crowd and to be willing to be slandered and to sacrifice for the sake of resisting this illiberalism, almost all of them are religious in some way or another. . . . Something deeper is rooting them. . . . One of the things that the atheist group maybe couldn't have foreseen is that robbing people of that religious impulse would soften the ground for the rise of this deeply illiberal ideology that functions in many ways like a new religion. . . . It's deeply connected to the rise of this new orthodoxy.[28]

Speaking of her return to Judaism, Weiss said, "The more deeply I connected to my own Judaism, Jewish history, the stronger my conviction has become. I am just extremely clear on who I am, what I'm about, and what I'm fighting for."[29]

Russell Brand presents another interesting case study. The well-known TV personality, actor, and comedian has also been on a journey of self-discovery in recent years. Having once been a party animal in the alternative comedy scene with a serious addiction to sex and drugs, Brand has since engaged in a spiritual quest that led him to renounce his previous lifestyle. He says that he now believes in God and that the practice of meditation and prayer has brought stability and a sense of the transcendent into his life.

While his spirituality is more influenced by an Eastern universalist philosophy than Christianity (the tattoo of a crucified Christ on his right arm is balanced by tattoos from multiple other religions across his body), Brand welcomes conversations with Christian theologians and is frequently critical of an atheistic view of the world that reduces meaning and purpose to matter and brain chemistry.

Brand also seems to be concerned by the self-inward turn of culture in the absence of a unifying story. In an interview with atheist comedian Ricky Gervais, Brand said, "When people think there's no purpose or meaning . . . it creates cultures that are oddly materialistic and nihilistic. And I feel like in the last twenty years we are seeing more and more worship of self, the worship of the individual."[30]

PHILOSOPHERS, FEMINISTS, HISTORIANS, AND SCIENTISTS

It's not just journalists, celebrities, and TV pundits who have moved in this direction. Secular philosophers such as John Gray and the late Roger Scruton have written at length about how New Atheism's religion-less utopia has proved to be a pipe dream. Why? Firstly, because human nature is irreducibly religious, and secondly, because many modern atheists fail to recognize the degree to which their vision of the good life is a product of the Christian culture that preceded them.

To this end, historian Tom Holland, author of *Dominion: How the Christian Revolution Remade the World*, has repeatedly pointed out this blind spot among secular humanists. "Humanism" has become the label for atheism's most recent incarnation as an ethical code for life. However, according to Holland, it is entirely constructed from the moral assumptions of the Christian West that it sprang from.

Telling how he came to this realization himself, Holland recounted to me the dawning of his own reevaluation of the Christianity he had left behind as a teenager. As a young historian he had presumed that the values of freedom, equality, and human dignity that he and his secular peers cherished were the natural product of any civilized society. However, his study of the ancient world quickly led him to recognize just how little he had in common with civilizations of the past. "I began to realize that actually, in almost every way, I am a Christian."[31]

The rise of new orthodoxies and their attendant cancel culture has also created strange bedfellows of religious conservatives and second-wave feminists like Germaine Greer. In common with other notable feminists, writers, and broadcasters such as Camille Paglia, J. K. Rowling, and Jenny Murray, Greer has caused controversy for her outspoken criticism of new gender ideologies. She and others have been labeled Trans Exclusionary Radical Feminists (TERFs) for their belief that the rights and experiences of women are intrinsically linked to their biology and cannot be conferred on those who have male bodies.

Ever since her bestselling 1970 work *The Female Eunuch*, Greer has never been afraid to lambast organized religion for its subjugation of women. But even she has spoken approvingly of the value of the convent school education she experienced in Australia. A self-described "atheist Catholic," Greer says that the strong example of the sisters in these female-only institutions sowed the seeds of her own feminism and that without them, generations of Australian women would not have had any education. In a similar vein, Larissa Nolan writes of how "nuns schooled today's torch-bearers of feminism."[32]

Scientists are also among those taking a fresh look at the value of religion. Bret Weinstein is an evolutionary biologist who, along with his wife Heather Heying, was a professor at Evergreen State College in Washington State. They both left their positions in 2017 after coming into conflict with student activists who had effectively closed down the campus amid protests over race and privilege. Like Boghossian, Weinstein has become a high-profile critic of politically correct ideologies on college campuses, which he says are stifling academic integrity and the free exchange of ideas that should characterize higher education.

But Weinstein is also increasingly well-known for encouraging a détente of sorts in the war between religion and science. As an athe-ist, Weinstein no longer believes in the Jewish faith he was brought up in but nevertheless engages in some of its rituals and commu-nity aspects with his family. When I hosted a discussion between the biologist and scientist-theologian Alister McGrath, we discussed Weinstein's contention that religion is "literally false and metaphori-cally true."[33]

Weinstein rejects the idea that religion is an unfortunate misfir-ing of the evolutionary process (as his scientific colleague Richard Dawkins believes) but says that the practice of religion has evolved as a beneficial survival strategy like any other aspect of biological adaptation. To that extent, Weinstein is willing to look for the good in religion whilst recognizing the limits of science's ability to convey meaning and purpose to humans.

Some of the thinkers listed thus far lean to the right (or at least away from the radical left) in their political and cultural outlook. This is perhaps no surprise. Conservative values often go hand in hand with an appreciation for the stability of the West's Judeo-Christian heritage. A subset of them, along with other thinkers such as Ben Shapiro, Sam Harris, and Bret Weinstein's mathematician brother Eric Weinstein, rallied under the aforementioned (and somewhat grandiose) moniker the "Intellectual Dark Web" for a while.

Yet even more left-leaning academics like Marxist historian Terry Eagleton have written devastating critiques of New Atheism. (He famously compared Dawkins's writing on theology to someone "holding forth on biology whose only knowledge of the subject is the *Book of British Birds*."[34]) And, like Holland, he has repeatedly pointed out to his secular contemporaries that Christianity's central story of self-sacrificial love is the revolutionary force that has most shaped the moral arc of the West, rather than the value-neutral project of science.

These are just some of the secular players who have been pushing back against the simplistic assumptions of New Atheism and who have begun a new conversation on the value of Christianity in an increasingly fragmented society. We will revisit some of their stories in future chapters.

Some of them still describe themselves as atheists; some admit to a soft spot for Christianity or even seem to be on a journey of reconnecting with faith. Others have invented their own labels. (Douglas Murray, as we've seen, has adopted the epithet "Christian atheist" for himself.) Either way, they are all convinced that a meaning crisis has overtaken the West that neither atheistic humanism, liberal progressivism, or any other variety of secularism is capable of responding to.

PETERSON AND GOD

As already mentioned, there has been feverish speculation about whether Jordan Peterson may yet embrace orthodox Christian belief. Throughout the debate I chaired between him and Susan Blackmore, you could have been forgiven for thinking that Peterson was already a full-blooded Christian apologist, so vigorously did he defend a Christian worldview against her atheism.

Yet Peterson has consistently refused to be pinned down on his personal religious convictions. When I pressed him on it, he described himself as a "religious man" who was "conditioned in every cell as a consequence of the Judeo-Christian worldview." The closest I could get to whether he really believed in God was that he lives his life "as though God exists," saying, "The fundamental hallmark of belief is how you act, not what you say about what you think."[35]

Peterson frequently applies the Jungian language of value hierarchy to this phenomenon. In our interview he insisted, "You have a hierarchy of values. You have to, otherwise you can't act, or you're painfully confused. Whatever is at the top of that hierarchy of values, serves the function of God for you."[36]

He's also openly critical of atheists such as Richard Dawkins, as their anti-religious polemic won't help anyone to actually live in the world. "The New Atheists have a hell of a time with an active ethic,"[37] he says. Indeed, Peterson has found more common ground with spiritual seekers like Russell Brand (both have appeared on each other's podcasts) than with his celebrity atheist interlocutors.

Which leads to the question of what Peterson actually believes about the unique claims of Christianity. During their debate, Susan Blackmore verbalized the frustration of her atheist peers. Peterson clearly believes in a scientific account of evolutionary psychology yet marries it with a fervent admiration for Bible stories that leaves many skeptics scratching their heads.

But Peterson was unapologetic, stating that "the biblical texts are foundational."[38] For instance, he believes the creation narrative in Genesis 1—in which God creates man and woman in his own image—is fundamental to our belief in the intrinsic dignity and equality of humans.

Likewise, he strongly endorses the effect of Christianity on the world, writing, "The Christian doctrine elevated the individual soul, placing slave and master and commoner and nobleman alike on the same metaphysical footing, rendering them equal before God and the law. . . . It is in fact nothing short of a miracle."[39]

Of course, recognizing the cultural and psychological debt we owe to Christianity is not the same thing as believing Jesus lived, died, and rose from the dead. Again, this is where Peterson becomes difficult to pin down. Christians don't just believe Christianity is socially useful; they believe it's true. But it's never quite clear where Peterson falls between those two options.

Similarly, a key question in the debate I hosted between Bret Weinstein and Alister McGrath centered on Weinstein's willingness to acknowledge the social and cultural benefits of religion even though he didn't believe in God. To that extent, he took the view that religion was useful rather than true. For many people, that is enough. They can get the benefits from practicing yoga without having to believe in the spiritual dimension of it. They can enjoy the feelings of goodwill that the Christmas season brings without believing that Jesus was born of a virgin.

But I'm not so convinced that we can forever enjoy the fruits of religion without the roots of religion, especially when it comes to Christianity.

Yes, we should be grateful for all that the Judeo-Christian heritage has gifted the West—human rights, democracy, and freedom of speech among them. However, as any student of history will tell you, these are rare fruits, uniquely cultivated in the soil of our specific Judeo-Christian heritage. How much longer will those concepts endure if the Christian identity of the West continues to wane and, in its place, multiple competing stories of identity and meaning continue to spring up?

These are the questions that also exercise many of the thinkers engaged in the new conversation on God. When Susan Blackmore confronted Peterson with the fact that once-Christian Scandinavian countries still lead the world in happiness and welfare despite their rapid embrace of secularism, he countered that these nations are still in the infancy of their post-Christian experiment. "They're stable to the degree that they're not secular," he said. "We're living on the corpse of our ancestors. But that stops being nourishing and starts to become rotten unless you replenish it. And I don't think we are replenishing it. We're living on borrowed time and are in danger of running out of it."[40]

Peterson recognizes the social utility of Christianity and fears for the future of the West in its absence. But again, recognizing something is useful doesn't make it actually true. Weinstein and Peterson seem to be willing to see Christianity as "metaphorically" true because it works. However, in the rest of this book I will be seeking to persuade you that the reason so many people are attesting again to the fact that Christianity works is because *it really is true.*

A NEW CONVERSATION BEGINS

So as we consider this new conversation that is happening, the question remains: Is Jesus really the divine Son of God? Or is Christ only a symbolic "archetype" (one of Peterson's favorite Jungian terms) who represents the perfection of the human condition? When asked by Catholic broadcaster Patrick Coffin whether he's ready to assert belief or disbelief in the historical resurrection of Jesus, Peterson replied, "I need to think about that for about three more years before I would even venture an answer."[41]

Peterson still seems to be thinking about it. Since his return to public life, the discussions he has chosen to engage in have increasingly focused on the realms of meaning, religion, and purpose. Perhaps the reason he continues to find such a large audience for these conversations is because he himself is still working out his own salvation in such a public way.

In conversation with Jonathan Pageau, an Eastern Orthodox Christian and sculptor of religious icons, Peterson struggled to contain his emotions as he spoke of his religious longings. Almost in tears, he described his growing comprehension that the "objective world" of history and fact and the "narrative world" of myth, meaning, and beauty seem to come together in the person of Jesus Christ, saying, "I'm amazed at my own belief, and I don't understand it."[42]

The psychologist is not afraid to wear his own emotions on his sleeve when he talks about such things, frequently tearing up in interviews or on stage. This too is part of his attraction.

He talks about people as though they have a soul. As if beauty, truth, and meaning really exist. Peterson has somehow broken through the intellectual firewall that often separates public thinkers from the "real world" of emotion, tragedy, and joy.

None of this means that Peterson should be hailed as the savior of the West or of Christianity (that job is already taken by Jesus Christ, as far as Christians are concerned). Some are also wary of the theological outworking of Peterson's take on Christianity. Practically speaking, it often boils down to a pull-yourself-up-by-your-own-bootstraps philosophy. One could argue there's more works than grace in such an approach.

Nevertheless, Peterson's reconnection of intellect, emotion, and spirituality is a powerful one. For a generation that has been starved of meaningful engagement with those faculties, it seems that a pressure valve has been released. "This is what I was looking for" is often the reaction from millennials who have been fed a meager diet of rationalism and science. And being given the opportunity to see the world in this new and unshackled way can often give people intellectual permission to explore Christianity.

Wherever the psychologist may personally find himself on the faith spectrum, he has been described as a "gateway drug" to orthodox Christian faith for others, and it's easy to see why. Indeed, his own wife Tammy and daughter Mikhaila Peterson have gone on record as having "found God" and an unprecedented peace through prayer and Bible reading.[43]

Peterson and the other public intellectuals who are following in his wake have identified the problem in the West: A lack of meaning. An identity crisis. The anxiety produced by living in a world without a story to live by.

But what can solve it? New Atheism has resolutely failed, but I don't believe the IDW and its cohort of new thinkers will successfully untangle this problem either. Yes, they are asking important questions, but they are far from having all the answers. Even someone with the cultural influence of Jordan Peterson—someone explicitly encouraging people to reconsider the value of Christianity—can't save the West from its meaning and identity crisis.

Why so? Because all these thinkers are pointing people back towards a story that is only useful if it is true. Yes, it may be "metaphorically powerful." But the power of a metaphor is contained in the fact that it ultimately points towards something that exists in reality. We cannot live on metaphors alone. We cannot use poetry, psychology, and myth to hold God at arm's length forever. What if this two-thousand-year-old story is only able to reconnect with our deepest desires for meaning, purpose, and identity because it is the true story to which all other stories point?

I sense that this generation is becoming primed to hear this story afresh.

CHAPTER 3

SHAPED BY
THE CHRISTIAN STORY

OCCASIONALLY I AM ASKED which of the conversations and debates I have hosted are my favorite. I often joke that the question is like asking me to choose a favorite from among my four children. But if I had to choose (a show, not a child!), then Tom Holland's dramatic clash with A. C. Grayling will always rank as one of the best.

Holland had just published his magnum opus, *Dominion: How the Christian Revolution Remade the World*. At over six hundred pages, it is a massive but extremely readable history of the way Christianity has shaped Western culture.

It is a magisterial piece of historical writing. The central argument is that, despite the protestations of modern secularists, the Western world's commitment to human equality, dignity, and value is intrinsically Christian in nature. Holland makes his case by galloping through two thousand years of history, from the Greek and Roman empires right up to the Beatles and the modern Me Too movement. Historical vignettes from across the centuries set the stage for the revolutions in politics, religion, science, and culture that are themselves aftershocks of the Christian revolution of the first century.

Needless to say, the faults and misdemeanors of the church down the ages are also laid bare. Yet time and again Holland returns to the "molten heart" of Christianity—the claim that God himself died the death of a slave.[1] That radical idea, says Holland, laid the foundation for the abolition of slavery, the modern welfare state, and even the freedom for people to reject religion in the modern world. Ironically, even modern atheism owes its origins to Christianity.

Consequently, it felt appropriate to bring A. C. Grayling—one of the world's leading atheist spokespersons—on with Holland. I knew it would be a showdown, and the intellectual sparks certainly flew.

Grayling, the master of the New College of the Humanities in London, is a respected philosopher and public intellectual. He turns his hand to a variety of subjects but has often been an outspoken and eloquent critic of Christianity. His books include *The God Argument*, in which he seeks to demolish a range of philosophical arguments for theism, and *The Good Book: A Secular Bible*, an alternative (and in his view superior) library of wisdom to the Hebrew and Christian Scriptures, compiled from secular sources.

In the run-up to the debate, Grayling had also recently published his own magnum opus, *The History of Philosophy*. As in Holland's book, Grayling sought to provide a narrative for the development of Western thought while cataloging the range of other philosophies that had emerged around the globe. Where they differed most sharply was in their assessment of the role of Christianity.

From the first page of the introduction, Grayling excoriated the church as a brake on progress historically. Having extolled the value of the art and literature produced by the Greeks and Romans, he turns to the Christians of the fourth century, writing,

> Christian zealots smashed statues and temples, defaced paintings and burned "pagan" books, in an orgy of effacement of previous culture that lasted for several centuries. . . . It is hard to comprehend, still less to forgive, the immense loss of literature, philosophy, history and general culture this represented.[2]

This particular claim proved to be the first of several dramatic flash points in the debate between Holland and Grayling. Holland, a meticulous historian, repeatedly challenged Grayling to produce actual evidence of this "orgy of effacement."

Grayling claimed the fact that we have, for instance, only seven of seventy plays written by the ancient tragedian Aeschylus is proof of the wanton destruction. But Holland pointedly repeated his request several times: How did Grayling know that "bands of Christians roamed around destroying copies of Aeschylus?" he asked. "We have no evidence for this whatsoever."[3]

On the contrary, said Holland, it was the monks of the early centuries that Grayling so readily dismissed in his book that we should thank for preserving almost all the copies of ancient literature and philosophy that continued to be the bedrock of classical education and learning into the Middle Ages.

According to Holland, Grayling was one more atheist who had bought into a myth primarily perpetuated by the eighteenth-century historian Edward Gibbon. Gibbon's highly influential *History of the Decline and Fall of the Roman Empire* had laid much of the blame for the loss of classical civilization at the feet of censorious, marauding Christians. It is an account which later historians, like Holland, describe as "to put it mildly, not exactly what happened."[4]

REASSESSING HISTORY

The version of history repeated by Grayling can be found in much of the literature of the New Atheists, for whom Christianity is perceived as having had a retrograde effect across the board. According to them, science, health, and ethics were all hamstrung by Christianity as it ushered in the Dark Ages and kept things dark for a long time. Only once the shackles of religion began to be thrown off during the Age of Enlightenment did rationalists, secular philosophers, and scientific pioneers get progress back on track.

But this popular narrative has increasingly been challenged by historians both within and outside the Christian fold.

One notable voice is Tim O'Neill, who runs the website *History for Atheists*. O'Neill is a nonbeliever himself but regularly critiques Internet skeptics who he says are mired in an "intellectually deadening and tone deaf combination of ideological bias and near total historical ignorance."[5]

As well as regular skirmishes with atheists from the "mythicist" tribe (he may not believe Jesus was divine, but O'Neill is certain he existed), he regularly writes to correct those who parrot the claim that Christendom was responsible for a thousand years of superstition, drudgery, and persecution. In fact, says O'Neill (along with almost every modern scholar of the period), the Dark Ages were a period in which art, agriculture, and learning blossomed in ecclesiastical centers of learning established by the church.

O'Neill also writes to debunk a related skeptical assumption: that the West's embrace of human values, rights, and democracy, and the accompanying rise of education, welfare, and science, are all the gift of a secular enlightenment that had finally managed to jettison its religious baggage.

Others have been telling a similar alternative story of how we got to where we are.

These include the late secular historian Rodney Stark, whose influential books such as *The Rise of Christianity* have reevaluated the countercultural nature of the early Christian communities. He has argued that Christianity was the pivot point that turned civilization in a radically new direction, from a culture in which many lives were regarded as cheap and expendable towards the valuing of every human life.

In recent years, works such as *The Evolution of the West* by Nick Spencer, *Atheist Delusions* by David Bentley Hart, and *The Air We Breathe* by Glen Scrivener have continued to press the ways in which Western culture's beliefs about human dignity, equality, and flourishing were shaped not by our Greek and Roman forebears nor by rationalist philosophers but by the Christian story that ultimately overtook the classical world and from which the Enlightenment itself was shaped and molded.

Holland, then, is hardly alone in championing a reappraisal of the influence of Christianity on the modern world. Perhaps the reason he has become such a prominent spokesperson is that he has straddled both the secular and Christian worlds in doing so. Like Jordan Peterson, Douglas Murray, and others, Holland has a story of being a secular thinker who has nevertheless become increasingly attracted to the moral and spiritual qualities of Christian faith.

A CHANGE OF MIND

Holland has been open about his own changing relationship with Christianity. When I invited him to a discussion with eminent New Testament scholar N. T. Wright, Holland explained where his love for ancient history began:

> I was the kind of child who loved dinosaurs. I liked them because they were big and they were fierce and they were glamorous, and they were extinct. . . . It was a seamless movement from Tyrannosaurus Rex to Caesar. The glamor

and the beauty and the power and the cruelty of the Greeks and the Romans I found very appealing.[6]

Having been raised and confirmed in the Anglican church, Holland explained how his childhood beliefs fizzled out in his teenage years as the "dimmer switch" of faith seemed to get turned down:

> I went to Sunday school and was very interested in biblical history, but I found them all a bit po-faced. I didn't like their beards. I preferred the clean-shaven look of Apollo. In a way I was seduced by the glamor of Greece and Rome, so the first books I wrote about history were about Greece and Rome.

The early books included *Rubicon*, *Persian Fire*, and *Dynasty: The Rise and Fall of the House of Caesar* and established his reputation as a bestselling author of popular historical writing.

But Holland's journey through the classical world also served as a stark reminder of how utterly different his own attitudes towards life, death, and human existence were to those ancient forebears for whom slavery, sexual exploitation, and a disregard for the weak and vulnerable were part of everyday culture. "The more you live in the minds of the Romans," he said, "and I think even more the Greeks, the more alien they come to seem. And what becomes most frightening is a quality of callousness that I think is terrifying because it is completely taken for granted."

By way of example, Holland described one of Caesar's campaigns:

> Caesar is, by some accounts, slaughtering a million Gauls and enslaving another million in the cause of boosting his political career and, far from feeling in any way embarrassed about this, he's promoting it. And when he holds his triumph, people are going through the streets of Rome carrying billboards boasting about how many people he's killed.

Holland summarized what was so troubling about this: "This is a really terrifyingly alien world, and the more you look at it, the more you realize that it is built on systematic exploitation. . . . In almost every way, this is a world that is unspeakably cruel to our way of thinking. And this worried me more and more."

This steadily growing awareness of how little he actually held in common with the culture of the ancient world was intensified when Holland turned his attention to late antiquity and the emergence of the Islamic empire for his book *In the Shadow of the Sword*: "There were aspects of Islam that were very familiar, but there were many aspects of it that again seemed deeply, deeply alien."

In fact, the book and his accompanying TV documentary *Islam: The Untold Story*, which questioned aspects of the historicity of Muhammad's life and the reliability of the Koran, led to intense controversy and even death threats from radical Islamists. As a liberal Westerner committed to concepts like freedom of speech and expression, Holland found himself again reminded of how peculiar his outlook was to many cultures both past and present.

It was obvious that the modern West's particular view of the world, so foreign to much of history and culture, had not appeared out of a vacuum. It was the product of one particular story. "I began to realize that actually, in almost every way, I am Christian," said Holland.

HUMANIST FAITH

Unsurprisingly, when Holland began publicly talking about his intellectual reorientation towards Christianity, his ideas were not met with universal agreement.

The historian (who is a keen Twitter user) would occasionally get into online spats with humanist spokespeople. They insisted that the concepts of human dignity, equality, and justice which framed their humanist morality owed more to classical civilizations and the secular enlightenment than Christianity. Holland on the other hand has increasingly insisted that the philosophy of secular humanism itself was a direct product of the Judeo-Christian heritage that birthed it.

He drove this point home during another flash point in his debate with Grayling (a vice president of Humanists UK) by pulling out a sheet of paper listing all the international cities where world humanist conferences had taken place since 1952. After reeling off London, Oxford, Miami, Washington, Oslo, Amsterdam, Brussels, Paris, Buffalo, Hanover, and Boston, Holland pointed out that, with the exception of Mumbai in 1999, all the locations were in "basically Christian countries." This, he said, was evidence that "humanism is a kind of godless Protestantism. It is in that sense as culturally contingent as everything else in the vast range and span of human civilization."[7]

Others have argued in similar ways that the very concept of human rights that undergirds the humanistic worldview is itself radically contingent upon a Christian understanding of what it is to be human.

For instance, the Universal Declaration of Human Rights (UDHR), drafted in 1948 and forged in the aftermath of two World Wars, enshrines in its very first article that "all human beings are born free and equal in dignity and rights."[8]

When I invited well-known humanist Steven Pinker to debate human morality and progress on an episode of *The Big Conversation*, the Harvard philosopher insisted that the document "has not a shred of Christianity in it."[9]

At one level, Pinker is correct. The UDHR is ostensibly a secular document, deliberately drafted to allow people of many cultures and worldviews to agree on the language used. But that doesn't stop the language from sounding almost religious in nature when it states that human beings are "endowed with reason and conscience and should act towards one another in a spirit of brotherhood."[10]

Pinker's discussion opponent Nick Spencer argued that much

of the document (which had been drafted in large part by Charles Malik, a Lebanese Christian) drew on the notion of a "person" as defined by Catholic social teaching.

The document goes on to list numerous fundamental rights and freedoms around belief, justice, health, race, and education. In Pinker's view, these concepts flow from the scientific fact that humans all share the same DNA along with their rational and emotional capacities: "The fact we're made of the same stuff, we're the same species, we all are sentient, we all have the capacity to experience pleasure and pain, we all have the capacity to reason. That is a pretty rock-solid foundation for universal human rights and universal human dignity."[11]

But Spencer was skeptical:

> I don't doubt that many of my atheist friends are committed
> to human dignity or human equality. But I can't see where
> the deep foundations for that are. I don't think reason, in
> and of itself, let alone science, acts as a sufficiently robust
> foundation for that commitment. . . . I would push back
> on the idea that simply being rational or being made of
> the same stuff is enough to justify our humanism.[12]

Like Spencer, I find it hard to justify the idea that such lofty concepts as the inherent freedom, equality, and dignity of all humans can be grounded in abstract scientific facts or our capacity for reason.

What exactly is it about being born with the genetic identity of Homo sapiens that suddenly confers the UDHR's long list of inalienable rights and freedoms upon an individual? Science itself has nothing to say on the matter. And when it comes to atrocities such as the Nazis' eugenics programs, science has frequently been employed to the detriment of these rights.

An even more famous document, the United States Declaration of Independence, states that "we hold these truths to be self-evident, that all men are created equal, that they are endowed by their Creator with certain unalienable Rights, that among these are Life, Liberty and the pursuit of Happiness."[13]

In this case, the framers of the Declaration were happy to employ religious language. But in reality, the "self-evident" nature of human equality and rights only seems self-evident to those who have inherited the same Christian assumptions that the founding fathers brought with them to the United States.

Contrary to the claims of contemporary humanists such as Pinker, the existence of these rights and freedoms is not at all self-evident in the absence of God. They do not present themselves simply by an act of rational reflection or by recognizing that we are made of the same stuff. For most of human history they were not recognized by the vast majority of cultures and are still not in many parts of the world today.

A notable atheist thinker who seems to have truly recognized the contingency of our embrace of human rights is Yuval Noah Harari. Commenting on the Declaration of Independence in his bestselling book *Sapiens*, he writes, "The Americans got the idea of equality from Christianity, which argues that every person has a divinely created soul, and that all souls are equal before God. However, if we do not believe in the Christian myths about God, creation and souls, what does it mean that all people are 'equal'? Evolution is based on difference, not on equality."[14]

As Tom Holland has stated, secular humanists who believe in the existence of human rights and treat them as sacrosanct are being just as theological in their assumptions about reality as the Christian who believes they are conferred by a divine Creator.

EXPLAINING MORALITY

So how do we explain the grounding for this widespread belief in the moral value of humans? When it comes to human morality and how atheism tries to account for it, there are two separate arguments to be parsed out. The first one concerns the notion of morality itself and whether it is even a coherent concept in the atheist worldview.

In my first book, *Unbelievable?: Why, after Ten Years of Talking with Atheists, I'm Still a Christian*, I spent a chapter explaining why I don't believe atheists have good grounds for believing in objective morality. Please note that this is not the same as saying that atheists are not moral. Most atheists naturally adhere to the same moral codes of behavior as the people around them. Indeed, some of my atheist friends are among the most ethical people I know.

However, in the absence of God, I don't believe there are grounds to believe that such moral codes amount to anything more than subjective opinions or the fashion of the age. In a godless universe there is no ultimate moral standard against which our efforts can be measured. We are all making it up as we go along. The atheist may be happy to agree with this. "Morality changes with the times," they may say, "just another subjective product of the socio-evolutionary forces that shape our cultures."

The problem with this account of reality is that none of us actually behave as though our moral beliefs are simply the latest instance of a constantly evolving moral zeitgeist. In fact, when it comes to the most heinous acts of evil and the most generous acts of goodness, we treat morality as having a very fixed and real nature. When we declare racism to be wrong, we aren't merely stating our current feelings about the issue; we mean that it has always been wrong and always will be. Our forebears who didn't recognize this in the past were gravely mistaken, and we know better now.

But this view of a fixed and objective nature to morality is at odds with the atheist worldview. In a purely naturalistic account of things there is no moral arc embedded in the universe, no "ought" to the "is" of physical reality. How do we square this circle? In summary, I argued that, if there is indeed a "true north" to our moral compass—a highest ideal towards which life should be lived—then it must find its home in something beyond ourselves. If there is a moral law, then there must be a moral lawgiver. And the best candidate for that job is God.

However, whether or not an atheist is convinced by that somewhat philosophical argument, there is a second and separate issue that needs addressing: How did we arrive at the morality we currently inhabit? This is a historical rather than a metaphysical question. But the answer, in my view, still points back to God.

As historians such as Holland have made clear, there is a very specific story of how modern Western values were shaped by the Christian revolution that took place two thousand years ago. For the sake of brevity, I will sketch out just two key moral beliefs in our Western culture, the development of which were profoundly influenced by Christianity. First, our belief in human dignity and equality, and second, the belief in our duty to protect the weakest in society.

HUMAN DIGNITY AND EQUALITY

The first moral belief we'll examine is the concept of the intrinsic dignity and equality of all human beings. Arguably, these are ideas that had their genesis (forgive the pun) in the very first page of the Bible. In its poetic opening chapter, Genesis 1:27 states,

So God created humans in his image,
in the image of God he created them;
male and female he created them.

Other ancient Near Eastern religions and pagan mythologies had their own creation stories too, but this one was different.

Old Testament scholar John Walton writes, "Mesopotamian literature is concerned about the jurisdiction of the various gods in the cosmos with humankind at the bottom of the heap. The Genesis account is interested in the jurisdiction of humankind over the rest of creation as a result of the image of God in which people were created."[15]

This uniquely Jewish idea—that humans, both male and female, bear the image of the creator God and exist to become cocreators within his creation—placed an unprecedented deposit of inherent value and dignity on the human race. No other origins account put humans at the apex of the creation narrative, nor invested them with this unparalleled status.

Again, Walton writes, "Since all people are in the image of God, all deserve to be treated with the dignity the image affords."[16]

Admittedly, many books could be filled with how inconsistently this ethic has been applied throughout history by those who claimed to be inspired by the Scriptures. Nevertheless, despite Christendom's frequent failures to live up to its ideals, the assumption of an "Imago Dei" residing in each human being has been foundational to today's secular framings of human dignity and equality.

However, the road from Genesis to our modern embrace of human rights didn't run through Rome or Athens; it ran through Bethlehem, Nazareth, and Jerusalem.

Slavery in the Ancient World

The belief that all people should be treated with inherent dignity and equality of status regardless of gender, ethnicity, sexuality, disability, economic status, or any other characteristic is so taken for granted by most people in the modern West that we barely question it. Yet to the majority of previous civilizations, it would have been regarded as bizarre in the extreme.

For most of human history the treatment of some types of people as less valuable than others has been the norm. The institution of slavery is one of the most obvious examples.

In the Greek and Roman world, slavery was regarded not only as essential to economic prosperity but also as part of the natural order of things. Aristotle summarized the attitude of his peers when he wrote, "For that some should rule and others be ruled is a thing not only necessary, but expedient; from the hour of their birth, some are marked out for subjection, others for rule."[17]

In the early Roman empire, as many as one in five people were slaves. The buildings, infrastructure, and commerce essential to its civilization would have been built upon the backs of slaves who did the jobs no one else wanted to do. The slave trade was a booming market, and successful military campaigns were commonly the entry point for whole swaths of people to become enslaved to the victors.

While some slaves held positions of authority and would sometimes be able to work towards freedom, in general a slave was regarded as less than a person. They were not allowed to own property, had little recourse to justice or basic rights, and were typically subject to corporal punishment and, in some cases, summary execution. When the senator Lucius Pedanius Secundus was murdered by one of his slaves, the senate approved the execution of all four hundred of his household slaves as punishment.

What to our modern ears and eyes seems unconscionable was, to the ancient world, simply the way things worked. The life of a slave was cheap. This was especially true of the sexual exploitation of slaves. Whereas women were generally expected to remain faithful to their husbands, a male master was at liberty to satiate his desires with as many prostitutes and slaves as he wished. During his debate with A. C. Grayling, Tom Holland graphically described the uses to which slaves were put:

> They were expected to be used as sexual objects. The Romans had the same word for "urinate" and "ejaculate," and essentially the mouths, the vaginas, the anuses of slaves were regarded as akin to urinals; these are objects in which bodily fluid can be ejected by the master. And that is their role, absolutely taken for granted.[18]

Spending time immersed in the world of Greek and Roman culture was what had caused Holland to begin to appreciate the radical distinctiveness of Christianity. Now, to see the apostle Paul write, "There is no longer Jew or Greek; there is no longer slave or free; there is no longer male and female, for all of you are one in Christ Jesus" (Galatians 3:28) struck home as a revolutionary egalitarian statement about ethnicity, gender, and social status.

Likewise, Holland believes that the early Christians' insistence on monogamy for both husband and wife and sexual abstinence for the unmarried was groundbreaking, especially because of the dignity it meant for slaves who joined the Christian community alongside free citizens:

> The doctrine on sexuality that Paul preaches is deeply founded in this idea that slavery is something to be overcome and that everybody has been liberated by the sacrifice of Christ. He is saying that every human being, by virtue of Christ's sacrifice and death, now has a value. And he specifically says that they have a bodily integrity. . . . That gave a dignity to a household slave that he'd never been given before.[19]

Many modern eyes have looked back on Paul's insistence on chastity, monogamy, and the longstanding Christian sexual ethic it birthed as repressive and puritanical. But set in the context of ancient Rome, it was a rule of life that offered dignity and stability both to women and to slaves. The fact that most secular societies now observe mutual consent and fidelity as a minimal expectation of sexual propriety is a reminder of how deeply entrenched that Christian ethic remains, even when societies have discarded its other prohibitions. Holland even makes the case that contemporary movements like Me Too, which denounce the sexual abuse of women, are still fundamentally appealing to the virtues and values of self-control and mutual person-hood that Christianity first brought to the table.

In recent years, other secular writers have also been recognizing the unique value of Christian monogamy in shaping the Western world. In his book *The WEIRDest People in the World*, evolutionary biologist Joseph Henrich argues that the Christian "Marriage and Family Program"[20] of the church was largely responsible for the development of the uniquely WEIRD (Western, Educated, Industrialized, Rich, Democratic) nature of Europe. Likewise, in her book *The Case against the Sexual Revolution*, feminist author and journalist Louise Perry has written a spirited critique of the porn-saturated, hyper-sexualized, hookup culture of the modern world. She argues that a return to a Judeo-Christian sexual ethic of chastity and monogamy is in the best interest of both men and women. At the root of all these books is a basic recognition that Christianity changed how we think about the value of men and women, slaves and free, and the way we should treat them.

Responding to an Important Objection

At this point a skeptic may naturally (and rightly) point out that Christian history and the Bible itself don't have clean hands when it comes to slavery.

In the latter case, the Old Testament certainly assumes slavery as part of the status quo in the ancient Near East and, at various points, affirms its place through the laws in the Torah. But as many scholars have pointed out, the regulations laid down for the treatment of slaves in the Hebrew Scriptures were leagues ahead of those adhered to by surrounding nations. This was not the chattel slavery of the trans-atlantic slave trade (which we shall come to) but something more like indentured servitude. Frequently, to sell oneself into this form of service was the only way of ensuring survival or economic stability.

Was this the ideal for humans envisaged by Genesis 1? Certainly not. But as many theologians have pointed out, in bringing about his purposes, God may choose to accommodate the cultural norms of a society as it is rather than move it immediately to where it should be. Much of the Old Testament is the story of God gradually drawing hardhearted and sinful people out of the practices of the pagan cultures around them towards a radical new awareness of his moral law and his perfect love. But the work of changing human hearts and human culture is a marathon, not a sprint—it takes time. This plays out throughout the whole story of the Jewish people. Having been slaves under the Egyptians themselves, they were reminded time and again that they were to be a light to the nations, bearing the promise of a future freedom. But that light would take a long time to break through in its fullness.

Fast-forward to the New Testament, and we still never receive an explicit denunciation of the institution of slavery. In some instances Paul seems to condone it by giving advice in his epistles on how relations between masters and slaves should be conducted. But it would be a mistake to assume Paul was advocating for the status quo. Certainly he would have entertained no illusions that within his lifetime the Christian community could disestablish the institution of slavery in the society they were part of. And yet his reworking of the household codes was remarkable for the way in which they commanded Christian masters and slaves to recognize each other as brothers and sisters in Christ. And when he sends the runaway slave Onesimus back to his master Philemon, it is with the instruction to receive him "no longer as a slave but more than a slave, a beloved brother" (Philemon 1:16).

But what about the horrors of the transatlantic slave trade and the fact that Christian slave masters and financiers often used Bible verses from both the Old and New Testaments to justify their actions?

From the sixteenth to the nineteenth century the transatlantic slave trade saw between ten and twelve million enslaved Africans transported to the Americas, many perishing in the inhuman conditions of the ships, while those who survived faced brutality and servitude. It was one of the greatest evils our world has ever known. The complicity of those who called themselves Christians is not something we can sanitize or wave away. The centuries-long subjugation of Black Africans is a scar that will always mark the conscience of Christendom.

With that in mind, it's worth remembering that the same Scriptures that were misused by those who plucked verses out of context to justify slavery on the plantations also inspired the Quakers and evangelicals such as William Wilberforce and Frederick Douglass in the abolition movement that would eventually bring an end to the transatlantic slave trade and ultimately outlaw slavery entirely. Likewise, the champions of the later Civil Rights Movement such as Rev. Martin Luther King Jr. were deeply inspired by the Israelites' own exodus from slavery in the Old Testament and Paul's vision in the New Testament of Jew, Gentile, male, female, slave, and free being united in Christ.

Paul was moving in the natural direction that Christ's own ministry had established—the Christ who in his incarnation took on "the form of a slave," according to Philippians 2; the one who lived among the poor and downtrodden, ministering to both masters and servants; the one who ultimately died the kind of humiliating death reserved for rebellious slaves and criminals. The trajectory for emancipation was established by the Christian revolution even though it took several centuries for it to be brought to completion. Slavery was first dissipated with the fall of the Roman empire in the fifth century, and then the impetus moved through Europe and Britain, until by medieval times, slavery in the Christian West was effectively a thing of the past.

Note, however, that this was something only achieved in Christendom. Slavery existed unchallenged for millennia in many other civilizations. It was only formally outlawed in many Muslim countries in the latter half of the twentieth century, and arguably in these cases because of pressure from the Christian West. As historian

Rodney Stark said, the "moral potential for an antislavery conclusion"[21] was only possible within Christian thought.

Sadly, there are still many parts of the world where slavery, while not state-sanctioned, still exists in practice through human trafficking, especially in the sex trade. Many Christians continue to work at the forefront of modern antislavery campaigns.

CARING FOR THE WEAKEST

Contrasting our own world with that of antiquity serves to highlight how radically Christianity has changed our view of human equality. The same is true—perhaps more so—of the second moral belief I want to sketch out: the importance of serving and protecting the most vulnerable.

Christ's repeated commands to his followers—to serve rather than be served, to love the outcast, to treat the poorest and weakest with special respect—were revolutionary in his own day but were backed up by his own example of compassion and love.

Jesus' description of a kingdom in which the first will be last and the last will be first still sounds topsy-turvy, even to modern ears. But we have at least become accustomed to the idea that no one should be left to starve when others have food to eat, that the sick or disabled should be looked after if there are people to care for them, and that those who are threatened by violence should be defended by those able to stand in harm's way.

These moral views manifest themselves in all manner of practical ways—the safety net of the welfare state; charities dedicated to serving the poor; hospitals and infirmaries; public vaccination programs, soup kitchens, food banks, and homeless shelters; international peacekeeping forces. The list goes on. All these humanitarian enterprises exist on the assumption that the lives of the poorest and most vulnerable deserve our compassion and respect. But, again, we didn't inherit these views from the ancient Greeks and Romans.

The ancient historian Rodney Stark is well-known for his thesis on why the early Christian church grew so quickly as it spread across the Mediterranean world. As already described, it naturally held an attraction for slaves and the underclass. But the number of women who committed themselves to Christianity, of both high and low rank, was also unprecedented.

This, says Stark, was because of the way women (commonly viewed as second-class citizens in the ancient world) were treated differently within the fledgling Christian community. "Christianity was unusually appealing because within the Christian subculture women enjoyed far higher status than did women in the Greco-Roman world at large."[22]

Stark posits another remarkable reason for the preponderance of women in the movement, stating that "an initial shift in sex ratios resulted from Christian doctrines prohibiting infanticide and abortion."[23]

"Exposure" was a common practice in the ancient world, one that was legal and advocated by the greatest minds of the day (such as Plato). Newborn babies were left on hillsides or refuse dumps to die of starvation or at the mercy of wild animals. Parents supposedly believed that because they were not directly killing the infant, they were innocent of their death. Fate, the gods, or a passerby could theoretically intervene to save them.

The most frequent victims of this practice were either baby girls or those born with physical deformities due to the economic disadvantages that their disability or gender carried in that culture. Stark states that "exposure of unwanted female infants and deformed male infants was legal, morally accepted, and widely practiced by all social classes in the Greco-Roman world . . . even in large families 'more than one daughter was practically never reared.'"[24]

While such a practice may appear utterly abhorrent to our modern instincts, it appears to have been almost entirely unremarkable to the ancients. A letter from a Roman soldier to his pregnant wife gives a sense of how cheap the life of a newborn was: "I am still in Alexandria. . . . I beg and plead with you to take care of our little child, and as soon as we receive wages, I will send them to you. In the meantime, if (good fortune to you!) you give birth, if it is a boy, let it live; if it is a girl, expose it."[25]

Rescue and Adoption

So what changed between then and now? In a word, Christianity.

"Thou shalt not murder a child by abortion nor kill them when born" was the command given in the early apostolic teaching of the Didache,[26] and it was embodied in the actions of Christians who scoured sites where infants were typically abandoned in order to rescue them. Christians became well known for the rescue and adoption of these children and, as Stark indicates, the number of infant girls rescued significantly contributed to the prominent place of women in early Christian communities.

Opposition to infanticide was not unprecedented. Jews were forbidden from the practice, and Jewish writers such as Josephus and Philo of Alexandria expressed abhorrence at the behaviors of their Greek and Roman counterparts. The significance of the Torah's doctrine that all people, male and female, were created in God's image ran deep in Jewish thinking.

However, it was that same view of the sacred nature of all human life as expressed in the activism and mission of the early Christian communities that actually changed the world. Gradually, the practice of exposure came to be seen as barbarous and was legally forbidden in the Roman world by the late fourth century. In due course, churches became the place where children who were unwanted or could not be cared for were left, and Christians founded the earliest orphanages. Many of today's leading fostering and adoption agencies have a Christian heritage that was founded in this tradition of rescuing abandoned babies.

Poverty and Plague

If orphaned newborn infants represent an obvious example of the most vulnerable form of human life in the early centuries, then so do widows, the poor, and the sick. In a patriarchal culture in which ownership of property and economic independence lay in the hands of men, the life of a woman who had lost her husband was precarious. If she had no independent means, her best hope was to be remarried as soon as possible or face economic destitution. Likewise, in the absence of a welfare state, the lives of the poor would have hung in the balance.

It's significant, then, to see that, from the birth of the Christian church as described in the book of Acts, provision for widows, orphans, the poor, and the sick was prioritized: "There was not a needy person among them, for as many as owned lands or houses sold them and brought the proceeds of what was sold. They laid it at the apostles' feet, and it was distributed to each as any had need" (Acts 4:34-35).

The remarkable thing about the almsgiving described is that, unlike the other cultures of the time, it was not predicated on ethnicity or familial ties (early disputes described in Acts involved ensuring the equal treatment of widows from different ethnic backgrounds) and was radical in its generosity. This marked out the nature of Christian charity from the beginning. It would go on to be expressed in the way Christians cared for the poor and sick outside of their own communities.

Another significant example of this is the way Christians responded to epidemics (something we've become all too familiar with on a global scale in recent years). When plagues swept through the cities of the Mediterranean world in the first and second centuries, the upper and middle classes fled for the safety of the countryside to escape disease. In contrast, the early Christians headed in the opposite direction—into the plague-ridden cities and towns to care for the sick and destitute. Rodney Stark writes,

Indeed, the impact of Christian mercy was so evident that in the fourth century when the emperor Julian attempted to restore paganism, he exhorted the pagan priesthood to compete with the Christian charities . . . noting that "the impious Galileans [Christians], in addition to their own, support ours, [and] it is shameful that our poor should be wanting our aid."[27]

N. T. Wright explains why the appeal of Christianity became so strong under such conditions:

[People] looked at these funny Christians who they'd always thought were weird, for all the usual reasons—and they said, "Why did you do that? Why did you come and nurse us? We're not your family. We're not your tribe." And [the Christians] would say, "It's because we follow this man called Jesus, who went about doing good and touching lepers and touching corpses and risking uncleanness in order to bring health."[28]

It's difficult to overstate just how radical this active commitment to the value of all human life was. Rich and poor, male and female, Jew and Gentile, slave and free were all included in the embrace of the new community of Christians. N. T. Wright has coined an extended description to encompass its unique nature:

It was known, and was for this reason seen as both attractive and dangerous, as a worship-based, spiritually renewed, multi-ethnic, polychrome, mutually supportive, outward-facing, culturally creative, chastity-celebrating, socially responsible fictive kinship group, gender-blind in leadership, generous to the poor and courageous in speaking up for the voiceless.[29]

In a word, it was the church.

In due course the church would go on to establish the earliest hospitals, almshouses, and centers of learning for medicine and nursing that would be the foundation for the modern health service in the West. Likewise, there is barely any other aspect of modern life and culture that has not been deeply influenced by our Christian past. Education and schooling; family and marriage; music, literature, and art; government and democracy; international law; and even technology and science (as we shall see in later chapters) have all been shaped in the wake of the Christian revolution.

More than anything, however, it was the fundamental moral instincts of the West that were shaped by this countercultural community, founded on the example of a messiah-king who lived among the poor and died the death of a rebel slave. When we exalt humility and compassion, or champion the equality and dignity of every human being, we are walking in the footsteps of Jesus Christ.

OUR MORAL INSTINCTS

This claim was at the center of Holland's debate with Grayling: that the rights and values espoused by secular humanism are not a product of the Greeks and Romans, or the enlightenment rationalism which Grayling stands in the tradition of, but are instead entirely dependent upon the Christian vision of the West.

Like the proverbial goldfish who fails to realize there is such a thing as water, we are all swimming in the moral water of Christianity, even if most people don't recognize it. It acts as a constant filter to our vision of reality, like the pair of spectacles we forget we are wearing on the end of our nose.

At various points in their debate, Grayling (quite justly) raised the failings of Christendom's history. From crusades and inquisitions to modern-day sex scandals, there is much that the church should be ashamed has happened on its watch. Yet ironically, to even recognize these events as moral failures is only possible because we are judging them on the basis of Christian values and virtue. When modern people rightly condemn the hypocrisy of Christian slave traders of the past, or even the morality of the Bible itself, they are doing so through the moral filter they have inherited from Christianity and the Bible.

This is why, when I later interviewed Tom Holland about his personal journey of faith, he likened the moral vision the West had inherited as more akin to a set of "instincts" than "values."[30] Today, the idea that all humans are equal in dignity and worth and are deserving of compassion and protection is simply assumed by everybody, not something that needs arguing for.

However, Holland's time spent in the company of the ancient Greeks and Romans made him realize that those instincts were entirely contingent on the Christian story of reality. They were not the instincts of other ancient civilizations, nor were they handed down through the rational observation of a materialistic universe, as many of his atheistic peers seemed to believe.

"The tenets of secular liberalism are as fantastical as the tenets of the Christianity from which it's emerged," says Holland. To that extent, "faith" in something supernatural is exercised by the atheist who believes in the existence of immaterial realities like human rights as much as by the Christian who believes in God, according to Holland.

But the historian's journey has not only been an intellectual one. He told me how his deep dive into Christian history had left him feeling "bored" with an "anemic" form of secular liberalism:

> I find abstract principles quite dull. Christianity is not only
> the source of these, but the explanations that it gives for
> why we believe these things are infinitely more dramatic and
> interesting and beautiful and complex. The experience of
> researching *Dominion* meant that I had to read an enormous
> amount of Christian writing from an enormous range of

sources and over an immense span of time. I found the process of doing this very, very seductive. I found them incredibly impressive.

ISIS, THE CROSS, AND THE ANGELS

Ultimately, it was a journey to the frontline of the Islamic State strongholds in Northern Iraq that most dramatically led Holland into a deeply personal appreciation of the Christian story of reality.[31]

In 2017 Holland presented a Channel 4 television documentary *ISIS: The Origins of Violence* covering the plight of the persecuted Christian and Yazidi minorities who had been overrun and forced to flee their homelands. At the time, ISIS was still in command of large swaths of territory. Bloodcurdling stories of atrocities against men, women, and children had regularly been in the news headlines. The documentary itself asked serious questions about whether the violence of the Islamic State was at odds with, or intrinsic to, Islamic thought.

Throughout the filming, Holland was by turns inspired, convicted, and sickened (literally) by what he encountered. He told me of a few particular incidents that left long-lasting impressions upon him.

The first was his encounter with Father Yousif Ibrahim, a Syriac Orthodox monk who oversaw the nearly 1,700-year-old Mar Mattai monastery perched on Mount Alfaf overlooking the Nineveh plains. Built like a fortress, it had provided a bastion of shelter for persecuted minorities fleeing terror. Holland described Father Yousif as "a man of palpable holiness and bravery." The way his faith led him to serve the most vulnerable struck Holland forcefully.

The second incident was a visit to Sinjar, a town which had only recently been liberated by Kurdish forces. It had been completely decimated by ISIS, whose frontline was still only a couple of miles away. The evidence of their campaign of persecution was everywhere: Body parts poking out from the rubble that lined the streets.

Blown-out doorways, daubed with the graffiti emblems that showed that Christians or Yazidis lived there. The homes of fathers and sons who had been rounded up to be shot; mothers and daughters captured to be sold as sex slaves.

It was also a town where ISIS had crucified people.

As a historian of antiquity, Holland knew all about crucifixion. It was an agonizing, brutal, and shameful form of public execution, used for centuries by the Roman empire to advertise the power they held over conquered peoples. Jesus was just one of hundreds of thousands of people who died by crucifixion under the Romans.

But walking through streets where "people had been put up on crosses and left in the burning sun like chunks of meat" suddenly transported Holland from something he had "understood in the abstract" to a far more concrete reality:

> It's possible to spend your whole life studying the Romans and never breathe in the dust of a town where people have been crucified. But when I did, I felt ashamed at the lack of historical empathy that I'd shown. And also the lack of curiosity in not wondering what it was that had changed since the time of Caesar and the time in which I was standing. To the Islamic State these crosses served as symbols of their power, and that's what they were to the Romans as well.
>
> Standing in Sinjar I realized that the existential abyss that I was feeling wasn't just my sense of dread and terror that I was close to the people who had done this. It was more profound than that. It was realizing the reality of a world in which the cross serves as a symbol of the power of the powerful to torture, torment, and kill the powerless, when instinctively to me, as someone who had grown up in a fundamentally Christian society, the cross served as the opposite.[32]

Seeing crosses used once again for the awful purpose for which they were first invented suddenly brought home to Holland the power of the cross, interpreted through the death of Jesus:

> We have to think ourselves into the sandals of the
> Romans to understand and properly appreciate just
> how unfathomably weird it is that today the cross, of all
> things, should instantly be the most recognizable cultural
> symbol that any human culture has developed. And that
> it symbolizes not power, but the opposite. That the victim
> will triumph.[33]

And finally, there were the angels.

While in Sinjar, Holland visited an Orthodox church originally built by refugees of the Armenian genocide a century before. The building had been gutted and the sanctuary "systematically desecrated" by ISIS, who had smashed statues, trampled icons underfoot, and even used power drills to destroy the stone altar.[34] Holland recalls picking up a picture lying in the rubble. It depicted the Annunciation—the angel Gabriel, wings unfurled, delivering the message to Mary that she would bear Jesus, Immanuel, God-with-us.

By his own admission, Holland says, "It was very hot. I was very jumpy, I was quite ill, and my mind was saturated with biblical stuff." But something strange happened:

> At that point I was open to the idea of there being angels.
> I was in a space where it didn't seem remotely impossible.
> It was a sweet sense of intoxication, that perhaps, actually,
> everything was weird and strange. And the moment you
> accept that there are angels, suddenly, the world just seems
> richer and more interesting.[35]

After his return home, and fully recovered, Holland says he was easily able to dismiss the experience on psychological grounds. But he found that he didn't really want to. "The memory of thinking that they might exist, was a really powerful one," he said. "It's like the memory of taking a drug. Everything seems more intense, more vivid, more beautiful, and you remember it wistfully. I think that was very transformative, because suddenly, I really wanted to believe it."

CHOOSE YOUR MIRACLE

To Holland, believing in the existence of human rights—the intrinsic equality of all humans and the duty to protect the vulnerable—is just as much an article of faith as belief in miracles, the existence of angels, and the resurrection of Jesus Christ. Finding himself unable to imagine a world without the former has led to an openness to a world that includes the latter.

So does Holland believe in Christianity—the story that God took on flesh in the person of Jesus Christ and through his life, death, and resurrection reconciled the world back to himself?

"Sometimes," he says with a wry smile. "Definitely at Easter, definitely at Christmas. At certain times and in certain places."[36]

Holland isn't being evasive or coy, just honest about the fact that integrating a "beautiful and complex" Christian faith into the less-contested but more mundane secular world around him is not without its challenges. He describes moments "when a bucket of cold water comes" and none of it seems possible. "There are times when I surrender to the power of this. And there are times when I just think no."[37]

Holland's hesitancy reminds me of the words of the man who comes to Jesus for the healing of his son and declares paradoxically, "I believe; help my unbelief!" (Mark 9:24). We are all a mixture of faith and doubt. Nevertheless, Holland seems to have become captivated by a story which speaks to his innermost desires and the nature of the world around him. "It makes sense in the most complete way of any metaphysics I can engage with."[38]

For Holland, the moments where belief seems most able to trump his doubts are when he enters into the story—not as an observer but as a participant in an ancient drama.

He loves old churches where the stones are soaked in the hopes, fears, and prayers of bygone worshipers. He has become a communicant member at one of London's oldest churches, where the choral tradition and Anglo-Catholic ritual seem to chime with his lifetime's work of imagining himself in the shoes (or indeed, sandals) of our ancient forebears.

"I want mystery. I want weirdness. I want strangeness. That's exactly what I want. I want everything that by and large, in its public manifestations, churches often seem to be a bit embarrassed about," he says.[39]

To that extent, Holland stands directly in the tradition of the earliest Christians. Their mysterious belief in the intrinsic dignity and worth of every human being—slave or free, male or female—was strange. By the standards of the day, their desire to serve the weakest and most vulnerable in society was weird. And all of this flowed from the strangest and most mysterious belief of all: that the Son of God had taken on flesh and surrendered himself to the humiliation of being crucified.

As Holland writes in *Dominion*, "The belief that the Son of the one God of the Jews had been tortured to death on a cross came to be so enduringly and widely held that today most of us in the West are dulled to just how scandalous it originally was."[40]

The citizens of the modern West have almost completely forgotten their founding story. Along with others, Holland has been helping them to remember the weirdness of the story that shaped their world. And, by comparison, how weird the world before the Christian revolution now appears to them.

In doing so, a world which (like Holland) increasingly finds itself dissatisfied with secular materialism and in which the foundations seem to be coming apart has perhaps begun to ask itself whether the story of Christianity could be true after all.

If the church is willing to risk being weird once more and to unapologetically tell its story of the God who became human, lived an exemplary life, suffered crucifixion, and was raised to life again, a new generation may yet find meaning in the midst of the rubble.

CHAPTER 4

REDISCOVERING
THE BIBLE

THE ACTOR DAVID SUCHET is most recognized for playing the role of Hercule Poirot. His portrayal of the plump Belgian detective became the definitive on-screen incarnation of the character for nearly twenty-five years across seventy TV and film adaptations of Agatha Christie's novels. Yet in person, Suchet is both slimmer (he wears a fat suit, apparently) and his voice much deeper than the character he portrays.

What many people don't know about the actor is that he is also a committed Christian. Even fewer know the story of his adult conversion.

When I interviewed Suchet about his stage and screen career, he told me how, while filming in the United States in 1986, a stray thought came to him while soaking in his hotel bathtub that would change the course of his life forever: "I was thinking about my late grandfather. He was for me very much alive, almost my guide. I used to talk to him. And I suddenly started thinking about the afterlife, because I said to myself, 'I don't believe in the afterlife. Why am I talking to my grandfather if I don't believe he's alive?'"[1]

Eureka moments happen in bathtubs, and it was this thought that led Suchet to get hold of a Bible and begin to investigate its claims.

Although the actor had grown up in a nominally religious household, none of it had stuck. The nearest he had come to religious practice was a fleeting interest in the Eastern spirituality embraced by the Beatles in the sixties and seventies. As far as Christianity was concerned, he wasn't even sure if Jesus was a strictly historical figure or not. However, from his dimly remembered divinity lessons, he recalled that the apostle Paul had written some letters. So he started with the book of Romans.

Suchet decided to employ the same technique he used when reading classic stage plays for the Royal Shakespeare Company, reading the book not as Scripture but as if it were the first draft that had ever been read—a letter written not just to those first readers but to him personally.

He admits that he struggled to comprehend the first several chapters of Romans. However, after reaching chapter 8, the apostle Paul's words seemed to speak across the two-thousand-year chasm in a powerful way:

> I suddenly found a way of existing, a way of thinking
> and behaving and caring and looking at the world, in a
> completely different way. By the end of that letter, I was very
> moved, very emotional. I believed I had found what I had
> been looking for. Forget the gurus, forget everything else.
> I'd found a new way of being, in the way he describes the
> Christian life.

That encounter in Romans sent Suchet back to the Gospels of Matthew, Mark, Luke, and John. There he met the figure of Jesus who had so captured the heart and mind of the zealous Jewish teacher Saul of Tarsus and who had tasked him, as the apostle Paul, to take the Good News to the Gentile world. In reading the Gospels, Suchet discovered the magnetic personality and sublime teachings of Jesus Christ, captured in a historically robust set of documents which, even at two thousand years' distance, were still capable of bringing another Gentile to the point of conversion. Suchet was baptized soon after.

STILL THE WORLD'S BESTSELLER

Today, the Bible has become such a culturally ubiquitous book that most people assume they know what it is about even if they've never actually read it. For that reason, many people dismiss its contents as outdated, irrelevant, and untrue on the basis of the background noise of a largely skeptical culture. Yet the Bible has a tenacious ability to surprise each new generation of readers when they actually open its pages.

Some three hundred years ago, one of the world's most famous skeptics of Christianity was the French writer and intellectual Voltaire. He is reputed to have said that "one hundred years from my day, there will not be a Bible on earth except one that is looked upon by an antiquarian curiosity-seeker."[2]

Of course, that is not what happened. In fact, the great irony of Voltaire's prediction is that, a century after his declaration, Voltaire's own home in Geneva, Switzerland, had become a storehouse for Bibles and tracts produced by the Evangelical Society of Geneva. Likewise, the same printing presses that had been used to print Voltaire's anti-religious pamphlets were being used to print their Bibles.

Similar sentiments to Voltaire's have been expressed by modern-day skeptics. All the horsemen of New Atheism have taken aim at the morality, historicity, and relevance of the Bible to a modern age.

Sam Harris has said, "I can go into any Barnes & Noble blindfolded and pull a book off a shelf which is going to have more relevance, more wisdom for the twenty-first century, than the Bible."[3] Other New Atheists such as Lawrence Krauss and Richard Dawkins disparage the Bible as the product of "Bronze Age peasants" or "desert tribes."[4]

Dawkins has famously taken aim at the Old Testament depiction of God as "arguably the most unpleasant character in all fiction: jealous and proud of it; a petty, unjust, unforgiving control-freak; a vindictive, bloodthirsty ethnic cleanser; a misogynistic, homophobic, racist, infanticidal, genocidal, filicidal, pestilential, megalomaniacal, sadomasochistic, capriciously malevolent bully."[5] It is a description the late Chief Rabbi Lord Jonathan Sacks condemned as "profoundly antisemitic."[6]

Dawkins has been similarly critical of the New Testament, dismissing its reliability by writing that "accounts of Jesus's resurrection and ascension are about as well-documented as Jack and the Beanstalk."[7]

Nevertheless, despite skeptics past and present predicting the demise of Christianity and its founding Scriptures, the Bible has a stubborn habit of refusing to die. Today the Bible remains the best-selling, most-published book in the world, bar none.

It dwarfs the book sales of the New Atheists themselves. Even J. K. Rowling's Harry Potter books—the bestselling novels of the twenty-first century at over five hundred million copies in print—pale in comparison to the estimated five to seven billion copies of the Bible that have been printed in its lifetime. Ironically, most of the world's Bibles are today produced in China, an officially atheistic country, where the Amity Printing Company churns out seventy Bibles per minute and celebrated printing its two hundred millionth Bible in 2019.[8]

Why has the Bible survived predictions of its death? Why does it still inform the lives of billions of people today? Like their forebear Voltaire, in their haste to cast aside the superstition of religion, the New Atheists have failed to comprehend that the Bible is not simply a moralistic history or science book to be picked apart and discarded when judged to be out of step with the modern world. It represents something far deeper than that.

In fact, I am convinced that this is another example of the turning tide of faith in our culture. As we shall see, many public intellectuals are no longer disparaging Scripture. Instead, they are recognizing that, regardless of its supernatural claims, the Bible contains a deep well of psychological, practical, and spiritual wisdom that has positively shaped culture in myriad ways.

THE BOOK THAT SHAPED THE WORLD

Some of the New Atheists themselves have been willing (albeit grudgingly) to grant the massive cultural debt owed to the Bible, especially William Tyndale's sixteenth-century translation and the King James Bible (also known as the Authorized Version) that followed it.

On the four hundredth anniversary of its publication, Christopher Hitchens wrote, "Though I am sometimes reluctant to admit it, there really *is* something 'timeless' in the Tyndale/King James synthesis. For generations, it provided a common stock of references and allusions, rivaled only by Shakespeare in this respect. It resounded in the minds and memories of literate people, as well as of those who acquired it only by listening."[9]

Likewise, even Richard Dawkins was prepared to fund a campaign to place a copy of the King James Bible in every school library across the UK, not because of any perceived moral value but because of its undisputed status as a "great work of literature."[10]

Indeed, no serious cultural critic, even those hostile to organized religion, can deny the cultural influence of the Bible.

First, there is the multitude of modern phrases it has given us: "salt of the earth," "good Samaritan," "going the extra mile." Even the self-styled moniker of Dawkins, Harris, Dennett, and Hitchens—"the four horsemen"—comes from the book of Revelation. Then there's the sublime poetry of passages such as Psalm 23 and the meditation on love in 1 Corinthians 13. In countless ways, the Bible's cadence, beauty, and rhythm has informed the poetry and literature of subsequent generations.

Dante, Milton, and Shakespeare are arguably among the greatest influences on Western literature, yet they all stand downstream from the Bible. Shakespeare himself was deeply influenced by Tyndale's translation of the New Testament. Directly or indirectly, all great works of Western literature have been fed by *the* great work of literature.

Pulitzer Prize–winning author Marilynne Robinson has described the Bible as "The Book of Books," writing, "Even when references to Scripture in contemporary fiction and poetry are no more than ornamental or rhetorical—indeed, even when they are unintentional— they are still a natural consequence of the persistence of a powerful literary tradition."[11]

When I interviewed veteran broadcaster Melvyn Bragg about his love of Tyndale's translation of the Bible (upon which the Authorized Version drew heavily), he explained why, despite no longer holding to the faith of his youth, he still had "Christianity branded into me somewhere" because of the pervading influence of the King James Version he had grown up with. And it wasn't only its literary impact. He described the "phenomenal social influence of the Bible" through "all sorts of culture, philanthropy, laws to alleviate poverty, in every way that you can think of."[12]

Bragg is dismayed that the Bible has been relegated to a subsection of Religious Studies and is no longer seriously read, listened to, or studied by most schoolchildren today (whereas Shakespeare remains a core part of most curricula):

I'm outraged by it. You wouldn't think of knocking down all the country's cathedrals because not that many people go. But we have knocked down cathedrals of language that are unique in the world. We should bring it back as a cultural force. They needn't believe if they don't want to, but as a cultural force, as something that holds this country together and did so for a lot of years—and could still—this is massively important.[13]

The Scriptures have also had an extraordinary impact beyond the English-speaking world.

Social reformer Vishal Mangalwadi, author of *The Book That Made Your World*, describes the far-reaching influence of the Bible globally, including in his own country of India. The missionaries who began translating the Bible into the mother tongue of thousands of different people groups were effectively responsible for the first official codification of those languages, leading to education and cultural progress that had never been available before. The biblical worldview that accompanied the missionaries led to the abolition of practices such as widow-burning and infanticide of baby girls. Mangalwadi even makes the case that when India forged an independent path from the British empire, it was largely because of the Christian worldview the empire's missionaries had brought with them: "We were always told that India's freedom was a result of Mahatma Gandhi's struggle; it was a surprise to learn that, in reality, India's freedom was a fruit of the Bible. Before the Bible, our people did not even have the modern notions of nation or freedom."[14]

Whether or not it's recognized or celebrated as it should be, there's little doubt about the cultural impact of the Bible in the English-speaking world and beyond. But the words which have shaped generations past have not simply done so on the basis of their literary genius. Those words were given their authority by the much older words they were translated from. The ideas they expressed were captured so poetically because they were intrinsically beautiful to begin with.

WHAT IS THE BIBLE, ANYWAY?

The Bible is, of course, not really a single book at all but a collection of books. The word *Bible* is derived from the Latin and Greek *biblia* for books or a library (like *bibliography* or *bibliothèque*).

The sixty-six books of the Bible (though Catholic and Eastern Orthodox Bibles include some additional books) were written in three different languages: Hebrew, Aramaic, and Greek. This collection of books, both Old and New Testament, were brought together over a 1,500-year span, with the origins of the most ancient texts going even further back. There were many different authors, living in different cultures and epochs of history, writing in many different genres of literature. In this library you will find wisdom literature, proverbs and poetry, prophecy and apocalyptic writing, as well as historical accounts, biographies, and letters.

Yet despite its variety of styles and multiplicity of authors over long periods of time, there is an extraordinary harmony and coherence that emerges from the collective whole. The claim of Christianity is that this is not just a happy coincidence but the work of a divine hand which links this story to the grand story of the cosmos itself.

In the public imagination, the Bible is often perceived as some sort of sacred reference book (and a long and complicated one at that) which religious people use to determine the rules for their ethical positions or doctrines. Others may vaguely recall Bible stories from Sunday school that functioned like morality tales in the tradition of Aesop's fables.

While the Bible contains some of those things, it would be wrong to mistake those parts for the whole. First and foremost, from Genesis to Revelation, the Bible is a story.

The Old Testament is the story of how the one God of the universe saw his good creation turn bad through human rebellion and so chose to call one particular group—the people of Israel—into a special relationship with him. His dealings with them would reveal his grand purpose and promise of redemption and renewal for the whole earth.

The New Testament is the story of how that purpose and promise was fulfilled in the life, death, and resurrection of Jesus Christ, the promised Messiah of the Jewish people. It documents the early years of the new Jesus movement as it spread from Jerusalem across the Mediterranean with the help of its most famous convert and evangelist, Paul.

Christians today believe they continue to swim in the stream of that grand story (it is sometimes said that the twenty-ninth chapter of Acts is still being written), which will yet have its fulfillment as predicted in both the Old and New Testaments—a renewal of all creation in which "he will wipe every tear from their eyes. Death will be no more; mourning and crying and pain will be no more" (Revelation 21:4) and where Jesus will reign, as the whole earth is "full of the knowledge of the LORD as the waters cover the sea" (Isaiah 11:9).

It is a grand narrative—often exciting and absorbing, sometimes complex and dense, occasionally disturbing and confusing, and frequently beautiful and inspiring. It's a story that has led to the rise and fall of nations, been used as a tool of oppression or as an instrument of liberation, been banned and burned by some and regarded as an object of veneration by others. To many it is a source of daily comfort, but it is left by many more to gather dust on a bookshelf.

But whether praised, pilloried, or passed over, the way this story has shaped the world and continues to do so cannot be ignored or blithely dismissed.

HOW NEW ATHEISTS READ THE BIBLE

This is why the New Atheist attacks on Scripture, while providing ample fodder for Internet memes about talking snakes and petulant deities, have entirely failed to appreciate the way the Bible continues to exert the influence it does. Why does it manage to rise phoenix-like from the ashes every time it gets literally or metaphorically burned?

Part of the problem is that the Bible's fiercest contemporary critics have tried to dismiss its credibility by reading it in the same way as the fundamentalist Christians they often find themselves at loggerheads with.

For example, they treat the early chapters of Genesis as though they are to be read as a strictly scientific and historical account of how the earth and all forms of life were created. Such straw men are erected in order to be swiftly knocked down when they point out the obvious differences between these readings and what our best scientific evidence tells us about the age of the earth and its evolutionary history.

But what if such critics (and the Christians who approach the Bible this way) were to stop and read Genesis on its own terms— engaging in the poetry, structure, and concepts it actually conveys?

For instance, there is pattern and purpose in the way the creation story unfolds. In each divine command, order is spoken into chaos and emptiness is filled with life. At its zenith, humans, who have been created in the image of God, are placed at the center of the story to comprehend, name, and cultivate this creation. In a prescientific age, this story communicated truths about our human origins and purpose that made sense of the world to its first hearers and did so across many generations. Remarkably, this story continues to resonate even in today's scientific age. The reason is not because it is a scientific account. It is because it is much more than that.

When I hosted a debate on whether the science of the universe provides evidence for God with Oxford professor Peter Atkins, an outspoken atheist scientist, he announced that the Bible might be able to authenticate its divine credentials if it contained an unmistakable scientific hypothesis, such as the second law of thermodynamics: "If I were looking in the Bible, heaven forbid, I would expect to see maybe 'increase in entropy is equal to Q reversible divided by temperature.' If there was an equation in the Bible rather than all this wishy-washy elastic writing."[15]

How generations of readers would have made any sense of these unintelligible words before nineteenth-century physicists came along to explain them is left unclear. Yet this idea—that the only way the Bible should be taken seriously by modern people is if its ancient writers had been inspired to include predictions about contemporary scientific theories and modern technology—is surprisingly common. In a similar manner, the inspiration of the texts is also called into question by commentators like Sam Harris and Richard Dawkins because its writers didn't explicitly advocate for our most recent standards of ethical and social behavior (standards which, as they both know from experience, are often updated and contested by their peers anyway).

The reason these critiques are so shallow is because they are based on a fundamental misunderstanding of the purpose of Scripture itself.

In his Lost World book series, Old Testament scholar John Walton helpfully distinguishes two audiences for ancient Scripture: those *to whom* the Scriptures were originally written (for example, a seminomadic people in the ancient Near East) and those of later generations *for whom* it is also written. Understanding what the text would have meant to the first audience will help later readers to properly interpret its significance for their own time and culture, rather than mistakenly reading their own modern assumptions into the text.

The fact that the books of the Bible weren't written in a way that satisfies the somewhat arbitrary level of contemporary scientific or moral knowledge demanded by New Atheists like Atkins, Harris, and

Dawkins is hardly a valid objection to a God who may have a much bigger picture in mind than only the concerns of early-twenty-first-century skeptics. C. S. Lewis coined the phrase "chronological snobbery" in reference to those who regard the thought and philosophy of the era they happen to have been born into as the only one worth listening to.[16]

But, once again, a new set of secular voices is reevaluating the Bible.

HOW THE NEW THINKERS READ THE BIBLE

The Bible hasn't been handed down, studied, and absorbed by billions of people through sheer luck or in spite of itself. There are reasons why it has survived and thrived. After the flurry of nay-saying and ridicule that the New Atheists heaped on the Bible, a variety of prominent thinkers are giving it a second look.

For instance, evolutionary psychologist Jonathan Haidt says that the Judeo-Christian Scriptures have provided an unequaled source of inspiration for human well-being and moral development, describing the Bible as "among the richest repositories of psychological wisdom ever assembled."[17]

Haidt is a bestselling secular author but came to appreciate the value of the Bible while researching his book *The Happiness Hypothesis: Finding Modern Truth in Ancient Wisdom*. When I interviewed him about the experience, he said it was spending time alongside religious people and in their texts that changed his mind:

> I was a standard American scientific atheist Jew. I was not predisposed to like religion. But in the course of writing that book, I came to see that religion is part of human nature. In America, religions as practiced make people better. They bind them into communities that try to elevate each other morally. When all the New Atheists were writing nasty

books about religion and the Bible and saying, "This is false," I was saying, "Actually, there's a lot of wisdom there."[18]

Speaking of our moral decision-making in his book *The Righteous Mind*, Haidt uses the analogy of an elephant and its rider, in which the rider has less control over the elephant than he would like to believe. Psychological research indicates that, whether we consider ourselves progressive or conservative, our moral beliefs are rarely the result of a purely rational process (the rider). Instead, we tend to use our reason to justify what our emotional commitments are already telling us (the elephant).

To that extent, says Haidt, our society has always depended on a shared stock of moral knowledge that has been handed down to us through means such as the Bible:

> The Hebrew Bible and the New Testament are full of insights. That really opened my eyes to the value of attending to our traditions, the words that get passed down to us. It's not that the ancients were smarter than us, but they wrote a lot down, they had a lot of insights. And what comes down to us is what has been filtered, tested, and found useful.[19]

In his follow-up book *The Coddling of the American Mind*, Haidt spelled out the psychological perils of raising children who are prevented from ever being hurt, offended, or challenged in their thinking. He questioned the proliferation of safe spaces and trigger warnings for an increasingly mentally fragile generation. In discussing the book, Haidt quoted Romans 5:3-4—"We also boast in our sufferings, knowing that suffering produces endurance, and endurance produces character, and character produces hope"—saying, "That's antifragility right there."[20]

Journalist and author Douglas Murray also finds himself to be a secular nonbeliever with a steadily growing appreciation of the significance of the Bible.

In our conversation on the direction of post-Christian culture, Murray described the "most striking failure of our time" as our inability to come up with anything better than the biblical ethic that all people are created equal in the eyes of God:

> People are struggling to maintain and hold onto this exceptionally important gift of the Christian inheritance. Without the idea of equality in the eyes of God and the value of every individual, you are left with these attempts to assert that, for instance, "everyone is the same, or can be." And it's clear that we can't be, and aren't.[21]

Murray went on to recount a story told by the late literary critic George Steiner about the way that a stable repository of knowledge in the "book" of Scriptures has given successive generations and cultures a sense of continuity and tradition. Steiner related a significant conversation he had late one night with Black activists in South Africa during the time of apartheid. One of them told Steiner, "But you don't understand. We don't have a book." Steiner, who as a Jew had the Torah to draw upon, said it was "one of the most distressing things he had ever heard."[22]

Asked where we can find such a foundational basis in the absence of the Bible, Murray referenced a quote by the philosopher Allan Bloom: "The Bible is not the only means to furnish a mind, but without a book of similar gravity, read with the gravity of the potential believer, it will remain unfurnished."[23]

"I've always thought this is a very important challenge," said Murray. "Because there are books that people might put forward to try to base it on, but they are never of equivalent seriousness. It's actually quite hard to think of a book of equivalent seriousness to the Bible. What would you base it all on?"[24]

HOW A PSYCHOLOGIST READS THE BIBLE

Foremost among the secular thinkers reevaluating the place of Scripture is Jordan Peterson, whose wonder and appreciation for the Bible only seems to grow with every passing year.

Peterson's rise to fame came in the wake of several sell-out theater lectures on the Old Testament, which have also received millions of views online. Talking for two and a half hours for fifteen nights on the book of Genesis isn't the most obvious way to build a fanbase, but thanks to Peterson's influence, his massive audience, many of whom are young men, are taking the Bible seriously.

One of them, Daniel James, who described himself as a "hardened anarchist atheist" in his late teens, has since gone on to be baptized in the Catholic church. James says that, as a young man, he thought the Bible was a "silly book," taking his cues from Lawrence Krauss's description of the Bible as written by "ignorant Bronze Age peasants." However, when he started watching Peterson's lectures, he found himself "blown away": "I'd never heard the Bible spoken about in that way. . . . Jordan really just opened the door for me to understand that, yes, it was written by people who lived in an era before science, but they were by no means ignorant."[25]

Peterson himself sees knowledge of the Bible as integral to "a deep understanding of Western culture, which is in turn vital to proper psychological health."[26] The psychologist frequently frames the stories of Scripture in Jungian terms—speaking of the archetypes and hierarchies that human life is patterned on. The stories that populate the Old and New Testament have immeasurable depths that bespeak their longevity and influence.

For instance, the creation story of Adam and Eve isn't merely a myth to explain where we come from. It's a story that tells us who we are and gives us a basis for human sovereignty, value, and equality. "In my estimation, that doctrine is grounded in the very deep and ancient Judeo-Christian proposition that men and women alike are made in the image of God, the very Creator of Being," writes Peterson. "There is likely no more fundamental presumption grounding our culture."[27]

Likewise, the story of Cain murdering Abel, which follows soon after in Genesis, is not simply a superstitious story about animal sacrifice and sibling rivalry. To Peterson it is "the manifestation of the archetypal tale of hostile brothers, hero and adversary: the two elements of the individual human psyche, one aimed up, at the Good, and the other, down, at Hell itself."[28] In fact, as we saw earlier, Peterson says the well of wisdom in this story is so deep that "it has no bottom"[29] (and he's only got to chapter 4 of the Bible's first book at this point).

This wonder grows as he explores the New Testament. Here, Christ is the preeminent archetype of the hero figure who must conquer through struggle and death. In *12 Rules for Life* Peterson describes Jesus' encounter with Satan as showing *"that Christ is forever He who determines to take personal responsibility for the full depth of human depravity. . . . It's no merely intellectual matter."*[30]

Of the Passion narratives he says, "You cannot write a more tragic story. It's impossible." He describes each element of the injustice and sorrow experienced by Christ as "the aggregation of everything that people are afraid of," and that each character in the story—Mary, Pilate, Judas, Barabbas, the mob—speaks to an aspect of our own human condition as we face death, destruction, and despair. And yet when we "look harder," we see "death and resurrection."[31]

To be sure, Peterson's account of the significance of Scripture is deeply symbolic and psychological. Questions of the actual historicity of the accounts seem almost irrelevant to him. Nevertheless, the psychologist is constantly amazed at the seemingly miraculous ability of Scripture to describe the human condition.

Peterson goes as far as to say that the Bible itself functions as the definitive text out of which all other texts and thoughts in the Western world flow. As he puts it, "It isn't that the Bible is true. It's that the Bible is the precondition for the manifestation of truth. Which makes it way more true than just true."[32] That means a modern Westerner can no more dismiss the Bible than someone standing on the twenty-fifth floor of a high-rise apartment can dismiss the foundation of their building, on the basis that it seems far away.

Peterson, Haidt, and Murray all approach the Bible as secular intellectuals with a growing admiration for its foundational contribution to our shared culture and human experience. That alone might be enough to send many back to the Bible to explore it as a psychologically profound and symbolically rich example of wisdom literature.

Yet once again, in my opinion, the new thinkers are still only halfway there. The Bible may well be the most extraordinary description of psychological and spiritual reality and nevertheless still remain a work of theological invention. Indeed, doubt about the historical reality of the Bible was one of the reasons Douglas Murray gave for losing his faith as a young adult.

However, I believe there need be no false dichotomy between the Bible's cultural and psychological impact and its claims to describe real, objective history.

A CLASSICIST MEETS JESUS

James Orr and I both attended the same college at Oxford University in the late 1990s. I was already a Christian when I arrived as an undergraduate, but James was not. His public school education had involved attending chapel, but it hadn't had much effect on him—he was fairly agnostic towards Christianity.

James and I didn't know each other as students (he was a year above me), but we've got to know each other in the years since— although James now has a much more impressive title than I will ever aspire to: Associate Professor of Philosophy of Religion at the Faculty of Divinity at Cambridge University.

How did someone with minimal interest in faith end up becoming a philosopher of religion at one of the world's most prestigious universities? It turns out that, soon after graduating, James experienced a dramatic conversion which had begun after encountering Jesus in the pages of the Bible while he was still a student.

At school James had studied Greek and Latin. He was almost fluent in reading Greek by the time he arrived at university for a degree in classics. Up to that point, James says he had only read the ancient works of the great playwrights and philosophers that were part of his reading list. But one day, a Christian friend gave James the New Testament in its original language—Koine Greek.

James says he vividly remembers the thrill of being able to read the Gospels in their original language. Of course, he had frequently heard English translations of the Bible being read in public before but had never really thought about it as a historical book.

James describes a "lightning bolt" moment, saying, "I became aware that this text was anchored in history. If you asked, 'Where did I think it had come from?' I don't know. But somehow up to that point it had occupied a part of my imagination that was siloed off from the warp and woof of everyday life and the concrete processes of history."[33]

As James started to read the Gospels for himself in Greek, he realized these accounts were written to be understood as real historical records just as much as any of the histories and annals he was familiar with from Thucydides, Herodotus, and Plutarch. James was also impressed by how well preserved these texts were compared to most of the ancient literature he was familiar with. Most significantly, the life of Jesus also suddenly came to life in a new way.

This was the beginning of the journey that eventually led to James becoming a Christian. As we shall see, there was more to his conversion than just this encounter with the Bible, but James's story illuminates an aspect of the Bible that is frequently underappreciated by many people: its historical pedigree, especially concerning the life, death, and resurrection of Jesus.

REASONS FOR RELIABILITY

When people think of the historical Jesus, a skeptical presumption tends to prevail in contemporary culture. Surely modern research shows the Gospels are just legendary accounts . . . right? According to one UK survey, 40 percent of the population either believe Jesus is a mythical character or are uncertain if he was a real person.[34]

Yet in reality, the trajectory of modern historical scholarship is consistently in the opposite direction to this widespread assumption. As research advances into the historicity of the documents and the time and place that Jesus lived, we are given ever more reason to trust that the Gospels are the product of real history.

Briefly, here are five areas where modern scholarship is confirming the reliability of the biblical accounts.

The Manuscript Evidence
New Testament historian N. T. Wright describes the crucifixion of Jesus as "one of the best attested facts in all of ancient history."[35] If you believe in ancient figures of the past like Julius Caesar or Alexander the Great, you shouldn't have any problem believing that Jesus existed.

It's well known that there are a number of extrabiblical sources that reference Jesus and the early Christian movement—written by ancient historians like Josephus, Tacitus, and Pliny the Younger. However, our main sources of information about Jesus are the four Gospels themselves. And those documents are among the most reliable we have from that era.

A rule of thumb when gauging historical authenticity is the closer to the events that the original texts were written down, the more reason we have to believe they are reliable. In addition, the earlier the extant copies of those texts are, and the more copies we have of them, the greater the likelihood we can reconstruct an accurate version of those first accounts. Naturally, most texts from the ancient world, written on papyrus, have crumbled to dust over the millennia. Yet early fragments of documents still turn up, even today.

So how do the New Testament documents compare in these terms to other ancient documents? As it turns out . . . extremely well. In fact, the New Testament outclasses most other ancient records of historical figures and events by a country mile.

When looking at other key historical figures of the ancient world, there are typically only a handful of existing documents that detail their lives. In addition, those accounts were usually written down many years or even centuries following the events.

In contrast, the four Gospel accounts are estimated to have been written within thirty to sixty years of Jesus' life, and many of the letters of the apostle Paul that witness to the same events were written even sooner.

Moreover, there are thousands of surviving manuscripts, many of which date to within a century or so of the events. Compare this to most other accounts from ancient history, where our surviving documents have gaps of hundreds, if not thousands, of years from the originals.

Critically, whereas the popular imagination assumes that the text we have today must have somehow been metastasized and mythologized in the course of time and transmission, in fact, the opposite is true. Through the science of textual criticism and the advent of digital technology, scholars have increasingly been able to cross examine a wide range of biblical texts and reconstruct what the original documents said with extraordinary accuracy.

These aren't merely half-remembered accounts, adapted, changed, and written down centuries later. The source material has a good historical pedigree.

Names in the Gospels

Turning to the content of the Gospels reveals a range of reasons to trust that they are reporting eyewitness testimony rather than second- or third-hand information. Research shows that the details of the Gospels confirm their accuracy and reliability in terms of their knowledge of geography, historical events and characters, and local customs and culture.

New Testament historian Richard Bauckham's book *Jesus and the Eyewitnesses* is a groundbreaking piece of scholarship in this regard.

His research communicates how the Gospels are filled with evidence that the authors were reporting eyewitness accounts of the very first followers of Christ. For instance, a strong case can be made that the Gospel of Mark is based on the firsthand accounts of the apostle Peter. Even the Gospel of John, often assumed to be a later, more theological account of Jesus' life, contains multiple clues to being the work of a direct disciple of Jesus.

Perhaps most fascinating is Bauckham's research on how the names used in the New Testament (think of Mary, Martha, Simon, Andrew, Bartholomew, and so on) are perfectly synchronized with the time and place of Jesus. The frequency of names in the Gospels was cross-checked with Israeli scholar Tal Ilan's comprehensive research from burial sites into the names being used during the time. A striking correlation showed that the Gospels are full of the same names that were common in the time and places where Jesus lived.

Any prospective parent who has looked up the most popular baby names that are published each year will know that the most common names change frequently. But the Gospel writers got it right for *their* time and place. It's a strong confirmation that these accounts were not made up in some other location at a later time. You can only get that sort of detail right if you were there and you knew the people you are talking about.

Geography and Customs

Likewise, further research by Cambridge biblical scholar Dr. Peter J. Williams, author of *Can We Trust the Gospels?*, has revealed a plethora of ways in which the Gospel writers show that they are clearly familiar with the times, places, and customs of Jesus' day, including the local geography.

Williams explains how remarkably reliable the Gospels are as a guide to the landscape of Judea and Jerusalem in the first century: "I'd say either the person has lived in the land, or they spent detailed conversations talking to people who lived in the land. And I'd say that about all four Gospels—that they know where the land goes up and down; between them they mention twenty-six town names; they know traveling times and so on."[36]

In the absence of Google or any sort of reference book, this is the sort of information you had to be a local to get right. Time and again the Gospel writers place their events in the right geographical and historical context. They also get the details right. They know the coinage, customs, and conventions of the day. Williams says the phraseology is distinctly local too:

> I can think of four verses in a row in Luke 16, where you get a dry measure and a wet measure, and then we get "the sons of light" as a phrase—which is a Palestinian religious phrase, and then "unrighteous mammon" in the next verse. Those are four bits of language which I would expect really reflects the land of Palestine. If we've got them in a row, it's because we actually have the wording somehow preserved.[37]

When you compare these sorts of details in Matthew, Mark, Luke, and John to later accounts of Jesus (sometimes called "apocryphal Gospels," like the Gospels of Thomas or Judas) from the second and third century, you immediately see the difference. Later accounts include very little detail of local custom, geography, or names. They are far vaguer, much less connected to real history, time, and place.

Undesigned Coincidences

Another line of evidence to show that the Gospels are the result of reliable eyewitness testimony has been explored recently by scholars including Dr. Lydia McGrew in her book *Hidden in Plain View: Undesigned Coincidences in the Gospels and Acts.*

Undesigned coincidences are details within stories across the different Gospels of Matthew, Mark, Luke, and John that seem to dovetail with each other, suggesting that the authors knew the truth of the events they describe. These "coincidences" are examples of natural corroborations between the separate accounts that could not have been manufactured.

To give just one example, when the story of the feeding of the five thousand is related in John 6, Jesus turns to the disciple Philip and asks him where they may go to buy bread for the vast crowd that has followed them into the countryside. In the story, Jesus is setting a test for his disciples and receives the answer he was expecting from a bewildered Philip: "Two hundred denarii [six months' wages] would not buy enough bread for each of them to get a little" (John 6:7). This brief dialogue sets the stage for one of Jesus' most memorable miracles, involving a young boy and his packed lunch of loaves and fishes.

However, if this story were being invented rather than recounted, why would the author have Jesus ask the question of Philip rather than one of the more senior disciples, such as Peter or John?

The answer may lie in other parts of the Gospels. We learn earlier in John that Philip is from the town of Bethsaida. As it happens, when the story is recorded in Luke 9, we are also told where the miracle happens: near the town of Bethsaida.

Furnished with this additional information, we can make sense of why Jesus asks Philip in particular. He's a local. Out of all the disciples, he would be most likely to know the answer to the question (however rhetorical it was). Luke's account of the story makes sense of John's account. In the process, we see that both accounts share the same underlying reality.

By itself, this single example is unlikely to convince a skeptic of the general trustworthiness of the Gospels. But the cumulative weight of the many additional examples that could be given should give a skeptic pause for thought. Like the pieces of a puzzle falling into place, the interlocking connections between multiple details in the Gospels can't be explained away by scribal ingenuity or later invention. As McGrew writes, all these undesigned coincidences are "marks of the truth of the Gospels hidden in plain view."[38]

Archaeology

Perhaps most impressive of all is to see the very places the Bible mentions being unearthed in Israel today, which continue to prove the authenticity of the Gospels.

For instance, in John 9 Jesus heals a blind man and tells him to wash at the Pool of Siloam. Until recently, the location of this pool had never been discovered, and skeptics assumed it probably did not exist. However, during construction work in 2004, the steps of the pool were unearthed, and eventually the site was excavated, revealing a grand pool that makes exact sense of Jesus' words and the story.

Biblical scholar Mark D. Roberts reports, "In the plaster of this pool were found coins that establish the date of the pool to the years before and after Jesus. There is little question that this is in fact the pool of Siloam, to which Jesus sent the blind man in John 9."[39]

The Pool of Siloam is just one example of many other archaeological finds that corroborate the New Testament accounts. These include recently excavated houses, settlements, and synagogues that have overturned previous skepticism about the cultural and religious significance of the towns where Jesus carried out his ministry, such as Nazareth and Capernaum. The remains of crucifixion victims also confirm the nature of Jesus' execution as related in the Gospels.

Many similarly exciting finds are confirming various aspects of Old Testament history and chronology too.

For example, there was the discovery of "Hezekiah's tunnel" under Jerusalem in the 1800s and an ancient inscription linking it to the biblical account of Hezekiah commanding the construction of such a tunnel to bring fresh water into the city because of an impending Assyrian invasion. Or the 1993 discovery of the Tel Dan stele—a stone slab which contains an ancient Canaanite inscription that provides evidence of the reign of King David outside the biblical accounts. And the finds keep coming. In 2022 archaeologist Dr. Scott Stripling announced the discovery of a "curse tablet" dated to between 1400 and 1200 BC, which appears to contain the earliest example of Hebrew writing and use of the name Yahweh. If verified (the find is still being peer-reviewed at the time of writing), it provides strong evidence that the historical accounts of Israel in the Old Testament may have been written down much earlier than critics have assumed.

Inevitably, most of the archaeological history of the Old and New Testament has been lost to the sands of time. Yet despite the skepticism that often exists towards the reliability of the biblical accounts, whenever new discoveries are made, they rarely contradict the Bible. On the contrary, every passing year seems to turn up further archaeological findings that confirm the biblical record.

These are just some of the reasons why new evidence and recent scholarship mean the Bible needs to be taken seriously, not only as a work of literature that has had a dramatic impact on the world, but also as a work of history. That means taking its central character—Jesus Christ—seriously too.

SOME IMPORTANT OBJECTIONS

Even though the New Atheists have undervalued the influence of the Bible and underestimated the historical nature of the Gospels, some of the general objections they have brought to the table are still worth responding to.

You Can't Trust the Gospels Because They Are Biased

This objection raises the question of whether the Gospels have a theological agenda at play. Aren't they simply pious fiction for the Jesus movement that began in the first century?

The first point to note in response is that the works of scholars such as Richard Burridge have established that the Gospels fall firmly into a category of Greco-Roman writing called "historical biography." It's the same kind of writing that Plutarch, Josephus, and other contemporary historians were doing in that era for other notable figures.

Whether or not you think they are accurate, these accounts were at least written to be understood as conveying real historical events, not simply pious fiction, as some critics have maintained.

So was there an agenda? My answer would be that, yes, of course the Gospels have an agenda. In fact, they are very explicit about it. John 20:30-31 reads, "Now Jesus did many other signs in the presence of his disciples, which are not written in this book. But these are written so that you may come to believe that Jesus is the Messiah, the Son of God, and that through believing you may have life in his name."

These stories of Jesus weren't recorded by detached, neutral observers. The Gospel writers believed Jesus was the Son of God and were writing down their accounts to persuade others to believe the same. But that doesn't mean the accounts are merely propaganda.

Having "an agenda" is completely normal for almost every piece of writing. Whether it be a newspaper that leans in a certain political direction, a brochure that wants to sell you something, or a work of history that wants to make a specific point about the world, you will hardly read anything in your life that does not have a purpose or agenda behind it, including the book you are holding in your hands.

So let's not get hung up on "agendas." Every writer has an agenda of some sort. The question is: Do they make a persuasive case? Does their evidence stack up? And, in the case of the Gospels, can we trust that we are getting a reliable account that supports their claim that Jesus really was the Son of God?

I believe we can trust that these documents are not only historically reliable accounts but that the Gospel writers had good reasons for conveying their belief that Jesus Christ really was the Son of God.

The story of a Messiah who was crucified as a criminal by the Jews' imperial oppressors and then discovered alive again three days later by a group of his female followers would have gone against all their prevailing Jewish cultural and theological norms. This would be a very odd story to invent. And yet this was the account they gave. It was a story they were willing to suffer persecution and death for, and which went on to change the course of history altogether.

What about All the Differences and Contradictions?

Many skeptics seem to believe that merely pointing out the fact that the Gospels contain differences between them is enough to dismiss the Bible's claim to be divinely inspired. But that's only true if we assume its divine pedigree is based upon how closely it mirrors modern literary conventions. What if, again, we are guilty of "chronological snobbery" in making such a judgment?

It's true there are differences between the accounts, but none of them are irreconcilable. Frankly, we should be suspicious if the accounts all lined up perfectly—that would suggest someone had rigged things. Any police detective will tell you that you never hear exactly the same account from two different witnesses at a crime scene. It doesn't mean they aren't telling the truth—just that they had different perspectives on it.

However, many of the supposed contradictions tend to evaporate once we understand that the Gospels' literary genre of historical biography adhered to different conventions than modern biography.

Certainly, if you line up the Gospels side by side, you'll frequently find a different timeline of events, mentions of different people in the same events, words and speeches recorded differently, and more besides. But that was just a standard way that biographers worked in that day and age.

In his book *Why Are There Differences in the Gospels?*, Michael Licona compares the Gospel accounts with the lives that the Roman biographer Plutarch recorded and finds a striking overlap in literary devices. Writers were simply more at liberty to reorganize and reorder their material or to spotlight certain characters to make their points. None of this diminishes Plutarch's contribution to history, and we should take the same approach with the Gospels.

The lesson for us today is that comparing the Gospels to a modern biography is going to be problematic—styles and literary conventions change a lot in two thousand years. It is a modern error, often committed equally by both Christians and skeptics, that weighs Scripture down with unreasonable expectations. However, understood on their own terms, these accounts do not contradict each other. If anything, they are noteworthy for the remarkable amount of correlation between them.

THE MIRACLE OF SCRIPTURE

In that sense, the Bible is not a magic book that floated down from heaven to earth fully formed, bound in a leather cover with index included. It doesn't exist independently of the historical circumstances and influences of the many hands that wrote it.

If God has chosen to convey something divine through this written word, then he has chosen to transmit it over many ages, through ordinary human authors and imperfect processes. That means serious work has been left for later generations to recover the most reliable manuscripts, piece together the original texts, and try to understand the historical and religious context into which they were originally written.

Nevertheless, once that work has been done (and it has been done *meticulously*), we find something quite astonishing.

What really marks out the Bible as unusual is that, despite being the end product of many different authors writing in times and places very different to each other and our own, it still tells a historically coherent and thematically unified story.

Perhaps even more remarkably, it has been able to unfailingly communicate the meaning and wisdom of that story to multiple generations in diverse parts of the world. Whole swaths of people whose lives have been soaked in the words of the Bible have consequently been able to locate themselves and their purpose within a grand narrative of what it means to be human.

This is the miracle of Scripture. Not some parlor trick of finding a scientific equation predicted in its pages (as a New Atheist like Peter Atkins might require). Nor some magical ability to exist hermetically sealed off from the normal processes of time and history (as some Christians might like to believe). The miracle of Scripture is that it has spoken, and continues to speak, to every generation, place, and time it encounters. In doing so, its message has transformed individuals, nations, and empires.

It is the reason why James Orr, having become intrigued as an undergraduate by the discovery of a real, historical Jesus of Nazareth, went on to test whether the Christ of history may also be the Christ of today.

Having graduated and embarked upon a promising career in law, James was nevertheless asking himself existential questions about the purpose of his life. On New Year's Eve 2002 he prayed a skeptical (and, he admits, fairly drunken) prayer, asking God, if he was there, to reveal himself. Remarkably, from the very next morning and over the following two months, James says he experienced a number of very specific and unusual answers to his prayers. "It got to the point where it was becoming irrational of me to deny the cumulative weight of these coincidences."[40]

These signs stopped almost as suddenly as they had begun but led to James investigating the evidence for Christianity with renewed vigor, devouring scholarly books alongside Bible reading. At this point he was not connected to a church community and knew no committed Christians, yet his lifestyle began to change dramatically. Any desire for smoking and drinking evaporated. People around him noticed the difference. His sudden change in behavior was "unsettling" to his family and friends.

Yet something had ignited inside James. The Jesus of history who had consumed his intellectual interest now began to come into focus as the same God who was leading him inexorably towards the Christian faith. James eventually became part of a church community, where he found others who had made similar journeys. They seemed to him to be "the real deal." "There was something self-authenticatingly true about this community," he says.

Through a further series of providential circumstances, James eventually felt called to leave his law career and begin a postgraduate degree in philosophy of religion at Cambridge. Ironically, the rise of New Atheism at that time also fueled his change in career. "I was amazed at the weakness of their arguments," he recalls.

Today James continues in his role as a member of the Divinity Faculty at the University of Cambridge. Incidentally, he is among a group of Cambridge academics who reissued the invitation of a visiting fellowship to Jordan Peterson (an original invitation had been controversially rescinded), allowing the psychologist to pursue his studies there in biblical literature.

MYTH BECAME FACT

Despite the Bible being widely available today in all manner of digital and physical formats, ours is the most biblically illiterate generation in several centuries. For that reason, it's encouraging to see that the shallow critiques of the New Atheists are now being replaced by a renewed appreciation of the Bible from secular quarters, through thinkers such as Peterson, Murray, and Haidt. Even if they don't believe in its divine inspiration (though Peterson comes pretty close to describing the Bible in miraculous terms), these figures are at least reminding their sizable audiences about the way Scripture has shaped culture and the debt we owe it.

But I want to push these thinkers a little further still.

The Bible is certainly a great source of ancient wisdom. It is also undoubtedly the distillation of thousands of years of myth[41] and meaning into one captivating narrative. And, as they point out, in its pages we find supreme psychological examples of sacrifice, heroism, and love that have been a source of inspiration to millions.

But what if, in the words of C. S. Lewis, in its central character, "the great myth became Fact"?[42] For it is only when we combine the psychological depth of Scripture with the historical bedrock of the person of Jesus Christ that we can truly explain the extraordinary impact this library of books has had on the world.

Think of those unforgettable stories about prodigal sons and good Samaritans; Jesus' unmatched teachings on forgiveness, grace, and love; the radical command to love enemies; his unique willingness to touch the untouchable and love the unlovable. It is the words and actions of Jesus in Scripture that have most shaped history.

But this amounts to more than just good moral teaching. The reason the Bible has changed the world is because its written word provides evidence of a personal "living Word" who can be encountered today.

During one of my conversations with Douglas Murray, I challenged him to give a reason why he remained an agnostic atheist, despite his appreciation for the cultural value of Christianity and the Bible. What would it take for him to believe? Murray replied, "I'd need to hear a voice."[43]

Many Christians would also appreciate a booming voice from the heavens to confirm their faltering faith from time to time. However,

I would argue that all of us, Murray included, do have access to the voice of God in a very powerful way. I hope that Murray will look again at the Bible, not just for its psychological and literary value, but at its historical pedigree. For there is ever-increasing historical evidence that the Gospels really do relay the real words and history of Jesus of Nazareth—words which, as Murray himself admits, have miraculously and irrevocably shaped everything in the world that he holds dear. What clearer voice could we ask for?

The stories of David Suchet, James Orr, and countless others demonstrate that this book cannot be picked up, admired, and then merely set aside. History itself hinges on the reality of the life, death, and resurrection of Jesus Christ. Somehow, in him, all the hopes, dreams, and fears of humankind once found their meeting place and continue to do so today. That, after all, is the radical claim at the center of the whole story.

CHAPTER 5

THE ALTERNATIVE STORY OF SCIENCE

IT WAS HAPPENING. The game was afoot. Richard Dawkins had replied yes to my email.

The name of the famous biologist has already been mentioned numerous times in this book. As one of the most prominent atheists of the twenty-first century, his name is also frequently invoked when I host discussions on science, faith, and belief. Yet despite some fleeting appearances in the past, I had never had the opportunity to bring him on my show for a proper interaction on science and faith. Until now. This time, he would be talking about his area of expertise in a long-form conversation on biology, belief, and COVID-19 with another star of the scientific world, Francis Collins.

Collins is every bit the equal of Dawkins when it comes to biology. A famed geneticist, he led the Human Genome Project, which first sequenced the DNA of the entire human body. He recently retired as head of the National Institutes of Health in the United States after leading their response to COVID and, at the time of our conversation, had just been appointed acting science advisor to the US president.

However, whereas Dawkins is the world's preeminent atheist, Collins is a committed Christian who founded BioLogos, an organization dedicated to showing the harmony of science and faith. His bestselling book *The Language of God: A Scientist Presents Evidence for Belief* was a counterpoint to Dawkins's *The God Delusion* and argued for the rationality of Christianity from science, reason, and experience.

Anyone expecting an explosive debate between the two would have been disappointed. Their mutual respect for each other as fellow scientists shone through, with Dawkins quizzing Collins for his expertise on specific matters of genetics while Collins approached the conversation as a friendly encounter between two old sparring partners.

Dawkins also warmly thanked Collins for the medical care he had provided their mutual friend Christopher Hitchens during his terminal illness. Collins was able to add several months to the atheist's life through genomic analysis and treatment of his esophageal cancer. No wonder Hitchens referred to him as "the best of the faithful."[1]

The conversation between Dawkins and Collins ran the full gamut of questions on science and faith—whether evolution can be reconciled with Genesis, why God allows suffering, how we developed our moral instincts, and whether a scientist can countenance the idea of miracles.

It was when they reached the biggest questions of cosmic purpose that the most fundamental differences between the two scientists emerged.

Collins raised the question of where the universe came from— indeed, why are there natural laws and physical reality at all? Why do the physical laws that govern the universe seem to be so perfectly set up to produce conscious living creatures like ourselves? Could there be an explanation in an ultimate designer?

Dawkins has often claimed that science and reason naturally point towards atheism. But when confronted with the appearance of design in the fundamental architecture of the universe, he admitted it was "the nearest approach to a good argument" for God. In responding to it, Dawkins acknowledged that his position was based more on his personal preferences than a purely scientific or rational response:

> I suppose perhaps we both come at it with a bit of
> emotional . . . emotional is the wrong word . . . a bit of
> presupposition. As somebody who's deeply steeped in
> evolution, I am in love with the idea that it's possible to
> explain complex things in terms of simple things. . . . And
> that's such a beautiful idea, that inventing a big complex
> thing (which God must be if he exists) throws a ruddy
> great spanner in the whole works of the beauty of that
> Darwinian concept.[2]

Whether God is a "complex" explanation in the way Dawkins envisages is highly questionable. But his admission of a presupposition about the way he feels reality *should be* and why he therefore excludes a divine explanation is an honest reflection of the fact that we all bring more than just our rational faculties to the table when we weigh the evidence.

Dawkins hesitated to label his feeling as "emotional." But some do go that far. In a frank passage about atheism and religion, the celebrated philosopher Thomas Nagel was willing to own up to the way his nonbelief was not a merely rational response to the evidence: "It isn't just that I don't believe in God and, naturally, hope that I'm right in my belief. It's that I hope there is no God! I don't want there to be a God; I don't want the universe to be like that."[3]

SCIENCE IS NEUTRAL, SCIENTISTS ARE NOT

Philosophers and scientists are as human as anyone else. When scientists step into the lab to conduct an experiment, they do not suddenly shed all the biases, assumptions, and preferences they carry with them in everyday life. While the scientific method they employ helps to make the results of their experiments objective (the pH level of pure water will always turn out to be 7, whether you vote Republican or Democrat), that doesn't mean their own beliefs about the way the world is—or ought to be—won't impact the way they interpret and apply those results.

In his landmark book *The Structure of Scientific Revolutions*, the philosopher of science Thomas Kuhn famously pointed out the way that scientists often stick doggedly to their favorite theories, even in the face of mounting evidence against them. One notable example is the way that the Newtonian model of physics gave way to Einstein's theory of general relativity in the twentieth century. Einstein completely changed the way we understand gravity at the very largest scales and paved the way for a new physics of the universe. However, at every stage, scientists wedded to the old order of Newtonian mechanics pushed against the new interpretations. Even in his day, Einstein rejected some ideas within quantum mechanics—such as the uncertainty principle—because he simply refused to believe the universe would behave that way.

Kuhn has pointed out that scientific revolutions only tend to take root once the level of evidence becomes overwhelming or when the old guard dies out. As the adage goes, science progresses one funeral at a time.

Likewise, at various points in the past, science has been used to justify racism, eugenics, and forced sterilization. Simply applying the scientific method doesn't eradicate the prejudices of scientists. As in any area of study, science is a very human endeavor, marked by the biases and presuppositions of those who engage in it.

So it's no surprise that, despite the frequent claim to be objective, neutral, and evidence-based, scientists also interpret the world through a set of quasi-theological spectacles.

In the previous chapter I introduced Peter Atkins, an emeritus professor of chemistry at Oxford University. The atheist is well-known for his brash style of debate which frequently involves deriding the faith claims of any believing scientist as "lazy thinking," "poppycock," or worse. The guests I bring him on with are usually braced for such theatrics and happy to shrug off any impolite remarks.

On one occasion, I invited him to debate the origin of the laws of the universe with Hugh Ross, a leading Christian astrophysicist. Ross, who founded the science and faith organization Reasons to Believe, argues that the properties of the universe—its beginning in time and the extraordinary degree to which it seems to be fine-tuned to allow life to exist—are evidence of a creator behind the cosmos. Naturally, Atkins disagreed and pushed back with his usual rhetorical bluntness.

I eventually asked Atkins what sort of evidence might come close to making him open to the concept of God. Was there any chink in his atheist armor? For instance, what if the stars in the sky lined up to spell out "Peter, please believe in me—it's about time"?

"I'd put it down to personal madness," Atkins responded.

"In that case it sounds like there's no evidence that would persuade you away from atheism," remarked Ross.

"To be honest, I think that's probably the case," replied Atkins.[4]

I think Atkins's honest answer is revealing. I could probably have given him a dozen more lines of hypothetical evidence for God and been met with similar naturalistic explanations. A Christian prophet predicts everything that happens to you over a twenty-four-hour period? A lucky guess. Someone is healed of lifelong blindness in front of you? Weird things happen. Jesus appears in the room and personally asks you to believe in him? I must be dreaming.

Even those who claim to "follow the evidence" may have erected invisible barriers that cannot be crossed. Some types of explanation are simply off the table.

The problem is not necessarily with the quality of the evidence produced; it is with the interpretive filter used to process that evidence. Like Dawkins, Atkins is a believer in scientific materialism—that all of reality is ultimately reducible to the impersonal forces of biology, chemistry, and physics. Atkins's worldview could equally be described as "scientism," in which the only plausible explanations are physical, scientific ones. His a priori commitment to a purely naturalistic worldview means that supernatural explanations are out of the question. Providing more evidence would not budge him an iota. For Atkins to stop being an atheist would doubtless involve something altogether different.

Yet if we can maintain an open mind and refuse to allow reason to be conflated with scientism, we may discover that the progress of science actually provides an abundance of evidence that points towards God rather than atheism.

SCIENTIFIC MYTHOLOGY

Science is the primary battleground upon which New Atheism mounted its attack on Christian belief. Admittedly, simplistic and fundamentalist forms of Christianity have given the New Atheists plenty of material to work with, and research shows that religious belief among scientists is generally lower than that of the general public.

However, the actual percentage of scientists who profess belief in God has remained relatively stable over the past hundred years. A 2009 Pew Forum survey showed that 51 percent of United States scientists believe in some form of deity or higher power.[5] The results were similar in polls conducted in 1914 and the 1990s.

Nevertheless, "the conflict thesis"—the story that science and religion have always been at odds with each other—seems firmly lodged in the public mind. Pew Research Center reported in 2021 that 56 percent of Americans believe there is a conflict between science and religion.[6] Likewise, a 2022 study showed that 57 percent of Brits think that science and religion are incompatible.[7]

Such statistics are unsurprising given how much airtime the "conflict thesis" gets in popular media. After all, didn't the church persecute Galileo for maintaining that the earth revolves around the sun? Aren't Christian views about creation and the age of the earth at odds with the theory of evolution? The list goes on.

However, some simple historical research soon reveals that these supposed conflicts are frequently misrepresented in the public sphere.

The trial of Galileo Galilei in 1633 is a case in point. Yes, Galileo was censured by the Catholic church for promoting the Copernican view of heliocentrism. But historians have pointed out that Galileo hardly helped his own cause.

The church was the primary sponsor of scientific research in Galileo's time. Pope Urban VIII had been a friend and patron of Galileo's and was prepared to allow him to publish his views on the condition that Galileo acknowledged it was still a hypothesis. Copernicus's theory was still in genuine dispute during this time, and the pope argued it should be represented as such. However, Galileo—who by all accounts was liable to make enemies where he didn't need to—chose to publish his work without any such caveats and provocatively placed the pope's objections in the mouth of a dullard called Simplicio.

Galileo's trial was as much about personality and politics as it was about science and faith. And far from being sentenced to languish in prison after an inquisitorial-style torture, as some imagine, Galileo's sentence involved being put under house arrest in the comfortable surroundings of his own villa, where he continued to enjoy receiving guests and to research and publish his scientific work.

In more recent centuries, the debate between evolution and the biblical account of creation has been paraded as a similar example of conflict between the church and established science. Yet again, the devil is in the details.

Darwin's theory was generally welcomed by the Church of England at the time. Much-publicized conflicts, such as the 1860 debate between Bishop Samuel Wilberforce and Darwin's protégé Thomas Huxley, owe more to larger-than-life personalities than a serious pushback by the church establishment. Even before Darwin's theory, there had been teaching as far back as Origen and Augustine in the third and fourth centuries that allowed for an allegorical interpretation of the creation story and a lengthy timeline for the appearance of life on earth. The young earth creation movement, which has been the focus of much New Atheist ire, is a relatively modern movement that only really gained prominence in the mid-twentieth century.

Many of these conflicts have been exaggerated by those who want to promote science as an ally of atheism rather than faith. But it's worth noting that neither Galileo nor Darwin embraced atheism. Darwin moved towards agnosticism during his life but objected to those who tried to forcibly connect atheism with science. And despite his disagreements with the church, Galileo remained a lifelong Catholic who saw no contradiction between science and faith, writing, "God is known . . . by Nature in His works, and by doctrine in His revealed word."[8]

THE REAL HISTORY OF SCIENCE

Just as new secular thinkers have been pushing back on New Atheism's simplistic critiques of the Bible, history, and the value of religion, so we will also find an alternative take on science among many critical thinkers, some of whom find themselves surprised by the direction in which the evidence seems to be pointing.

The first and most obvious place to begin is with the history of science itself. Many skeptics assume that the scientific revolution came about as the Enlightenment allowed reason to break free from the shackles of religious superstition. But this notion is as prejudiced and unhistorical as the exaggerated stories about Darwin and Galileo we have already touched on. In reality, both those men were building on the foundations of a scientific revolution that was a direct product of the Judeo-Christian tradition. And all the chief architects of that revolution firmly saw their science as a gift from God.

When it comes to devout believers who spearheaded the scientific revolution, there are too many to choose from. To name just a few from the seventeenth century, we could begin with Francis Bacon (arguably the founder of the scientific method) along with Johannes Kepler, Robert Boyle, Isaac Newton, and Blaise Pascal. Then there were Gottfried Leibniz, Antoine Lavoisier, and Carl Linnaeus in the eighteenth century. Michael Faraday, James Maxwell, and Louis Pasteur are among the many from the nineteenth century. The history of science is replete with pioneering scientists who were devout believers.

Importantly, historians of science agree that these men were not simply parroting a faith handed to them by their culture but genuinely perceived the universe and the scientific enterprise through Christian eyes. John Hedley Brooke writes,

> When natural philosophers referred to *laws* of nature, they were not glibly choosing that metaphor. Laws were the result of legislation by an intelligent deity. Thus the philosopher René Descartes (1596–1650) insisted that he was discovering the "laws that God has put into nature." Later Newton would declare that the regulation of the solar system presupposed the "counsel and dominion of an intelligent and powerful Being."[9]

Rodney Stark writes,

> The Christian image of God is that of a rational being who *believes in human progress*, more fully revealing himself as humans *gain* the capacity to better understand. Moreover, because God is a rational being and the universe is his personal creation, it necessarily has a rational, lawful, stable structure, *awaiting increased human comprehension*. This was the key to many intellectual undertakings, among them the rise of science.[10]

Even the avowed atheist philosopher Friedrich Nietzsche, who despised Christian belief, wrote,

> There is no such thing as science "without any pre-suppositions" . . . a philosophy, a "faith," must always be there first of all, so that science can acquire from it a direction, a meaning, a limit, a method, a *right* to exist. . . . We men of knowledge of today, we godless men and anti-metaphysicians, we, too, still derive *our* flame from the fire ignited by a faith millennia old, the Christian faith.[11]

C. S. Lewis summarized it pithily: "Men became scientific because they expected Law in Nature, and they expected Law in Nature because they believed in a Legislator."[12]

Lest we think that examples of scientists who believe in God are relegated to centuries past, we could compile an equally long list from the twentieth and twenty-first centuries, including Arthur Eddington, Werner Heisenberg, and John Polkinghorne. Happily, with the advent of greater equality and opportunity for women in academia, we can also add many female names to the roster of believing scientists, such as mathematician Katherine Coleman Goble Johnson, whose calculations were critical to spaceflight; NASA astrophysicist Dr. Jennifer Wiseman; and AI technology pioneer Rosalind Picard.

Indeed, the vast majority of Nobel Prize winners in the sciences during the twentieth century have either identified as Christians or were from the Jewish faith.[13] Only a tiny minority have identified as atheist or agnostic. In addition, many of the Christians working in science were not simply "born" into their beliefs but came to a considered faith as adults. We shall explore some of their stories later.

In fact, the idea of an age-old battle between science and faith is largely a nineteenth-century invention promulgated by John William Draper and Andrew Dickson White, two quirky historians whose pamphlets on the "conflict thesis" became wildly popular, despite most of the historical details being completely false. Sadly, their version of history is still uncritically regurgitated by many modern-day critics of the faith, despite having been debunked by historians.[14]

The undisputed Christian roots of the scientific revolution and the fact that most scientists of faith report a complementarity between their work in the lab and the God they worship in church show that the conflict is not between science and faith at all but rather between two worldviews—naturalism and theism. Adherents of both can practice perfectly good science. The question is, which of those two worldviews makes the most sense of what science tells us about the world we live in?

THE ICEBERG UNDER OUR FEET

This question brings us to the second place that we can look for an alternative story of science—the results of scientific research itself and the scientific thinkers who are asking hard questions of a purely naturalistic view of the universe.

The progress made by science has always been the New Atheists' greatest showpiece, the place where they were able to safely say the need for God had been eliminated. The deities that had once functioned as explanations for the seasons, harvests, and weather events that superstitious farming cultures depended on had been banished as science explained where the wind, rain, and sun actually came from. Even the apparent design and varied complexity of life in all its forms no longer needed a divine creator. As Richard Dawkins put it, "Darwin made it possible to be an intellectually fulfilled atheist."[15]

And yet the fact that science has given us physical explanations for so much that our forebears attributed to a divine hand does not mean that God has been explained away. Far from it.

If God were merely a "God of the gaps"—a divine being who was once used as an explanatory filler for all manner of phenomena but who was eventually made redundant as physical explanations were discovered—then that God would indeed be "explained away" by scientific progress. This is the sort of God the New Atheists usually seem to have in their sights.

Yet the advance of science is a double-edged sword. Every time we acquire more knowledge about the world, we suddenly perceive how little we actually know about physical reality. Like an arctic explorer who suddenly realizes they are standing on an iceberg, mapping out our physical surroundings only makes us realize how much more there is below our feet that we do not yet comprehend. But can the depths of reality that science points to be answered by a purely scientific-materialist account of the universe?

THE ORIGIN OF LIFE

Take, for instance, deoxyribonucleic acid. Every part of you is built from this blueprint called DNA. Its famous spiraling helix, identified by Francis Crick and James Watson in the 1950s, contains the microscopic building blocks of life—vastly long sequences of code written in four base letters: A, C, G, and T.

Every cell in your body contains billions of these tiny instructions which, through a remarkable and complex process, can store, copy, and transcribe the information to develop new cells, organs, and body parts. These long sequences are coiled so tightly that each cell contains two meters of code. If you unraveled it all, the DNA in an average human body would stretch around the entire solar system twice.

Naturally, Charles Darwin had no concept of DNA or modern genetics when he proposed his theory of gradual change and adaptation over long periods of time. With the tools at his disposal, a cell under a microscope looked like a blob of simple jelly. He could not have known that, within it, future generations would discover a vast world of microscopic machines, delivery systems, and production factories. The complete DNA code for the cell is itself stored in the central nucleus, containing more information than any library Darwin had ever walked into.

In popular culture most people assume that Darwin's theory explains all this complexity. There are numerous reasons why, in fact, Darwin's original theory is increasingly contested in academic circles. But its most glaring limitation is that it cannot explain where life came from in the first place. To have a process of biological evolution at all requires a self-replicating DNA molecule for it to go to work on. Where did the source code originate? This is the mystifying problem of abiogenesis.

A significant secular voice in the debate about the origins of life is eminent physicist Paul Davies, who runs the Beyond Center at Arizona State University. Davies has been a thorn in the side of the New Atheists for decades. Like many of them, he is a bestselling popularizer of science, but he rejects their materialist analysis of the universe and why it has produced us.

Davies often speaks with almost reverential awe about the way the universe seems to be "primed" for life to develop. When I interviewed him about how life got started on planet Earth, he was clear—even as a firm advocate of the evolutionary process—that evolution is incapable of explaining the origin of life and that Darwin himself steered clear of trying to explain it:

> Darwin gave us a theory of evolution about how life has evolved over billions of years from simple microbes to the complexity of the biosphere we see today. But he didn't want to tangle with how you go from nonlife to life. And for me, that's a much bigger step.
>
> The transition from the earliest microbes to what we see today is an enormous amount of complexification. But it's got nothing on that first step of going from a mishmash of chemicals to the first living thing, because almost all the complexity in the biosphere is in the individual organisms, not in the subsequent ecology and everything else.[16]

The complexity involved for the first form of life to come into being is indeed mind-boggling. When Stanley Miller and Harold Urey conducted experiments in the 1950s to replicate the "chemical soup" of early Earth's atmosphere, they managed to produce amino acids by passing electricity through a mixture of water, methane, ammonia, and hydrogen. This was considered a step towards solving the mystery of abiogenesis. After all, amino acids are the building blocks needed to give rise to proteins and, ultimately, DNA.

But it quickly became apparent that the problem was not producing the amino acids; it was getting a string of them in the right order. It's the difference between having a pile of bricks and constructing St. Paul's Cathedral out of them. Calculating the odds of this complex string of information assembling spontaneously results in a number so large that it competes with the number of atoms in the universe. Chance isn't an option.

While a number of inventive naturalistic hypotheses have been suggested for how the beginnings of a sequence might have originated, most scientists will admit that we don't currently have a clue.

As chemist and nanotechnologist Dr. James Tour has written, "Those who think scientists understand the issues of prebiotic chemistry are wholly misinformed. Nobody understands them. Maybe one day we will. But that day is far from today. . . . The basis upon which we as scientists are relying is so shaky that we must openly state the situation for what it is: it is a mystery."[17]

Paul Davies is convinced that the exact conditions required to produce the first living thing defies our present understanding of physics. He's also skeptical of scientific colleagues who assume that life must exist elsewhere given the vastness of our universe. Even with billions of Earth-like planets in the universe, the odds are still massively stacked against spontaneous abiogenesis. In order to have that hope, he says there must be a "life principle" at work in our cosmos that pushes against a purely naturalistic view of chance working over time: "From my point of view, I would like to believe that we live in a universe which is rigged in favor of life, where there is a life principle that coaxes matter to life against the raw odds that you will get just from shuffling molecules, but we haven't found it yet."[18]

Davies is not a religious person, and he strongly disavows the idea of God tinkering with the nuts and bolts of amino acids and nucleotide bases in order to create the first form of life. But Davies nevertheless borders on religious language when he speaks of this "life principle"—a deeper structure that pushes the universe towards order, complexity, and conscious life:

> If there is this sort of pro-life principle, then there is a coherent scheme of things of which our existence is a part. So, it embeds us in the cosmos in this broader context. Now, that's not quite the same as religion, though some people say it's got a religious flavor to it. But I think it's something that gives human life meaning in a rather abstract sense. It gives us a cosmic meaning.[19]

When I hear such statements, I am reminded of the Greek word *Logos*. It can convey "reason," "order," or a "meaning-giving principle." Our word *logic* comes from it. Famously, it is also the term used in the opening chapter of John's Gospel to describe the pre-existent Christ of the Godhead as the creative, life-giving "Word" through whom all things were created.

Given that the DNA code itself is equivalent to a language that you and I and every living thing are written in, perhaps it's no surprise that, the more we learn of the way our origins defy a purely naturalistic account of time and chance, the more we may lean towards a "religious flavor" in expressing it.

THE FINE-TUNING OF THE UNIVERSE

For life to have developed on Earth requires a universe capable of producing our planet. This takes us to the next great mystery of what science is revealing about how we got here. Paul Davies is also among a number of physicists pointing out that the universe appeared to "see us coming." He has described "broad agreement among physicists and cosmologists that the Universe is in several respects 'fine-tuned' for life."[20] But what does a universe being fine-tuned for life look like?

It is generally accepted among astrophysicists that the forces and laws that have existed since the earliest moments of the universe are exquisitely finely balanced in a way that has allowed life to develop in the cosmos.

If we zoom further into the DNA molecule, we find that each amino acid is itself composed of several chemical elements, the key constituent of which is the carbon atom. Indeed, carbon is critical for innumerable aspects of the basic chemistry that can sustain life. But how was carbon itself formed in the history of our universe?

You may have heard the phrase "we are all made of stardust." It's often used in a semi-mystical way to denote that the elements that form the chemical basis of everyday life first emerged from the centers of burning stars. Physicists tell us that carbon is the result of a fusion reaction at the core of stars in which three helium nuclei, forced together by the incredibly high temperatures, fuse to become a carbon nucleus.

However, in order for this reaction to efficiently produce the large amounts of carbon needed, the resonance of the energy levels in this fusion process must be very precisely matched, each taking very specific values. Had these numbers been slightly different from what they are, then far too little carbon would have been synthesized to form the basis of life in the future.

Such a happy coincidence may be impressive, but it doesn't end there. If we drill down even further than the carbon atom to the fundamental particles it consists of—the protons, neutrons, and electrons—we discover a yet deeper level of fine-tuning.

For there to be any sort of chemistry at all, the mass of protons and neutrons need to be precisely calibrated to each other. If neutrons were slightly heavier, then stars that burn hydrogen could not exist. If they had slightly less mass, we would have a universe full of black holes. No life would be possible in either case. Likewise, the ratio of electrons to protons in the universe is also exquisitely finely balanced, giving us an overall neutrally charged universe in which matter can clump together instead of being pushed apart by electrical repulsion.

With each of these progressively more finely tuned aspects of chemistry and physics, science is showing us that there are vastly more configurations that the universe could have taken which would be incapable of yielding life. And yet here we are.

At the most extreme end are the fundamental forces of the universe, such as the strong and weak nuclear force, the electromagnetic force, and the force of gravity. The extraordinary precision of these forces shows that the existence of our life-permitting universe is balanced on the most razor-sharp of knife edges.

For instance, if the force of gravity varied from its actual value by just 1 part in 10^{60} (a 1 with 60 zeros after it), then life could not exist. If the force were slightly stronger, then matter would collapse back in on itself. If slightly weaker, then matter would spread out so thinly that no stars, planets, or galaxies could form.

Various analogies have been given for the chances of these numbers falling out the way they do by accident. One of my favorites by astrophysicist Michael Turner likens the odds to throwing a dart from one side of the entire universe towards a dartboard on the other side and scoring a bullseye.

The most impressive of these cosmic phenomena is referred to as the initial entropy of the universe. This refers to the distribution of matter and energy in the early universe being organized in just the right way so that, once the universe began its rapid expansion, it would permit life. The vast, vast majority of ways it could have been organized would result in a sterile universe of black holes. Just how finely balanced was this initial state? Nobel Prize–winning physicist Roger Penrose has calculated the tolerance at 1 part in $10^{10(123)}$. That number is so large that to write it down would require more zeroes than there are subatomic particles in the universe.

It was this apparent fine-tuning of the universe, which seems to defy any naturalistic explanation, that Dawkins admitted would be most likely to persuade him that a God may exist. However, plenty of objections (most of them better than Dawkins's complaint about a "complex" creator) have been raised to counter any supernatural explanation for the phenomenon.

The most frequent counterargument is the "puddle" objection, beloved by fans of science fiction writer Douglas Adams, who coined it. To claim the universe has been designed for us is as misguided as the puddle who assumes the hole has been created to fit its exact shape, they say. Like the water that fills a hole, life simply shapes itself to the conditions it is presented with. But the objection is itself misguided. Without fine-tuning, there would be no chemistry for life to evolve from in the first place. To return to Adams's analogy, there would be no puddle to speculate on its good fortune, since there would be no water to fill the hole.

Another, more sophisticated objection to fine-tuning is also a favorite of sci-fi fans—the multiverse hypothesis. What if our universe is just one of a potentially infinite number of universes, each with its own set of physical laws and parameters? We've won the lottery by being in one that supports life.

However, while it makes for enjoyable plotlines in Star Trek, multiverse theory is highly speculative. It's also probably untestable, leading some to question whether it should be treated as a *scientific* theory at all.

Most problematic to the theory is that the enormous, long-lasting, and highly ordered cosmos we find ourselves in is not the sort of universe we would expect to observe if the multiverse exists. Probabilistically, we should expect to find ourselves in a small patch of order in an otherwise disordered cosmos. That we don't is a significant strike against multiverse theory. In the end, a multiverse would only knock the question back a stage anyway. As others have shown, the proposed mechanism for generating a multiverse would itself need to be exquisitely finely tuned.[21]

Fred Hoyle, one of the most influential physicists of the twentieth century, was the person who first proposed the fusion hypothesis for carbon in the 1950s. When he realized how precise the resonance levels needed to be, he famously stated, "A common sense interpretation of the facts suggests that a superintellect has monkeyed with physics, as well as with chemistry and biology, and that there are no blind forces worth speaking about in nature. The numbers one calculates from the facts seem to me so overwhelming as to put this conclusion almost beyond question."[22]

The "overwhelming" facts that Hoyle referred to have only increased in number and specificity over the decades as physicists continue to discover just how incredibly unlikely our life-permitting universe appears to be. As science progresses, our existence becomes ever more remarkable. The fact that we are here, against all odds, seems to be crying out for an explanation.

BIG BANG COSMOLOGY

The next, and perhaps greatest, mystery brought to light by the progress of science in the past century is how there came to be a universe of any sort at all.

In 1927 Belgian physicist-priest Georges Lemaître first proposed the concept that the universe had not always existed in its present form but had expanded over time to its present size from an infinitely small, dense, hot point in the distant past that he termed a "primeval atom." Soon afterwards, Lemaître's mathematical predictions were confirmed by the observations of Edwin Hubble, who showed that the galaxies were moving away from each other—that the universe was in a state of expansion.

Despite his wonder at the nature and implications of the fine-tuning of the universe, Fred Hoyle, a lifelong atheist, was unsettled by this new theory about the universe's origins. Hoyle was a defender of steady state theory—that the physical universe had always existed eternally in the past. Hoyle was invested in his own theory and disturbed by the potential divine implications of a universe that appeared to have "popped" into existence.

Yet even when the observation of the cosmic microwave background in the 1960s provided clear empirical evidence of the heat signature left by the early expansion of the universe, Hoyle refused to embrace it. He held that position until his death in 2001, another example of the way in which science often progresses one funeral at a time. One thing Hoyle did contribute was the name we commonly associate with this phenomenon. The derisive term he coined for it in 1949—the "big bang"—has stuck.

Big bang cosmology went on to become the consensus view in

astrophysics. In time, the bright minds of physicists such as Stephen Hawking would develop "singularity theorems," showing that, if we wound the clock back some 13.8 billion years, we would find that the universe had a "first moment" when all of space, matter, and even time itself first appeared.

The questions raised by such momentous scientific discoveries have naturally revived interest in the classical arguments for God's existence. Long before the advent of big bang cosmology, theologians and philosophers such as Aquinas and Leibniz argued for the existence of a divine "first cause" for anything to exist at all. As Fred Hoyle feared, big bang cosmology seemed to have put the God hypothesis back on the table.

Like the mystery of the fine-tuning of the universe and the nature of DNA's information, the question of what preceded the big bang— where our universe came from—has exercised scientific, philosophical, and theological minds ever since it was proposed. After all, the idea that the universe began to exist at a certain point in the past seems to dovetail remarkably neatly with the Christian view of God creating the universe ex nihilo.

Christian philosopher William Lane Craig has been the most prolific voice arguing for the theistic implications of the big bang. Craig has married the evidence from contemporary cosmology with a philosophical argument, first proposed by medieval scholars, that the universe cannot logically exist infinitely into the past. In short, Craig's kalam cosmological argument contends that space, time, and matter coming into existence requires a first cause that transcends space, time, and matter. Additionally, that cause would be both powerful (to be able to create a universe) and personal (to be able to choose to create). The only logical candidate, says Craig, is God.

Naturally, such theological conclusions are hotly debated. The question of whether the universe can be said to have had a beginning at all is what most divides opinions.

In defense of the scientific evidence for a beginning, Craig has championed the Borde-Guth-Vilenkin theorem, which states that any universe which has on average been expanding must have a past space-time boundary. The framers of the theorem themselves seem to be split over its implications. While Guth denies that it necessitates a beginning of the universe, Vilenkin seems certain that it does.

Some physicists such as Caltech cosmologist Sean Carroll have proposed alternative theories that avoid such a beginning to physical reality. However, critics maintain that these exist only as mathematical models and don't satisfy the physics of our actual universe. Others have proposed arguments that our universe began as a fluctuation in a preexisting "quantum vacuum." But such theories only tend to push the questions back a stage: Why is there a quantum vacuum? Where do the laws that govern the quantum and classical realm of physics come from? And, as Hawking once asked, "What is it that breathes fire into the equations?"[23]

"BRUTE FACTS" AND GOD

Few people are in a position to judge the mathematics and theoretical physics involved in these debates. However, it's not difficult to grasp the intuition that science is constantly revealing a universe that is stranger than we could ever have imagined and more intriguingly suited to our existence than we could have ever predicted.

When I interviewed Sean Carroll about these ultimate questions,[24] he stated that he accepts that there are some "brute facts" in his own account of reality. Unlike many of his atheist peers who simply assume a naturalistic account of reality, Carroll says he has come to the conclusion by looking at the evidence. He thinks the existence of God is improbable and that naturalism is a more likely hypothesis. Nevertheless, he acknowledges that it leaves some potentially unanswerable questions about why the laws of physics exist or why there is a physical reality at all:

I am more or less convinced that we are always going to bottom out our series of explanations—they will end somewhere. There is this temptation to think, "There must be an explanation." But in the context of modern physics that's not the right way to think. The language of causes and explanations is inappropriate when we are talking about the fundamental nature of reality.

I had brought Carroll into conversation with Australian astrophysicist Luke Barnes. Barnes is a Christian and sees the evidence of fine-tuning and the origin of the universe as consistent with the idea that there is a mind behind the cosmos. He sees no reason why explanations should "bottom out" at the level of Carroll's naturalism.

As a thought experiment, he envisaged a futuristic scenario in which Alberta, the great-great-great-granddaughter of Einstein, has written down the ultimate principles of reality on a blackboard for all the top physicists of the world. In Barnes's words, "Physicists totally nail this universe. We solve the crossword puzzle. It's all done." After some high fives all around to celebrate this achievement, Barnes asked Carroll whether the gathered scientists would have any more questions:

> Would we be okay with just saying, "Those are the ultimate principles of reality. If you have any questions that go deeper than the blackboard, then just swallow them. We've reached the end. That's all"? Or are there questions raised by the blackboard that you would still want answers to? "Why is there a universe that is described by the stuff on this blackboard?" "Why is there stuff at all?" "Why does it obey scientific laws at all?" "Why is it presumably rather elegant and beautiful mathematical principles?"

Carroll responded that Barnes had his own "brute fact"—God. And since Carroll doesn't think the evidence is in favor of God, he'd rather live with the mystery of his own brute facts.

Either way, it seems that whether we call ourselves theists or atheists, there is a stopping point for physical explanations of physical reality. The universe can't completely explain itself. So do we simply accept that we have hit a bedrock of mystery at the level of naturalism, or are deeper explanations needed at this point? Barnes says that God provides a deeper level of explanation that "helps us deal with why there is a blackboard at all."

THE MIRACLE AND MYSTERY OF MATHEMATICS

It should already be apparent by now how extraordinary it is that we are here to observe the universe we find ourselves in. So many things had to happen in just the right way that any scientific-materialist account of our existence that boils down to dumb luck begins to look remarkably unpersuasive. But the most noteworthy thing is not only that the universe cannot explain itself but that the very science we use to fathom the universe cannot explain itself either.

One of the most significant voices in cosmology is that of mathematical physicist Sir Roger Penrose, who was awarded the Nobel Prize in Physics in 2020. Among the many stellar achievements of his career was working alongside Stephen Hawking to develop the singularity theorems for gravity and black holes in the 1960s. Since then, Penrose has developed his own (much contested) theory of cyclical universe formation and has also turned his attention to theories of how consciousness interacts with quantum physics.

Penrose says he has no religious beliefs. At the same time (rather like Paul Davies), he resists being associated with his anti-religious peers who reject any sense of ultimate meaning in the cosmos, saying, "There is a certain sense in which I would say the universe has a purpose. It's not there just somehow by chance. . . . I think that there is something much deeper about it—about its existence—which we have very little inkling of at the moment."[25] Likewise, when I spoke to him about the nature of reality, he spoke at length about how mysterious it is that our limited human minds possess the ability to map out the universe (and our own unlikely place in it) in the first place.

Penrose identifies three separate realms of existence—the physical world (think of rocks, planets, and the universe), the mental world (our thoughts, feelings, and consciousness), and the abstract world (mathematical laws and numbers). Simply in naming these as real, separate entities, Penrose has already stepped apart from the naturalism of his peers such as Sean Carroll and Richard Dawkins, who claim that only one of them—namely, the physical realm—exists.

Penrose goes on to specify three "great mysteries" about the way these separate realms overlap and interact with each other. First, the fact that the physical world is described so precisely by the abstract realm of mathematical laws. This allows us to plot the precise movement of planets and galaxies using equations and numbers. "The mathematical theories . . . when we really understand them and when we get them right, the precision is extraordinary,"[26] says Penrose.

Second, the fact that we gain access to the mental realm when the physical world is arranged in certain ways—producing things like conscious human brains. How does such a world of experience and thinking arise? "It's not just a matter of complicated computations; there's something much more subtle going on."

And third, the fact that we can use our conscious experience to access, understand, and harness the highly complex abstract realm of mathematics. We can send people to the moon because we have discovered a world of pure mathematics that we can apply to the physical one we live in. "It's so indirectly connected with our existence and how we get along in the world and how natural selection has helped us to survive and so on—it's really hard to see how these things come about from that."

In short, Penrose is asking why reality has been arranged in such a way that the universe can be precisely mapped out in the language of mathematics. And why do our fragile human minds happen to be equipped to comprehend that map in such a remarkably fruitful way? To put it even more briefly: Why can we do science in the first place?

It's a question that has been repeated in various ways by other great minds. Another Nobel Prize–winning physicist, Eugene Wigner, remarked that "it is difficult to avoid the impression that a miracle confronts us here." In an article titled "The Unreasonable Effectiveness of Mathematics in the Natural Sciences," he wrote, "The miracle of the appropriateness of the language of mathematics for the formulation of the laws of physics is a wonderful gift which we neither understand nor deserve."[27]

Einstein himself famously summed up the sense of fortuitousness by saying, "The most incomprehensible thing about the universe is that it is comprehensible."[28] Elsewhere, in a letter to his philosopher friend Maurice Solovine, he wrote,

> You find it strange that I consider the comprehensibility of
> the world . . . as a miracle or as an eternal mystery. Well,
> *a priori* one should expect a chaotic world which cannot
> be grasped by the mind in any way. . . . The kind of order
> created by Newton's theory of gravitation, for example,
> is wholly different. Even if the axioms of the theory are
> proposed by man, the success of such a project presupposes
> a high degree of ordering of the objective world, and this
> could not be expected *a priori*. That is the "miracle" which
> is being constantly reinforced as our knowledge expands.[29]

Paul Davies echoes Einstein's comments on the comprehensibility of the universe, saying,

> The directionality in the universe going from matter, to
> life, to consciousness—I would add comprehension to that.

There's an arrow of time in the direction of comprehension. And if that is the case—if this is not just an enormous fluke, a happy series of accidents—then that to me comes very close to something like a meaning or purpose in nature. . . . I think that's a sort of religious feeling. What Einstein called "a cosmic religious feeling."[30]

ATHEIST HERETICS

Terms like "miracle," "mystery," and "religious feeling" are not the sort of words we normally associate with science. Yet the questions that present themselves at the boundaries of physical explanation seem to force us to reach for a vocabulary that transcends science. Perhaps we shouldn't be surprised that other prominent thinkers appear to be turning away from the stark reductionism of the New Atheists. In fact, the last several decades have produced a fascinating roll call of scientists and philosophers who find themselves at different points along the spectrum between atheism and religious faith.

For instance, in his 2012 book *Mind and Cosmos*, influential philosopher Thomas Nagel (whom I quoted earlier as saying, "I don't want there to be a God") argued against a purely materialist view of life. Recognizing the fine-tuning of both the universe and biology for the emergence of life, Nagel says that nature manifests a "teleology" (a goal-directed purpose) in the way it produces life and consciousness, which can't be accounted for by chance or physical laws alone.

Nagel doesn't offer a divine solution to this mystery—he seems to prefer a view that consciousness itself is the primary driving force in the universe. Nagel continues to identify as an atheist (inasmuch as he doesn't believe in God), yet one who nevertheless observes a mysterious and as yet undefined principle of purpose and progress that is embedded into the physical stuff of nature.

Further along the spectrum sits the curious case of Antony Flew. From the 1950s to the 1980s, Flew was one of the most influential philosophers in the world, spearheading an analytic approach that increasingly placed scientific materialism as the de facto position in the academy. Flew was one of the best-known intellectual defenders of atheism in the world—until his shock announcement that he had converted to deism.

He spelled out the reason for his dramatic conversion in the 2007 book *There Is a God: How the World's Most Notorious Atheist Changed His Mind*. Like Nagel, Flew's reasons were directly linked to the evidence he had been exposed to regarding the order and complexity required for life to emerge. Flew wrote, "How can a universe of mindless matter produce beings with intrinsic ends, self-replication capabilities, and 'coded chemistry'? Here we are not dealing with biology, but an entirely different category of problem."[31]

While Flew went beyond Nagel in ascribing a divine intelligence to the universe, he rejected any suggestion he had converted to Christianity (although he latterly also seemed to concede the power of some arguments for Jesus' resurrection). His acceptance of deism was in the mold of what he described as the "Aristotelian God"—an intelligence who was responsible for investing the cosmos with order and complexity but did not intervene personally in human affairs, a God who had lit the blue touch paper but then stood back to allow nature to take its course.

Both Nagel's and Flew's views led them into protracted conflicts with the New Atheists, who treated them as heretics for stepping outside the orthodoxy of scientific materialism. Steven Pinker dismissed Nagel's book as "the shoddy reasoning of a once-great thinker,"[32] while science popularizer Jerry Coyne wondered "if Nagel is losing his critical abilities, or simply is plagued by a nagging desire to go to church."[33]

Antony Flew was in for even more personal attacks. Between his announcement in 2004 and his death in 2010, he was accused numerous times of being the victim of duplicitous Christians preying on a senile old man. Flew repeatedly rebutted such accusations, writing, "I have been denounced by my fellow unbelievers for stupidity, betrayal, senility and everything you could think of and none of them have read a word that I have ever written."[34]

When I phoned him myself shortly after the publication of his book, he repeated the same frustration to me. He did not have the time or energy to debate his critics on my show, but he was angered by their insistence that the only reason for his change of mind was that it had grown feeble in his advanced years.

SCIENTIFIC CONVERTS

Whereas Nagel and Flew represent examples on the spectrum of thinkers who have stopped short of embracing Christian faith, many notable philosophers and scientists have ended up converting to Christianity as adults after encountering a world that could not be explained by scientific materialism alone.

Rosalind Picard was raised in a nonreligious household and grew up believing that "people who were religious had thrown their brains out the window."[35] Today, as a leading expert in artificial intelligence research and a pioneer in lifesaving wearable tech, she credits her passion for science to God. So what changed?

Rosalind's adult conversion began when a Christian couple asked her to babysit. She evaded their invitations to church but was intrigued that two such intelligent people could be believers. When they challenged her to read the Bible, she accepted. "I started to realize there was a lot of wisdom and intelligence in that book and that it wasn't just a bunch of goofy, made-up stuff."[36]

A straight A student with a career in science ahead of her, Rosalind took a logical approach to the evidence for Christianity. To her surprise, she found the evidence was stronger than she had expected. "I became somebody who started to believe not only in the possibility that God existed, but maybe it was more probable than not."[37]

Eventually Rosalind went to church and was challenged to make a decision about Jesus. "I decided to run it as a scientific experiment: if it's really stupid, it won't make any difference, it doesn't really matter. And if it makes a difference, wouldn't it be better to have the mind of the whole universe, who knows everything, as Lord of my life?" She took that step, and it made "an enormous difference." She felt "amazing peace."[38]

Rosalind has gone on to have a significant career as founder of the Affective Computing Research Group at MIT, where she and her colleagues have developed lifesaving wearable technology that can monitor emotions and seizures. She says her work has only served to increase her awe of God: "The more I learn about how the human mind works and how the human emotion system works, I'm just in awe. I'm in awe of how fearfully and wonderfully we are made, and it inspires me."[39]

Another famous convert, introduced at the beginning of this chapter, is Francis Collins. Before he began his prominent career in genetics, he studied physical sciences as an undergraduate student. With no family commitments to faith or church, he described himself as an agnostic, saying, "By the time I got to graduate school in physical chemistry, I became deeply sceptical of anybody who wanted to talk about spiritual matters; it was all very reductionistic in my head. I guess at that point, I was an obnoxious atheist."[40]

In due course, after switching his scientific education towards human biology, Collins decided to pursue a career in medicine. However, as a medical student, Collins found himself confronted by questions of purpose and meaning in the stories of the patients he met on his rounds.

One elderly woman, suffering from advanced cardiac disease and coming to the end of her life, left a lasting impression on the trainee doctor:

At one point, after being very open about what she believed, she simply asked in the most straightforward way: "Doctor,

I've shared my faith with you, what do you believe?" And it totally threw me. I was supposed to be a thoughtful, rational scientist who looks at important questions and collects evidence and decides what the right answer is, but I hadn't done any of that.

Instead of running away from these questions, I realized I had to run towards them and figure out: what was a reasonable position for a thinking person to take? And, to my surprise, that reasonable position was ultimately to see all the pointers for there being a creator God; to ultimately recognizing that God was interested in me; and then, on top of that, getting to know the historical person of Jesus Christ in a way that became utterly compelling.

That happened over about two years, with a lot of kicking and screaming on my part. But ultimately, age 27, I became a Christian, and ever since, that has been the rock upon which I stand, in terms of trying to deal with any of these profound issues of the meaning of life; what is good and what is evil and how we make moral decisions and how we love each other.

Many others have made similar journeys. Oxford professor Alister McGrath also describes himself as having been an "aggressive atheist" in his younger years. He was as surprised as anyone by his own conversion while studying biochemistry at Oxford University:

To my disquiet, I began to realize that the evidence for atheism was much weaker than I had thought. I also began to talk to Christian friends, read Christian books, attend some Christian lectures. The intellectual case for faith was much stronger than I had realized. I don't think I had fully understood the Christianity that I had rejected as a younger man.

What drew me to faith initially was this very deep sense that it made much more sense of the world and my experience than anything else. Certainly much more sense than atheism. Faith makes sense in itself but it makes sense of everything else as well.[41]

GOD-SIZED QUESTIONS

These are just a few examples of the many scientists who have crossed from atheism to religious belief. Many others find themselves more comfortable with the fuzzy agnosticism of Davies, Wigner, Nagel, and Penrose—convinced that there is something more than the material universe but unwilling to describe it in terms of a personal creator. Yet the labels they prefer—such as "transcendence," "teleology," or even "miracle"—still point in a similar direction to those who have decided to name the mystery "God."

Why do the greatest minds working at the limits of our knowledge about the universe resort to such terms? Not just because of the extraordinary complexity involved in humanity's coming to exist but also because of the way that nature seems primed to be probed by the human minds it has birthed. Not only was it set up to produce us; it was set up to be understood by us too.

Richard Dawkins famously wrote that "the universe we observe has precisely the properties we should expect if there is, at bottom, no design, no purpose, no evil and no good, nothing but blind, pitiless indifference."[42] But the evidence from science doesn't seem to agree with Dawkins's statement. On the contrary, our scientific discoveries seem to reveal a universe that is teeming with order, purpose, and meaning.

Thousands of years ago a poet compared the cosmos to a royal herald announcing news of a king who rules it:

The heavens declare the glory of God;
   the skies proclaim the work of his hands.
Day after day they pour forth speech;
   night after night they reveal knowledge.
They have no speech, they use no words;
   no sound is heard from them.
Yet their voice goes out into all the earth,
   their words to the ends of the world.

PSALM 19:1-4, NIV

The psalmist intuitively sensed that the grandeur of the universe points beyond itself. Our awe at the size, scope, and complexity of our home in the cosmos has only increased in the intervening centuries as science has unfurled before us the universe that we are part of. We have discovered layer upon layer of dazzlingly serendipitous features.

In the big bang we see time, space, and matter come into existence. In the mind-bogglingly specific fine-tuning of the universe's fundamental parameters, physical matter was primed for the conditions that allow life to exist. Then, in the extraordinarily complex and efficient information system of DNA, that inert matter somehow turned into living, replicating organisms. Those first forms of life eventually led to a sentient, self-aware consciousness like ours—intelligent, thinking humans, capable of asking the kinds of questions that have filled this chapter so far.

These extraordinary facts leave us with important questions: Why does inert physical matter go to all the bother of becoming complex, conscious, living beings at all? Is this just the ultimate coincidence? Are we really the fluke happenstance of a mindless, unguided physical process? Or is the synchronicity that led to our existence best explained by a mind that transcends the time, space, and matter of the universe and its physical processes?

So far, the staunch materialists remain unconvinced.

They will often invoke the same objection voiced by Dawkins at the beginning of this chapter. By positing God as an explanation, am I merely replacing one mystery with another? As Douglas Adams famously quipped, "Isn't it enough to see that a garden is beautiful without having to believe that there are fairies at the bottom of it too?"[43]

That objection may be true when it comes to believing in fairies, but we might still want to find and thank the gardener who arranged and tended the garden for our enjoyment. That is the better analogy for God's role in the process. And even if we may struggle to describe the gardener, or where he himself came from, it does not diminish the fact that there is evidence such a person has been at work.

What about the related "God of the gaps" objection? In positing God as an explanation for the mysteries of our universe, am I simply guilty of sneaking God into another convenient gap in our scientific understanding? Again, I don't think so.

Certainly, when it comes to storm clouds and rainbows, we should be grateful for scientific explanations about the air pressure and pre-cipitation that causes rainfall or the refraction of sunlight that creates a rainbow. These are physical questions that the toolkit of science is equipped to address. But such explanations do not exclude the idea that God is behind the physical processes and order in our universe that allow the scientific method to do its job.

If I switch the kettle on and you ask, "Why is the water boiling?" I can give an answer about the water molecules' movement being excited by the energy from the heating element. Or I can equally answer, "Because I want a cup of tea." One is a physical, scientific answer; the other answer has to do with purpose. Both are valid and do not compete with each other. It's not a question of "gaps"; it's a question of appropriate explanations.

The same goes for the ultimate questions: Why is there a physi-cal reality at all? Why does it take the very specific nature it does? Whence come the physical laws and logic that nature is invested with?

These questions cannot be answered by the toolkit of science. Just as the universe cannot explain itself, it also turns out that our ability to do science cannot explain itself either. Just as a microscope cannot be trained upon itself, the "brute facts" of naturalism cannot be explored by naturalistic processes, since we are asking why such processes exist in the first place.

To claim that every kind of question must be answered with physical scientific explanations is to assert a naturalism of the gaps as fallacious as any "God of the gaps" argument. When the New Atheists close ranks against heretics like Nagel and Flew who question their materialist orthodoxy, they aren't doing so on the basis of science or reason. They are already committed to an a priori naturalism that has excluded God as an explanation. Blind faith comes in many forms.

However, for those willing to keep an open mind, the questions haven't gone away with the progress of science. Far from closing down the God question, the advance of science only seems to open it up with each new discovery. And, in the end, the questions we are left with seem to require God-sized answers.

A saying attributed to Nobel Prize–winning physicist Werner Heisenberg puts it well: "The first gulp from the glass of natural sciences will turn you into an atheist, but at the bottom of the glass God is waiting for you."

What if the "brute facts" of Sean Carroll's naturalism have a deeper explanation in an Ultimate Fact? What if Roger Penrose's "three great mysteries" of the overlapping mental, physical, and mathematical realms can be unified by a Divine Mind? What if Paul Davies's wonder at the directionality of our universe is best explained by a Great Director? What if Thomas Nagel's goal-directed universe has a Grand Purposer behind it? And what if Flew's disinterested deity is in fact a personal God who cares about the creation he has brought into being?

This has been the conclusion of those such as Rosalind Picard, Francis Collins, and Alister McGrath, who have journeyed all the way from atheism to Christianity. They see the evidence for God in the universe they examine as scientists. But they also believe that this God was so invested in his creation, he chose to cross the cosmos and step into it in person.

Such a conclusion inevitably requires more than a merely scientific approach, yet it may still be a perfectly reasonable inference to draw. Evidence from history, philosophy, theology, personal experience, and the testimony of others will all play their part in drawing thinking men and women towards Christian faith. But for many, an awed wonder at the complexity of the very smallest building blocks of life—and at the very largest aspects of our cosmos—may be the place where such journeys begin.

CHAPTER 6

MIND, MEANING, AND THE MATERIALISTS

ONE OF THE GREAT PRIVILEGES of hosting the *Unbelievable?* podcast has been hearing from a wide range of listeners who share their spiritual journeys and explain how the conversations from the show have helped to illuminate their path.

Many have a story of "deconstructing" as adults from the straitjacket of an oppressive form of faith they once inhabited but then failing to find satisfaction in an atheistic account of reality. Many of these are tentatively reexploring Christianity. Others have lived in a skeptical mindset for their whole lives but have begun to find a new appreciation for Christianity in more recent years.

There are a wide variety of reasons for this change of mind.

There's Nico, who, having been raised in a nominally Catholic home, grew up believing that Christianity was a made-up religion. He remembers approving that Bibles had been filed under "mythology" in a bookstore he worked at. His college professors confirmed what he had already imbibed from pop culture: "Religion was the opiate of the masses, a lie concocted by the patriarchy to justify their bigotries and control people."[1]

After graduating from law school, Nico and his wife decided to try for a baby. However, he didn't want to decide the God question on behalf of his child, so he determined to look into religion again. He "did what any millennial would do" and began listening to podcasts.

When Nico stumbled across the *Unbelievable?* podcast, he found the show perfectly suited to his background as an attorney, as both sides made their case. "Not only was I blown away by the fact that the Christians in these debates weren't the indoctrinated idiots I'd been led to believe, or the fact that there were logical arguments for the existence of God, but I found myself siding with the Christians in these debates, having expected the opposite to happen."

As Nico began to question his atheism, he picked up a book by Catholic philosopher Peter Kreeft, whom he'd heard about on the show. That turned into an email exchange with Kreeft in which Nico's final defenses were brought down. "There was no hope for me to remain atheist at that point. A few exchanges later, and I told him I'd go to church."[2]

Then there's Tamara, a New Yorker now living in Scotland who has recently converted to Catholicism. She comes from a "very secular family," her husband is an atheist, and she frequently experiences doubt. Sometimes "every single New York skeptic is screaming in my head!" she writes.

So why has Tamara converted? "The person of Jesus; the fact that everyone I know wants love, relationship, connection; the fact that everyone I know is often living somewhere between angst and misery and wanting 'more' (mixed with times of happiness); because people create and because beauty matters; because of morality."[3]

Or there's Jacqui, in her early seventies, who says the tide of her faith had completely receded after walking away from thirty years in fundamentalist Christian circles, leaving her feeling "like a stranded starfish." Mercifully, she says, "the tide has come back in" during the "second half" of her spiritual life, thanks in part to the contributions of secular thinkers like Douglas Murray. She ends her email, "It seems that, at 71, I am lucky enough to have the chance of another half when I thought it was all but over!"[4]

There are also plenty of *Unbelievable?* listeners whose journeys have not decisively led to a commitment to Christianity. But they also know they aren't atheists any longer.

Dean, a listener from Australia, got in touch with me shortly after Jordan Peterson appeared on the show. He is one of many people who discovered the podcast because they follow the work of the psychologist and have been influenced by his own grappling with Christian faith.

Dean is a talented novelist who works as a nurse in an intensive care unit and has appeared on the show to talk about his own search for faith. Christened in the Anglican church as a baby, he was exposed to a nominal form of Christianity in childhood but was dismissive of any form of organized religion by the time he reached adulthood.

However, the writings and lectures of Peterson on the Bible and the way Christianity has set the moral compass of the West led to new questions. Dean's own battle with spinal cancer and his work on the front line of life and death in the ICU had led to soul-searching over the nature of suffering. Hearing responses to these topics via *Unbelievable?* gave Dean a new perspective on faith. He describes it as "one of the richest learning experiences I've encountered, and it is encouraging me to see the world and my place in it more considerately than I have before."[5]

Every story is unique, but they all have something in common: a search for a meaningful account of life and purpose that New Atheism was unable to provide.

Dean says he has moved far beyond his atheist phase. He now devours philosophy and theology books but hasn't yet felt able to embrace Christianity. "Intellectually I'm kind of there. But there's something missing. There's a spiritual and an emotional ingredient that I'm looking for. And I wrestle with that."[6]

LIVING IN A DISTRACTED AGE

Dean is not alone in struggling to connect the intellectual and experiential dimensions of Christianity. Ever since the Enlightenment, Western culture has created an ever-widening gap between reason and religious experience. We trust the dispassionate use of science, data, and logic, and we are suspicious of feelings, instincts, and emotions.

But this is a false dichotomy. The analytical part of our mind exists alongside a broad array of sense-making faculties that allow us to function in the world. These are the parts of our personality that respond to art, music, love, and relationships. This can encompass the spine-tingling awe we experience when we walk into an ancient cathedral or the pit of fear in our stomachs when we encounter genuine malice. Or it can be found in the many day-to-day experiences where we just know things without necessarily understanding how.

All these phenomena can be given a level of explanation that involves the firing of neurons in our brain, but we also know that such a reductive explanation falls far short of the meaning these experiences actually involve. This awareness sometimes comes under the label of "emotional intelligence" or "intuition." But we are in danger of losing this side of our sense-making faculties in modern society.

Until recently, our forebears always conceived of humans as a mixture of mind, body, and soul. In fact, they rarely distinguished between those things. Modern society, in its rush to understand everything in terms of material explanations, has radically undermined this holistic aspect of human experience. As our feelings, intuitions, and even sense of self have been increasingly "explained away" by biology, chemistry, and psychology, so we have increasingly been cut adrift in a spiritual vacuum where everything has an explanation but none of it necessarily means anything.

We know far more than our forebears did about how the world works and possess a hitherto unimaginable ability to control it through technology, medicine, and science. Yet today's skyrocketing rates of anxiety and depression suggest we know far less about how to live happily in such a world.

This is not to disparage the advance of science and technology. In his books *The Better Angels of Our Nature* and *Enlightenment Now*, Steven Pinker convincingly shows how life expectancy and freedom from violence, hunger, and poverty far exceed previous ages. Yet such facts and figures don't necessarily tell us much about how well we "fit" into the more prosperous world we have created for ourselves. Material prosperity can mask spiritual poverty. We already noted in chapter 2 the massive increase in the numbers who commit suicide each year[7] (especially of men) and the unique stresses induced by our technologically connected culture. These tell a different story to Pinker's facts and figures.

Indeed, many contemporary thinkers such as Jonathan Haidt have recognized that "the meaning crisis" is partly a product of the rise of social media platforms and technology that prevent us from communicating in natural, human ways and instead lead to polarization, conspiracy theories, and cancellation in the echo chambers of both left- and right-wing culture wars. But, as Haidt writes, the greatest victims are the "digital natives" being raised in this not-so-brave new world:

> While social media has eroded the art of association
> throughout society, it may be leaving its deepest and most
> enduring marks on adolescents. A surge in rates of anxiety,
> depression, and self-harm among American teens began
> suddenly in the early 2010s. (The same thing happened to
> Canadian and British teens, at the same time.) The cause

is not known, but the timing points to social media as a substantial contributor—the surge began just as the large majority of American teens became daily users of the major platforms.[8]

We live in a hyperconnected age of shallow relationships and constant distractions. Our minds are not designed to cope with the multiplicity of devices, choices, and concerns that crowd our waking hours. Our ancestors only needed to worry about immediate threats to their lives and liberty. If they did receive news of international wars or catastrophe, it was usually long after the fact and far removed from their world. Nowadays we feel the full force of the daily news cycle and are often intimately engaged with the tribulations and injustices of a billion other individuals we will never meet in person.

Life in previous centuries was not without its own challenges, but it was also predictably boring and made sense when lived alongside those in the same circumstances. Today, especially through social media, we are constantly confronted with images of success and achievement that urge us to accomplish more, do more, *be* more. Of course, the actual reality of the average Instagram influencer is very different to the curated image they present. Nevertheless, numerous studies show that any length of exposure to social media on average leaves people with heightened feelings of envy, inadequacy, and social isolation.[9] It's hard to miss the irony of comparing how these platforms market themselves as tools of empowerment and connection to the reality of the feelings they actually engender.

Alan Noble, author of *You Are Not Your Own: Belonging to God in an Inhuman World*, delivers a bleak but honest analysis of how our culture is self-medicating its way through this present time:

> Ask an honest parent, student, or employee and they'll tell you that their goal for the day is to survive—to "get through the day," or "make it through." Existence is a thing to be

tolerated; time is a burden to be carried. And while there are moments of joy, nobody seems to be actually flourishing—except on Instagram, which only makes us feel worse.

Strikingly, even as our standard of living in the West continues to rise, our quality of life doesn't.[10]

Yet the pressure to make a success of our lives only creates an intolerable burden that fuels the rampant anxiety and increasingly esoteric search for identity in modern culture. Noble writes, "This burden manifests as a desperate need to justify our lives through identity crafting and expression. But because everyone else is also working frantically to craft and express their own identity, society becomes a space of vicious competition between individuals vying for attention, meaning, and significance, not unlike the contrived drama of reality TV."[11]

In reality, technology is only exacerbating a problem that already existed. The seeds of our modern malaise were sown long ago. Social media is simply accelerating their growth. The foundational problem is that we no longer possess the common story that Christianity once gave people to identify themselves as part of. Instead, we have all become free-floating entities in an indifferent universe, forced to make up our own story as we go along.

But as we'll see in this chapter, while we have largely lost the story of Christianity as a way to define our lives, the tide is turning once again. Dissatisfaction with a naturalistic framework of the mind (and the despair it inevitably leads to) is pushing even secular thinkers to consider whether there might be more to what it means to be human than the New Atheists believed.

LIVING IN A MATERIAL WORLD

As new generations seek to carve out identity and meaning in a world devoid of both, they are often unaware that an alternative narrative has replaced the Judeo-Christian story. It is the background hum, the assumed fact, the white noise of our present-day culture. It is the *materialist* account of reality. This particular story goes under other names too, such as *naturalism* and *physicalism*. But whatever the name, it is ultimately a story which says, "There is no story."

In this nonstory, the universe came from nowhere and is heading towards extinction. Its order and complexity do not require any explanation beyond their own existence. Energy and matter are the fundamental reality. Everything that does exist can ultimately be explained in terms of physical stuff—atoms, electrons, and energy. Human life and consciousness are the chance result of favorable conditions on a fortunate planet and an unlikely combination of chemical and physical processes.

In such a nonstory, any concepts of purpose, meaning, beauty, and morality are the inventions of human minds, selected for their survival value by the blind forces of evolutionary biology. As such, they are ultimately illusions, imposed on us by forces we have no control over. There is no ultimate meaning to life when we are the happy (or sometimes unhappy) accident of an indifferent universe.

And what is the final ending of this nonstory? There will be no happily ever after. Even if humanity escapes the bounds of earth before our sun incinerates the planet, we can't outrun nature forever. As our universe expands, its energy will continue to dissipate, and the cosmos will gradually cool down. Granted, it will take a long time, but one day all of our human plans, purposes, and beliefs will be extinguished in the heat-death of the universe. All that will remain is a cold, sterile void, stretching on into infinity.

C. S. Lewis likened this account of nature to a "sinking ship," writing, "If Nature is all that exists—in other words, if there is no God and no life of some quite different sort somewhere outside Nature—then all stories will end in the same way: in a universe from which all life is banished without possibility of return. It will have been an accidental flicker, and there will be no one even to remember it."[12]

Lewis's contemporary Bertrand Russell, one of the twentieth century's most famous atheist philosophers, was brutally honest about the consequences of the materialist view:

> That Man is the product of causes which had no prevision
> of the end they were achieving; that his origin, his growth,
> his hopes and fears, his loves and his beliefs, are but the
> outcome of accidental collocations of atoms; that no fire, no
> heroism, no intensity of thought and feeling, can preserve
> an individual life beyond the grave; that all the labours of
> the ages, all the devotion, all the inspiration, all the noonday
> brightness of human genius, are destined to extinction in the
> vast death of the solar system, and that the whole temple of
> Man's achievement must inevitably be buried beneath the
> debris of a universe in ruins—all these things, if not quite
> beyond dispute, are yet so nearly certain, that no philosophy
> which rejects them can hope to stand. Only within the
> scaffolding of these truths, only on the firm foundation of
> unyielding despair, can the soul's habitation henceforth be
> safely built.[13]

Whether expressed as explicitly as Russell or simply imbibed as the implicit worldview of science and academia, materialism is the background story that now frames many people's existence.

Russell's "unyielding despair" is not the sort of bumper-sticker sentimentality that characterizes most modern forms of humanism. I am much more likely to hear atheists respond, "But at least we can enjoy our moment in the sun and make the most of our brief lives. Perhaps they are all the more significant because we won't be around forever. In a world with no ultimate meaning, we must make our own meaning in life."

However, there is one more bitter pill that the committed materialist must swallow which undercuts even this sunny optimism. But to get there we must take a detour into the depths of another slightly mind-boggling concept—determinism.

A CLOCKWORK UNIVERSE

Perhaps it's no surprise that scientific materialism rose to prominence at the same time that combustion engines and the industrial revolution got going. Just as a child can dismantle a clock in order to find out how it works, so the scientists of the Enlightenment were pulling apart the universe and concluding that the cogs and pulleys they found there explained the whole show. When nature and all its workings can be fully described by their constituent parts—those atoms and electrons mindlessly banging around—then we have essentially described a machine.

But if nature is ultimately a machine, then its mechanisms, once set in motion, need no external intervention to do what they do. The cogs and wheels of the machine run automatically. Likewise, in a universe that consists entirely of physical causes and effects, there is no freedom to maneuver or change the outcome. Every molecule in existence has a path it will necessarily follow from the beginning of time until the end.

This doctrine of "determinism" is the twin sister of materialism. In short, it states that every single physical event—from the orbits of the planets to the movements of electrons in our brains—follows predictable laws of cause and effect. Therefore, the way that everything in the universe is now is a direct result of the way it was when it first began.

What does this mean in practice? An awful lot, it turns out.

When I spoke to atheist philosopher Daniel Dennett, a committed determinist (and one of the famous "four horsemen" of New Atheism), he gave the example of lining up a putt on a golfing green. A golfer who misses their putt may say, "If I could take it again, I'd get it in the hole." Certainly, Dennett says, if they simply lined it up and tried again, they may be successful the second time around. However, if there were some way to rewind the clock by several seconds to the exact same moment, with the exact same external physical conditions on the course and the exact same physical arrangements of atoms in the golfer's body and brain, then exactly the same miss would occur . . . every time.[14] By the same token, on a cosmic scale, whether you rewound the clock by thirteen seconds or thirteen billion years to the exact same physical state of affairs, events would roll out in exactly the same way they already have.

This is what it means to live in a clockwork universe. The whole show is running according to a predetermined script which cannot be changed no matter how much influence we think we have. The only reason we can't predict what will happen (whether Tiger Woods will miss that putt or not) is because we know only a tiny fraction of the variables that affect outcomes. But in principle, if we had knowledge of the position and activity of every particle in the universe, we could predict every outcome in the future.

Determinism has become an increasingly widespread belief, not just among philosophers like Dennett but also among their followers, especially in the world of technology and computation. Predicting the outworking of a deterministic universe was the intriguing premise of the sci-fi series *Devs*, which envisioned the creation of an all-knowing computer that could map the past and future with unerring accuracy.

There are, of course, several major consequences of this worldview. For one thing, the concept of human choice evaporates. When you become one more constituent in a predetermined process, you are no longer the operator at the wheel but simply a cog in the machine. Every thought, feeling, or decision you have ever made was not really made by you at all. It was made by the inevitable outworking of a series of physical events involving the interaction of atoms and electrons in your brain over which you have no control. If you wound the clock back a minute, a day, a year, or a lifetime to the exact same physical state, then every thought, feeling, and decision you have ever made would play out in exactly the same way.

Hence why (according to a deterministic view) free will no longer exists. You could not have done anything differently than you actually did. If you are leading a happy, prosperous, and morally upright life, then congratulations! You happen to be the lucky recipient of a good set of cards dealt from the beginning of time. But you did nothing yourself to earn such a life. The universe delivered it to you. Likewise, if you have led an unhappy life marked by poor choices and tragedy, then bad luck. You got a bad deal from the universe. But there is nothing you could ever have done to change that reality. Whether happy, sad, or something else, your destiny was determined from the outset. Every aspect of your existence was predestined by a cosmos blindly following the laws of cause and effect.

It should be noted that Dennett and some other philosophers who believe in determinism have tried to avoid these bleak consequences by positing the idea of "compatibilism." This is the claim that there are first-order and second-order forms of freedom. Even in a fully causally determined universe, humans are still free in a meaningful sense, they say, just so long as we are not being forced to act against our own will by anybody else. That the golfer can at least take the putt again and get a different outcome means we don't have to worry that the result of the second attempt is just as inevitable as the first.

I've never understood this logic (nor has Sam Harris, another notable determinist, who had quite the public falling out with Dennett over this philosophical question[15]). It seems to me that the compatibilist view is (to quote Kant) a "wretched subterfuge."[16] All it hands us is the illusion of freedom. It's like saying that Keanu Reeves's character Neo should have just accepted that he was living in a computer-generated virtual reality in *The Matrix*. After all, it seemed real enough, right? But once you've seen through the illusion, you can't unsee it. Our will is never truly free if determinism is still the bottom line.

WHY DETERMINISM CRUSHES HUMANISM

And so we return to the plucky secular humanists who cheerfully advise us that we must simply strive to make our own meaning in life. Why does the doctrine of determinism undercut such sunny optimism?

For this reason: How can we begin to speak of making our own meaning in life when we have no control whatsoever over the physical processes that actually deliver the thoughts, habits, and life that make us who we are? How can we aspire to develop the noble values of justice, compassion, and humility that humanism espouses when all such virtues are predetermined to either manifest or be absent from our lives depending on the physical conditions that the universe happened to produce in our circumstances, body, and brain at any given moment?

You don't have to look far to find the strange paradox of those who insist on meaning in a meaningless world. I stumbled upon one such epithet in a book of inspirational quotes by leading humanists. It reads, "The meaning of life is to live it, as wholly as we can, as abundantly as we can, as bravely as we can, here and now, sharing the experience with others, caring for others as we care for ourselves, and accepting our responsibility for leaving the world better than we found it."[17]

This beautiful quote comes from educational pioneer James Hemming, a former president of the British Humanist Association. As I argued in chapter 3, I believe the noble sentiments expressed in this quote owe more to the inheritance of Christianity than to any secular philosophy. However, quibbling over the source of the wisdom is only half the problem.

I do not know precisely what Hemming's metaphysical commitments were, but if he did believe in a purely material universe, it is difficult to see how such an unequivocal description of the "meaning of life" can amount to anything more than his personal preferences about how he would like people to behave. In a world which can be reduced to the blind process of physical causes and effects, the moral beliefs a person holds are entirely a product of their brain chemistry. All this heartwarming stuff about living as "wholly," "abundantly," and "bravely" as we can becomes meaningless in a world where none of us have any direct control over our thoughts, attitudes, or direction in life.

Likewise, nor can Hemming or anyone else demand that others abide by their moral worldview. In a materialistic account of reality, there are no "shoulds," "oughts," or "responsibilities" that any of us are subject to. There is simply what happens when nature takes its course. If a self-centered person disagrees with his philosophy, Hemming cannot take the moral high ground. Their selfish viewpoint is as fixed and predetermined as his generous vision for "leaving the world better than we found it."

This is another major concern raised by the determinist perspective. The concept of morality itself becomes incoherent if our behavior is wholly decided by a combination of nature, nurture, genetics, chemicals, and atoms that irrevocably determine who we are and what we do. The axe murderer cannot be blamed for their actions any more than the person who volunteers weekly at the soup kitchen should be commended for theirs. We "deserve neither such praise nor such censure" (to quote Elizabeth Bennet) when it comes to the good or evil we do.[18] It was never our decision in the first place.

This raises all sorts of ethical dilemmas. In such a world, how can we punish people for their choices (sending them to jail, imposing fines, etc.) when they had no agency in their decisions? Why should we reward those who make great sacrifices for the common good (with accolades or medals of honor) when they likewise had no real choice in their actions? How on earth do we order a society in which "good" and "bad" actions are no longer . . . well, good or bad? They just are.

Many committed materialists either seem unaware of these contradictions between their worldview and the values they espouse, or they choose to embrace them as a paradox they must live with. But for some, as we will see later, it becomes the catalyst for a complete change of worldview.

WHY DETERMINISM IS FALSE

But what if—whether we like it or not—determinism is simply true?

For instance, there have been claims that scientific experiments prove that determinism is a fact of nature. Famously, trials conducted by neuroscience researcher Benjamin Libet in the 1980s appeared to show that subjects who "chose" when to tap a finger were not, in fact, acting from free will. Brain scans of the subjects showed a faint blip of activity (supposedly the brain's "readiness potential") milliseconds before they consciously chose to move their finger. This, argued Libet, proved that our choices are in fact a product of our brain chemistry acting independently of us before we are even aware of our own desire to do something.

However, Libet's conclusions (which were already contested by many) were debunked in 2012 by another brain researcher, Aaron Schurger.

Schurger showed that the blips of neural activity Libet had identified were not evidence of the brain gearing up to tap the finger. Rather, they were the natural peaks and troughs that arose in the background noise of the brain's activity. With no other external cues to influence their choice of when to tap, people tended to act on these internal cues, hence the correlation on the charts. But the brain activity was not predetermining the choice; it was merely prompting the decision.[19]

Nevertheless, even in the absence of experimental evidence for determinism, there are many who still believe in it as a logical out-working of their naturalist worldview. (And I agree with them—if materialism is true, then so is determinism.) But there is one more significant challenge for the twin doctrines of materialism and determinism. And in my view, it is fatal.

While many materialists are willing to concede that concepts of justice, morality, purpose, and beauty lose their meaning in a deterministic world, they still tend to satisfy themselves with the fact that they have at least worked out the way things are. Even if we must accept the harsh reality that—as Bertrand Russell so eloquently put it—our origin, growth, hopes, fears, loves, and beliefs are "but the outcome of accidental collocations of atoms," at least we can comfort ourselves that we are still in the position of being able to work out our place in the universe using reason and evidence. There is certainly no need, they say, for any religious notion of a God-given purpose or meaning to life.

But hang on . . . let's look at that quote from Russell a little more closely. Among the products of the accidental collocation of atoms he lists our beliefs. Now, this presents a serious problem.

If our beliefs are themselves the result of an undirected, predetermined process that boils down to the movements of atoms in our head, then how can we claim to have based those beliefs on reason or evidence? Surely any process of reasoning requires the freedom to be able to associate one idea with another, to weigh the evidence, and, using logic and inference, come to a considered belief. Most atheists I know say that this process is precisely why they are atheists and why they believe in determinism. They reasoned themselves into their naturalism.

But if the thoughts we have and the reasoning process itself are completely outside of our control, being instead the inevitable result of a deterministic physical process, how can any of us claim to have used reason or logic to arrive at our beliefs?

In a purely deterministic understanding of ourselves and our universe, no one arrives at their beliefs through a process of reason. The atheist believes in atheism simply because their brain chemistry fizzes one way, and the Christian believes in theism because their brain fizzes another way. But there's nothing true or false about the fizzing of brain chemistry. Therefore, the idea that we choose our beliefs on the basis of reason and evidence is yet another illusion. In fact, our beliefs were handed to us by the universe from the moment the great clockwork machine was set in motion. It could never have been otherwise.

So when an atheist confidently affirms their belief in determinism, they are rather like the person who has climbed a tree and is now confidently sawing away at the branch they are sitting on. It is a self-defeating philosophy that radically undercuts itself. We are supposed to believe things on the basis of reason and evidence. Yet if determinism is true, then anyone who professes such a belief only holds to it because they were predetermined to do so.

This vicious circle seems inescapable for the materialist. As far as I can see, the only way we can trust in the concept of rationality is if we live in a universe in which free will actually exists and in which materialism is false—a universe in which there is something (or someone) beyond the physical world that acts as a guarantor of reason.

C. S. Lewis put it succinctly:

Supposing there was no intelligence behind the universe, no creative mind. In that case nobody designed my brain for the purpose of thinking. It is merely that when the atoms inside my skull happen for physical or chemical reasons to arrange themselves in a certain way, this gives me, as a by-product, the sensation I call thought. But if so, how can I trust my own thinking to be true? It's like upsetting a milk-jug and hoping that the way the splash arranges itself will give you a map of London. But if I can't trust my own thinking, of course I can't trust the arguments leading to atheism, and therefore have no reason to be an atheist, or anything else. Unless I believe in God, I can't believe in thought: so I can never use thought to disbelieve in God.[20]

Lewis seems to have hit the nail on the head, and such arguments have persuaded some atheists to abandon materialism. However, there is far more at stake here than scoring philosophical points against the atheist position.

Whether it is consciously recognized or not, I believe the materialist view of reality is the background assumption that many people in the West live by: that nature is a machine and we are insignificant cogs within it; that there is no ultimate meaning to the choices we make; that we are simply being herded along by a vast, undirected, and uncaring universe in which, as Richard Dawkins famously put it, there is "no design, no purpose, no evil and no good, nothing but blind, pitiless indifference."[21]

But what we believe about reality has real-world consequences. In such an environment, it's no surprise that a meaning crisis exacerbated by the dehumanizing effects of modern technology has begun to surface in our culture. When we are cut adrift from the shared story that invested our lives with significance and agency, and instead conceive of our place in the universe as meaningless and arbitrary, it shouldn't surprise us when we collectively slip into distracted, anxious, and even nihilistic directions.

So is there any hope? At first sight it may seem that the Christian story has lost all its ground in the battle against the materialist philosophy being propounded in academia by intellectual popularizers like Dennett and Harris. But as we have already seen in other areas of science and culture, reinforcements can often join the battlefield from unexpected quarters.

A NEW CHALLENGER

Iain McGilchrist has a graying beard and wears a pair of spectacles that are balanced carefully on the end of his nose. When he peers over them and fixes me with a quizzical look, I am transported back to my undergraduate days at Oxford University, being interrogated by professors in one-on-one tutorials.

The associations are apt since McGilchrist is an Oxford don who has been researching psychiatry and brain science for decades, studying the nature of the human brain and the illnesses that can affect it. However, before turning to medicine, his interests lay in literature, philosophy, and theology. Consequently, his wide perspective on science and culture has led him to diagnose a far more serious problem in the world.

I had invited McGilchrist to an episode of *The Big Conversation* with Christian neuroscientist Sharon Dirckx to talk about his influential theory that the two hemispheres of the human brain are no longer cooperating as they once did. In his bestselling books *The Master and His Emissary* and *The Matter with Things*, McGilchrist takes the popular notion of the split between the left and right brain and applies it at a whole new level.

In popular psychology, we often speak of left- or right-brained people. The left hemisphere of the brain is typically associated with analytics and reasoning (think of logical, scientific types) and the right hemisphere with creativity and feelings (think of artsy, imaginative types). In fact, says McGilchrist, their roles are actually far more nuanced than this popular caricature. Ultimately, however, the left side of the brain does most of the work of analysis and dissecting the world piece by piece, while the right side of the brain is concerned with big-picture thinking that also encompasses intuition, context, and understanding relationships.

This is why McGilchrist refers to the right hemisphere as "the master" and the left hemisphere as "his emissary." They are not equal partners. The left brain is supposed to serve the right brain by doing computation of the individual pieces of data it has gathered. The right brain then fits this information into a larger sphere of sense-making. For millennia we have been guided by the harmony of this relationship, with the right brain taking precedence.

However, McGilchrist's thesis is that, with the prolific rise of science and technology in the last few centuries, this cooperative relationship has become inverted. Now left-brained thinking rules a culture in which the world can be explained mechanistically and where the role of intuition and imagination has been sidelined. So when atheistically inclined scientists reduce the world to a set of physical constituents and, in doing so, believe they have explained the nature of reality (to the exclusion of purpose, meaning, and design), it is yet another sign of the left brain dominance in our culture.

Many of our modern problems, says McGilchrist, stem from the fact that the left side of our brain has overtaken its right counterpart in culture, science, and education. More worryingly, McGilchrist believes that historically vibrant cultures have always imploded when the left side of the brain took over. "They became more and more bureaucratic, devitalized, categorical rather than subtle. Effectively the life, the magic, the imagination, the spirit went out of the civilizations, and they collapsed."[22]

The polarization, alienation, and social ills we are experiencing in the modern West are evidence of a similar fall and decline:

What I see very, very vividly in the last couple of hundred years and particularly accelerating in the last thirty or forty, is that we are moving into a world in which things are atomistic, static, certain, known, black-and-white in their nature, disembodied, abstract, categorical, and really only representations of the reality.[23]

THE GOD INTUITION

McGilchrist was raised, like many of his peers, in a Christian culture but claims no particular religious affiliation. Yet his theory about the brain's influence on our modern world has attracted admirers from both the religious and the secular world.

When *The Master and His Emissary* was published, it gained glow-ing endorsements from voices as diverse as atheist philosopher A. C. Grayling, secular novelist Philip Pullman, comedian John Cleese, and then-archbishop of Canterbury Rowan Williams. A book that traverses the religious-secular divide is worth taking notice of and is one of the reasons why McGilchrist strikes me as another bellwether of the new intellectual attitude towards faith emerging in our culture.

In his most recent two-volume work *The Matter with Things* (not a short read at more than three thousand pages), McGilchrist tackles the God question head-on. Knowing how much baggage is associated with religion, he was nervous about including a chapter that argues for a divine source underlying our minds and the cosmos, saying, "Many of my colleagues begged me not to include it."[24] However, McGilchrist felt compelled to name a divine "something" behind material reality, "something very powerful, of ultimate importance, of great beauty and the source of life and creativity, which is behind this cosmos."

Even in attempting to categorize and name it, he admits we are engaging in a typically left-brained activity but says our culture needs to be directed back towards this divine source as experienced by the right brain through art, literature, music, and yes, even meditation, prayer, and religion.

When forced to place a label on his belief in God, the psychiatrist describes himself as a "panentheist," distinguishing it from panthe-ism, saying, "Pantheism is the belief that all things are God and that God is all things. But panentheism is really importantly different—that little syllable 'en' in the middle means 'in.' So God is *in* all things and all things are *in* God, but neither of these things exhausts God."

McGilchrist's panentheism is not necessarily incompatible with Christianity (I received a scholarly telling off from him for creating a "false dichotomy" when I suggested it). The Eastern Orthodox tradi-tion has always focused on the "immanence" of a God who is deeply involved in and through his creation. St. Paul himself endorsed a similar description of God by ancient philosophers, saying, "In him we live and move and have our being" (Acts 17:28).

However, McGilchrist does not describe himself as a Christian. He struggles with the concept of a divine hand that directly intervenes in history and with the exclusive truth claims of Christianity, preferring to see God expressed in many religions. Nevertheless, he describes the Christian story of Jesus' incarnation, death, and resurrection as "the most powerful mythos about God that I can think of."

Like many of the other new thinkers who straddle secular and Christian culture, McGilchrist has been deeply critical of the New Atheist approach to science and reality. He says that the reductionist perspective of these rationalists and scientists is a prime example of the pernicious left-brained way of seeing the world.

The way we end up shaping the world is radically determined by the way we attend to it, according to McGilchrist. If we go the left-hemisphere route of reducing everything to discrete atoms and electrons, we will end up with a mechanistic view of reality in which dead matter is all that ultimately exists. This results in technocratic, soulless cultures in which people are no longer connected to anything beyond their immediate concerns and circumstances.

Only by attending to the bigger picture that our right hemisphere inspires—taking seriously the religious impulse, being willing to admit the transcendent significance of beauty, morality, and our relationships with each other—will we find our way back to the kind of meaning that allows humans to flourish. Likewise, the reality of God will only make sense to our culture when we allow our intuition, imagination, and emotional intelligence to inform our thinking once again.

ABANDONING MATERIALISM

The fact that we can think, feel, and reason is itself one of the greatest challenges to materialism.

McGilchrist is among a number of thinkers who take issue with the "emergent" theory of consciousness, popularized by atheist philosophers such as Daniel Dennett. Dennett and other physicalists argue that the phenomena of our mind can be fully explained by the physical processes going on in the brain. In this view, consciousness is on a sliding scale—as the brain gets physically more complex, it gives rise to our ability to experience greater levels of awareness and mental ability. Effectively, we are our brains.

Indeed, in Dennett's view there really is no "you" or "me" to speak of. The concept of a continuous independent "self" is itself an illusion foisted on us by this process of consciousness. "You" are simply a set of experiences fused together by a brain. And there isn't even such a thing as "experience" in the sense of a private, first-person sensation. Consciousness really isn't anything special at all, says Dennett; it's just a function of the brain.

For his part, McGilchrist is perplexed by Dennett's insistence on this physicalist view: "I think his position is wholly incoherent: he says that consciousness is an illusion, but I would point out that for it to be an illusion, there must be a consciousness to be 'illuded.' It's one of the most remarkable statements by an obviously rather intelligent man."[25]

Like many other philosophers such as David Chalmers and Thomas Nagel, McGilchrist also recognizes the so-called "hard problem of consciousness" as a significant challenge to a materialist account of the mind. It asks how a purely physical understanding of the brain that boils everything down to electrical impulses and chemistry can possibly explain the actual experiences they give rise to.

For example, could you explain to someone who had never felt any physical sensations what pain is like by showing them a brain scan of what happens when you step on that piece of Lego dropped by your child? Could someone who exists in a world of purely black-and-white visual perception understand what the color red looks like, even if they fully understood the neurochemical activity that accompanies that experience?[26] Could the smell of freshly brewed coffee be described through a comprehensive knowledge of the way the chemicals from the brewing process interact with our brain's synapses? Of course the answer to all these questions is no. These experiences ("qualia" in philosophical jargon) are qualitatively different to the physical brain processes that accompany them. While our conscious experiences are clearly connected to brain activity, they are also clearly not the same thing as the brain activity itself.

These and other considerations about consciousness have led many to abandon the hard reductionism preferred by New Atheists and have prompted a revival of interest in more open-minded perspectives, such as panpsychism, the view that consciousness is the primary nature of reality and that every atom in the universe is ultimately conscious in some simple way. Rather than creating the illusion of consciousness, as Dennett claims, a brain "permits" the consciousness that already exists in the universe to be manifest through humans in a unique way.[27]

What was once viewed as an anti-scientific trickle of resistance to the materialist view of reality now seems to be turning into a surging river as more and more philosophers such as David Chalmers, Galen Strawson, Rupert Sheldrake, and Philip Goff argue for panpsychism. This has happened alongside a revival of interest in the use of meditation or even psychedelics to induce altered states of consciousness, popularized by well-known personalities such as Jordan Peterson, Russell Brand, and Joe Rogan.

Even bestselling atheist author Philip Pullman, whose His Dark Materials trilogy is highly critical of organized religion, has become an enthusiastic supporter of McGilchrist. I was made aware that Pullman's own views on consciousness had been turning away from strict naturalism when he was a guest on my *Unbelievable?* show and revealed that he was a panpsychist, admitting that it put him "in a very odd position"[28] compared to his secular peers.

Whether it is the panentheism of McGilchrist or the panpsychism of these alternative thinkers, the tide certainly seems to be turning away from the purely material understanding of nature that has dominated academia for some time. Some of these thinkers seem to be traveling in the direction of recognizing a Mind behind the cosmos. Others are simply recognizing that the universe is stranger than a materialist perspective allows, even if they haven't yet opened the door to God as a possible explanation.

While the philosophical questions around consciousness may seem complex, the actual experience of it is not. That we are conscious beings is one of the most obvious things we can ever know. Yet it is an aspect of our experience that resolutely refuses to fit into the box of atheist materialism. Perhaps the evidence for God is, quite literally, staring us in the face.

MEANING MAKES CONVERTS

For many, the stark mystery of consciousness and a growing dissatisfaction with the materialist account of reality has resulted in a search for meaning that has led them all the way to Christianity.

There's Robbie's story, an Australian listener who told me of how he lost his faith as a university student after being confronted with a variety of arguments against religion. He still clung to the value of Christianity's ethical principles but became an atheist as far as belief in God was concerned.

However, Robbie is philosophically inclined, and he soon began to realize that the materialist worldview failed to explain his direct experience of the world. The popular view that his sense of self was an illusion and his experiences were explicable by brain chemistry alone seemed to continually jar with the meaning he met in music and art. "I remember one occasion when I nearly lost my atheism simply whilst listening to a Beethoven symphony and watching the sunrise over Sydney Harbor," says Robbie. "I couldn't understand how such an experience could be explained by a material world without some form of independent conscious awareness."[29]

It was the "hard problem of consciousness" that convinced Robbie that materialism was false and, in conjunction with other philosophical arguments, set him on an intellectual path, first to deism (belief in a God behind nature) and finally to Christianity.

Jen Fulwiler, an American author, comedian, and podcast host, tells the engaging story of her own adult conversion, which was sparked by an existential crisis about meaning.

Growing up, Fulwiler had neither experience of nor respect for Christianity, seeing religious people as gullible and deluded. "I was a true atheist materialist," she says. "I believed that the physical world around us that we can touch and observe is all that there is."[30]

However, it was the experience of having a child that first shook Fulwiler's worldview. She describes a moment, while looking at her firstborn son, in which she had an epiphany:

> I looked down and thought, "What is this baby?" And I thought, "Well, from a pure atheist materialist perspective he is a collection of randomly evolved chemical reactions." And I realized if that's true, that all the love I feel for him, it is all nothing more than chemical reactions in our brains. And I looked down at him and I realized, "That's not true. That's not the truth."[31]

This was the experiential jolt that sent Fulwiler on a journey to investigate the intellectual arguments for faith. Her disdain for Christianity began to dissolve as she met intelligent believers and realized that many of the greatest minds in history—such as Augustine, Aquinas, and Descartes—had been Christians. "I was really surprised when I actually found these very intellectually rigorous books where people talked about their faith from a place of reason and not a place of emotion."[32]

From being a happy "lifelong atheist" in her midtwenties, Jen Fulwiler, along with her husband, entered the Catholic church in her early thirties—a convert whose journey began because she recognized the conflict between the materialist story of reality and her own experience of love.

A similar pattern emerges out of many of these conversion accounts. Before the full embrace of Christianity and its historical creeds, there is first an intellectual metamorphosis that takes place as the materialist worldview gets chipped away. There is often a growing sense that purpose, beauty, right, and wrong really do exist and that our emotions, thoughts, and feelings can't be reduced to the movements of electrons in our brain.

The idea that the love we feel for a newborn child or the intensity of emotion that accompanies a stirring piece of music is fully explained by a series of chemical reactions in our brain stops making sense. This is not to deny that these physical phenomena are linked to those experiences. If we were being monitored by an MRI scanner, we would certainly see the appropriate parts of our brain light up during these moments. But that doesn't mean that's all that is going on. That would be like looking at the notes written on the page of a Beethoven concerto and thinking we understood it, without ever having heard the notes played. Meaning cannot be contained by such one-dimensional explanations.

Perhaps these conversion stories are only the first ripples of a forthcoming tide of people looking for the source of meaning that they sense must exist somewhere over the horizon.

SYMPTOMS OF THE MEANING CRISIS

"Humans are storytelling creatures" is a widespread dictum that probably originated with Jerome Bruner, a pioneer of cognitive psychology in the twentieth century. He emphasized the importance of storytelling for the healthy development of children. But seeing ourselves as part of a meaningful story is important throughout our lives.

Jonathan Gotschall's book *The Storytelling Animal* emphasizes how important it is for humans to create a narrative for their own lives, rather than seeing themselves as simply bouncing around chaotically with no plotline or destination. "We all have a story that we tell about ourselves—about who we are, what our formative experiences were, and what our lives mean," says Gotschall.[33]

The psychologist admits that the stories we tell ourselves aren't always trustworthy. We habitually overrate our own qualities. "Yet," he says, "crafting these stories—and believing them—seems to preserve our mental health."[34]

For centuries Christianity gave people in the West a story to measure their lives by—a story in which they had been created for a purpose within a universe which, although it was broken, was headed for redemption. True or not, it was a story that gave people meaning even in the midst of misery and helped make sense of suffering. Shakespeare wrote that "all the world's a stage, and all the men and women merely players." Yet even if the roles seemed insignificant in the scheme of things, there was still nobility in being part of a larger story. The narrative may have included many twists and turns, but it was heading towards a grand conclusion.

For many years now, that story has been replaced in the West by an account of reality in which there are no plotlines or cues, no scripting or directions, and certainly no playwright to bring it all together in the end. This is the all-pervasive materialist worldview, where we are but one cog in a mindless machine. Indeed, even the belief that we are in some small way the master of our own destiny has been extinguished by its wholly deterministic account of the universe.

There are many potential factors contributing to the rise in anxiety, depression, and distraction in our culture, especially the pressures of living in industrialized urban communities that make us less connected with nature and with each other. But the modern materialist story is, in my view, the overwhelming reason for today's meaning crisis.

As I mentioned near the start of this book, the term "meaning crisis" was coined by psychologist John Vervaeke. It describes the sense of alienation people experience when they move through life feeling disconnected from each other and the world. Most especially they feel disconnected from a purpose to live for, or a story that makes sense of who they are. It ties into the description of the world becoming atomized, disembodied, and abstract that McGilchrist identified.

Vervaeke sees a range of symptoms to this crisis, including "the rise in suicide, even suicide independent of clinical depression right now, which is a very telling sign. A loneliness epidemic, the mental health crisis . . . depression and anxiety disorders, the addiction crisis, the opioid crisis."[35]

Vervaeke is also concerned by "the virtual exodus"—the attempt by many to distract themselves from real life by immersing themselves in technology and gaming. Indeed, with the proliferation of immersive multiplayer online role-playing games, the existence of "gaming widows"—those who have lost partners to video game addiction—has been well-documented. But now many young men are surrendering any aspirations of career or family to begin with.

These are the increasing numbers of adults who have given up on pursuing "real life" goals because the rewards of the online gaming world are so much easier to attain. Writing for the *Economist* on "game drain," Ryan Avent states that "today's games seem to be displacing careers, friendships and families, and thus stopping young people (particularly men) from starting real, adult lives."[36]

Again, for Vervaeke this is yet one more symptom of a world in which people have lost connection with a meaningful story. "People are explicitly declaring that they prefer to live in the virtual world rather than the real world. . . . They're finding something in that world that's missing from the real world."

Gotschall expresses similar concerns. "If you had a technology that allowed you to live any story you wanted, why would you ever come out? Why would you ever want to stop being god?"[37]

TURNING THE TIDE

Faced with this burgeoning meaning crisis, many have tried to find solutions in the form of the mindfulness revolution. There has been an explosion in pop psychology books, courses, and apps aiming to soothe our anxiety and develop positive habits for mental health, often drawing on ancient forms of wisdom to do so. These are welcome developments insofar as they help stressed and anxious people to find a sense of equilibrium. Even Sam Harris has reinvented himself in recent years as a mindfulness guru with his own popular meditation app and podcast.

But these attempts to redeploy ancient wisdom through modern technology and psychology still feel like a temporary fix rather than a solution. The optimistic slogans of humanists who insist that we must "make our own meaning" are well-intentioned. But as long as their best minds are also reminding us that we are "accidental collocations of atoms" for whom personhood and free will are an illusion, their efforts will always be a placebo rather than a cure.

Is there a way back from this crisis? I am confident there is and that we are beginning to see the turning of the tide. It begins with recognizing that we have been living in the wrong story for too many years. The materialist-determinist paradigm is an atheistic assumption supported by neither science nor philosophy. We need not be compelled to live in such a nonstory.

I welcome the growing influence of thinkers from the secular world such as the panpsychists, who are pointing out the problems with materialism, or the psychiatrists and psychologists like McGilchrist and Vervaeke, who are encouraging us to return to holistic ways of thinking about the world. At the same time, I don't want to settle for anything less than the true story of reality.

The way forward must involve recovering the power of story-telling. We are all searching for a story to live our lives by. Stories allow us to see ourselves as part of something much bigger than ourselves. But the purpose of storytelling is not to be led off into fairy tales or the simulacrum of a virtual world but to recover the true story that all other stories are ultimately pointing towards.

If there is a story that makes sense of who we are, then we must inquire of the Playwright to find out what it is and how we can play our part in it. If there is a path we are meant to take, then there must be one who can show us the way. If there is a meaning to be discovered out there, then there must be a source of truth. If there is a way to be truly human, then there must be one who can show us what fullness of life consists of.

Having been starved of meaning, purpose, and a story to live by, the West is, I believe, beginning to recover the story of Christianity and its central protagonist's claim to be the personal embodiment of the way, the truth, and the life. Throughout this book I've tried to spell out the ways we are seeing that happen intellectually in culture, history, and science.

But perhaps more importantly, it will happen as we begin to overcome the false dichotomy of the left and right brain, of scientist and storyteller, of reason and imagination. I see it already happening in the stories of the heterodox thinkers pushing against the prevailing paradigms and the converts finding God as they reject the machine of materialism to explore the meaning of a great Mind behind it all. These are early signs that people are giving themselves permission to live in a different story.

It is the story of the one described as the *Logos*—the Word—who created a world out of love, placed humans at the center of it, and when it all went wrong, entered the story himself to redeem and restore the creation he had made. It is a grand story that declares that every individual story matters. Far from being one more product of a mindless, purposeless universe headed towards oblivion, we have each been offered an integral role in a cosmic drama. What you do with your part is up to you, but you are nevertheless invited into a story that is being woven through time and space, a story in which you are intended, purposed, and loved.

This is the story that shaped and fed us for almost two millennia. Its power has not gone away, even if it is often only dimly remembered now. But when people do embrace it today, it continues to transform individual lives and whole civilizations in turn.

What if the tide is due to turn?

In the final chapter of this book, I will explain why I think we may see it happen in our own generation. The surprising rebirth of belief in God is underway, and we may yet live to see the rebirth of our culture in the process.

CHAPTER 7

THE SURPRISING REBIRTH OF BELIEF IN GOD

I BELIEVE WE ARE ALL MADE TO WORSHIP. That instinct runs so deep within us that, if we don't worship God, we will end up worshiping something else instead.

The object of people's worship is whatever preeminent thing they build their lives around. There are the usual glamorous contenders—money, sex, power. And the less obvious idols too—career, family, fitness. Not that any of these things are bad in themselves, but, as Tim Keller says, idolatry usually involves "turning a good thing into an ultimate thing."[1]

Secular forms of worship frequently involve the pursuit of a righteous cause. A noble campaign, social ideology, or political calling can often become the conduit for a sense of the sacred in people's lives. We want to believe in and work towards that which is truly good, righteous, and beautiful.

For Paul Kingsnorth, nature was the object of his veneration from a young age, and the wild countryside was his place of worship. Kingsnorth's love of the natural world inspired his adult involvement in environmental activism:

> I used to go on a lot of walks with my dad when I was young. We'd spend weeks walking and camping in wild places. I think he accidentally made me a pantheist. When you see society systematically destroying creation in order to make money, it makes you an activist. I had a sense that something very sacrilegious was happening to the living world.[2]

Kingsnorth is an award-winning poet and novelist living in Ireland, and for many years, he was a campaigner in the environmental movement. News of his conversion to Christianity began to circulate in 2021 after the publication of his online essay titled "The Cross and the Machine."

When I invited him to tell his story in a conversation with the former archbishop of Canterbury Rowan Williams, Kingsnorth described growing up in a household where religion was regarded as largely irrelevant. Exposure to school hymns and occasional visits to church during childhood gave way to a short-lived period of rebellious teenage atheism. "For a couple of years, I was trying to be a teenage Richard Dawkins," he recalls.

But his flirtation with atheism was "never very convincing," he confesses. "At the same time as mocking religion, I was a real lover of fantasy literature and a great believer in ghosts and the supernatural. I was never one of these people who thought the world was disenchanted. I always knew it was enchanted, but I didn't know what to do with that."

This sense of the sacred evoked by nature led Kingsnorth on "a fumbling spiritual quest" towards some sort of religious expression to his longings. For a number of years he practiced Zen Buddhism but finally admitted that, rather than looking inward for the answers, he wanted to look outward. He wanted to worship . . . something.

So he tried nature worship by joining a Wiccan coven. Despite its claim to ancient origins, Wicca is, according to Kingsnorth, a new age religion invented in the sixties ("Wiccans would get very cross if you called them new age, but they basically are") involving a mixture of goddess worship, mystery traditions, and occult teaching. "You mix it all together, and the whole thing is an excuse to worship nature in the woods," says Kingsnorth. "On one level, it was quite satisfying because it met my need to find a name for the divine."

Yet something was still missing. In his professional life, Kingsnorth had become increasingly disillusioned with the corporate nature of an environmental movement that had been "hijacked" by the forces of technological industrialism it had once opposed. He had also come to realize the limits of human power—even the laudable desire to save the planet could end up making tyrants out of good people. Nature needed a savior bigger than itself, and so did humans.

FROM WICCA TO ORTHODOXY

Kingsnorth says he was taken by surprise on the night his wife predicted that he would become a Christian:

> My wife is much more spiritually intelligent than me and is very good at quietly prophesying things. One day we were out for dinner, and she suddenly said—out of nowhere— "You're going to become a Christian." We weren't even talking about religion. I said, "What are you talking about?" And she said, "I don't know, I just knew I had to say it." And she was right, as she usually is.[3]

He describes what it was like to move from Wicca to Christianity:

I felt like I was physically dragged out of Wicca, actually. There's all sorts of strange forces at work that people are not necessarily aware of. I had really been looking for God—and Christ had come to find me. I'd gone looking for Buddhism and I'd gone looking for Wicca because I thought they fitted with how I saw the world. But I didn't think Christianity fitted how I saw the world at all! And I didn't want to be Christian.

Kingsnorth isn't the first person to describe himself as a reluctant convert. Despite his skepticism about Christianity, he started to see an increasing number of "God-incidences" that all seemed to point in the same direction:

I started having very strange experiences that are difficult to describe. I was having dreams and meeting Christians every five minutes. I used to run a writing school and, suddenly, I had vicars asking me to read their sermons and give them feedback. People I'd known for years suddenly told me they were Christians, and I hadn't known. I felt like I was being hunted by Jesus! This was not the plan. But it was happening. . . . If I'd listened to this sort of thing five years ago, I'd have thought it sounded absurd.

This journey eventually led Kingsnorth to Eastern Orthodoxy, arguably the most ancient branch of the Christian church. He acknowledges that an Englishman in Ireland attending a Romanian Orthodox church is not the most obvious combination, but from the first moment, he was "swept up" in a form of liturgical worship that finally felt connected with the God he had been searching for:

The integration of all the senses is so strong in the
Orthodox tradition. It's not just a matter of your intellectual
engagement—everything happens at once. And things
really did happen in that liturgy. . . . In Orthodoxy the
emphasis on God being both transcendent and immanent—
"everywhere present and filling all things," as it says in
the Trisagion Prayer—is very, very real. This wasn't why I
became Orthodox, but it satisfied the need I had for a God
that was in creation, as well as beyond it.

I see Paul Kingsnorth's journey as a sign of the times we are living
in. People are searching for a story that makes sense of their lives.
Perhaps it's no surprise that a novelist would embark on such a quest.
But even Kingsnorth was surprised to arrive back at the Christian
story, a religion which he'd discounted in his youth as a "hang-up
from a time that it was real, but we didn't believe it any more" and
which he'd assumed was just another form of social control. Now,
from the inside, he sees things very differently:

We can't deny the realities of some of the bad things that
have happened in churches—the abuses of power and
the rest of it. But the actual path—the way, the faith—is
enormously freeing, and that was again a shock to me.
You grow up with these unquestioned assumptions
about how Christianity is a thing that just wants to
take stuff away from you and somehow control you—
but it isn't.

Why return to the Christian story after looking into so many other
options—atheism, Buddhism, and new age? I believe it's because all
stories ultimately point to the story of Christianity.

Some are more derivative of it than others. "Looking back, I see
Wicca—and a lot of new age stuff—as a Christian heresy," says

Kingsnorth. "There's a lot of playing around with bread and wine and altars. They're satirizing Christianity."

But, as we have seen, we also find the Christian story embedded in the moral assumptions inherited by secular humanism and the myriad causes and ideologies that have sprung up in recent decades. Moreover, I believe that even precursors like Buddhism, Hinduism, and the nature religions are echoing the story of Christianity in ways that point towards its eventual fulfillment in Jesus.

We all worship something—even in a time when religion (and especially Christianity) is thought to be in decline. But I believe that the reason we are beginning to see a rebirth of belief in God is because the story of Jesus still makes the best sense of our own stories.

RELIGION BY NUMBERS

The decline of Christianity in the West since the 1950s onwards has been well chronicled. Each new survey reminds us of the downward trend.

According to Pew Research, 63 percent of the US population identified as Christians in 2021, down from 75 percent a decade earlier. Meanwhile, 3 in 10 US adults identified as "nones"—people who describe themselves as having no religious affiliation. That figure leaps up to almost half among millennials (born 1980–1996) and Gen Z (born 1997–2012).[4]

The trend is even more pronounced in countries that are more post-Christian than the United States. Over half of the UK population now identify as nonreligious, with almost a quarter of people never having been brought up in any kind of religious setting to begin with.[5]

It's worth noting that these Western statistics do not represent the whole picture. In other, less secular parts of the world such as the Global South, belief in God remains part and parcel of every-day life. In fact, because religious people tend to have more children than their secular counterparts, the number of people who identify as nonreligious is actually shrinking as a proportion of the global population.[6] And even in the West, there are notable exceptions to the overall picture of decline. The growth of the African Caribbean community has swelled churchgoing in many UK cities, while the church-planting activity of Holy Trinity Brompton, home of the Alpha Course, has revitalized hundreds of churches that were on the brink of closure.

Nevertheless, the overall picture in the West is one of steady decline in churchgoing. While a good number of Protestant evangelical churches have held relatively steady in recent decades (though even they have begun to slip), most of the mainline denominations in Europe and the United States are shrinking at an alarmingly rapid pace,[7] a trend that two years of COVID-19 restrictions only served to reinforce. Some predict that the Anglican and Methodist denominations may go extinct within a few decades if the terminal decline is not reversed.

Yet the same statistics that confirm a decline in religiosity don't necessarily show that atheism is on the rise. Those who self-identify as atheists in the United States rose by just 1 point—from 2 percent to 3 percent—between 1991 and 2014,[8] suggesting that New Atheism's prominent evangelistic efforts were not matched by an embrace of antisupernaturalism among the public.

The "nones" may have rejected organized religion but are more likely to describe themselves as agnostic or "spiritual but not religious" than atheist. Indeed, a mishmash of quasi-religious practices, supernatural beliefs, and mystical new age ideas often typify the nonreligious. For instance, a quarter of the UK's nonreligious population say they pray at least occasionally,[9] while one in five "nones" in the United States say they pray every day.[10] In the secular West our religious instincts continue to run deep, even if we can't name who or what we are praying to.

It is the "organized" part of religion that people have rejected in the last half century, rather than spirituality itself. And it's not only organized religion feeling the effect. The rise of individualism and a rejection of traditional forms of community in general mean that the church is in the same boat as political parties, social clubs, and civic groups, who have also seen a similar drop in membership. The fact that local village pubs are closing faster than rural churches is a reminder that wider demographic changes are afoot.[11]

Ironically, those who reject being part of a religious community in favor of retaining a semblance of personal spirituality are losing out on most of the social benefits that religious affiliation brings. Research shows that people who regularly attend church report stronger social support networks and less depression. They smoke less, have happier marriages, and lead healthier and longer lives than people who don't go to church. Actively religious people are proven to give both more money and more time to charities (including secular ones) than nonreligious people. They even donate more blood.[12]

Over the years there have been efforts by some secular groups to replicate the benefits of a religious community for nonbelievers. The late nineteenth century saw the establishment of "Ethical Societies" in the United States and UK—gatherings of people who wanted to disentangle morality from religion. The movement gained adherents for several decades but experienced steep decline from the 1920s onwards, with only a handful of congregations remaining today. As referenced in chapter 1, a more sprightly incarnation of "atheist churches" took off more recently when the first Sunday Assembly began in London. It resembles a typical church service but with God removed.

As is the case with many religious groups, it is the community life that primarily attracts people to these gatherings. But churches have something extra that an Ethical Society or Sunday Assembly doesn't. They don't simply gather around a shared set of ideals or the fun of singing Queen songs together. Churches gather around a person,

Jesus Christ, and believe that in their diversity they are held together by the living presence of the Holy Spirit. It's hard to beat that, no matter how good the singing is.

After an initial flurry of publicity, a number of Sunday Assembly congregations formed in other parts of the world. However, the growth stalled following a split in the network, and a number of congregations folded. COVID has also taken its toll and, at the time of writing, the website lists many of the assemblies as dormant.[13] It seems that godless churches are prone to many of the same challenges as regular churches.

In summary, organized religion (and nonreligion) is out of favor in the West. But many people are still seeking meaning and spirituality where they can find it.

WE'RE ALL BELIEVERS

Even if more of us are choosing to stay in bed on a Sunday morning rather than go to church, and even if belief in God is less widespread than it used to be, I'm convinced that none of us are actually any less religious than we used to be—we're just religious about different things.

I was reminded of this when an atheist on Twitter scornfully denounced my belief in God, saying it was ridiculous to believe in immaterial things that you can't prove scientifically. I pointed out that his Twitter bio declared his firm belief in human rights, women's rights, and LGBT rights—all immaterial things that you can't prove scientifically.

Our innate religious impulse is also manifest in the quasi-religious devotion (already mentioned in chapter 2) to various ideological causes, whether it be the issues of sexuality, race, and gender on the left or political nationalism on the right, with its belief in sacrosanct liberties such as, in the United States, the constitutional right to bear arms.

Even the most nonreligious people can still demonstrate a single-minded devotion to a holy cause: think of the righteous anger of Extinction Rebellion activists willing to blockade traffic and sabotage public transport for their convictions or the devotion to absurd QAnon-style conspiracy theories that have typified parts of conservative culture. There are often ritual ceremonies: think of those who take the knee at public events to protest racism or swear allegiance to a flag to demonstrate their patriotism. There are sacred symbols too: think of the ubiquitous rainbow motif that decorates so many public spaces and corporate logos during Pride month. And there are even heretics: think of J. K. Rowling.

It turns out we're all believers deep down. We all believe that good must conquer evil and that justice really matters. We may have inherited those beliefs from our Christian past, but as that story has faded from view, we're left with a set of quasi-religious beliefs that have become detached from their original moorings. As Glen Scrivener puts it, "We're all standing on the Bible, hurling verses at each other. We've just forgotten the references."[14]

The problem is that the acolytes who congregate around the new totems of LGBT rights, environmentalism, feminism, anti-racism, and patriotism often inherit the worst aspects of religious fundamentalism in their zeal for justice. However worthy these causes may be, their proponents often come across as self-righteous crusaders who, if they cannot convert those around them, will use the power of the mob against the unrighteous.

The drive for ideological purity has even led to the woke being out-woked by their peers.

When young adult fiction author Amélie Wen Zhao, a Chinese female immigrant to the United States, received her first offer of a book deal, she was ecstatic. Publishers were excited by her series of fantasy novels set in a mythical empire where a group of people with magic powers are enslaved and demonized. But her joy was short-lived. Early review copies of her debut novel *Blood Heir* were savaged by readers accusing her of racial stereotypes, cultural appropriation, and a disregard for the experience of African American slavery. The outrage mill quickly swung into action, and within days a mortified Zhao had published her apology and the book had been withdrawn.

One of her chief critics was another young adult novelist, Kosoko Jackson, a queer Black writer who was very vocal about diversity and representation in the genre. His own debut novel, *A Place for Wolves*, told the story of two boys falling in love during the Kosovo War. Yet even his politically correct pedigree could not protect Jackson from his own public shaming after a negative review of his treatment of the war and portrayal of Muslims in the book led to a backlash on social media. Like Zhao, he withdrew the book from publication and wrote an apology, promising to learn from his mistakes.

Jesus' words "Judge not, that ye be not judged" (as the Authorized Version puts it) seem apposite. Sadly, judgment is frequently the modus operandi of this new religious movement, in which there is no atonement, no forgiveness, and no restoration of the sinner.

Lest the above examples make us imagine that these problems exist only on the progressive left, it's worth noting that both sides have their sacred causes. "The madness of crowds"—a phrase coined by the Scottish writer Charles Mackay and later used by Douglas Murray for the title of his book critiquing woke culture—can often apply to those on the right too.

The invasion of the United States Capitol on January 6, 2021, by crowds of people who believed the presidential election had been stolen was motivated by a quasi-religious belief that the future of America hung in the balance and that Donald Trump was its designated savior. People who prior to that day had never been charged with more than a parking ticket were swept into civil insurrection in the fervor of the moment. Perhaps, in the humdrum disappointment of daily life, this felt like a great mission, an adventure—something to believe in.

In a world where we have lost sight of the grand adventure of the Christian story of reality, we are liable to settle for much smaller stories. We replace a drama of cosmic significance, written across the pages of Scripture and history, with political battles and culture wars that will likely puzzle future generations in terms of how much heat was generated, yet how little was achieved.

The irony is that the motivations of both left and right are usually good—the pursuit of truth and justice. But religion without grace is unsustainable. It quickly degenerates into culture wars and cancellation. When religious zeal gets disconnected from the one true source of justice and peace, burnout and resentment are inevitable.

There is a reason why the greatest moments of cultural and systemic change throughout the centuries have been wrought by those whose eyes were turned to heaven rather than earth—people like William Wilberforce and the Clapham Sect pursuing the abolition of slavery and Rev. Martin Luther King Jr. and his fellow church leaders pursuing civil rights in the United States. They saw a bigger picture that transcended power and politics. They were committed to the slow and patient work of sowing the seeds of a different kingdom. They were willing to show grace, to love their enemies, to turn the other cheek, and to bless those who persecuted them. Why? Because they lived by the story of the one who had walked that path already.

LITERARY CONVERTS

As the New Atheist story of scientific materialism begins to wear thin and as people tire of the quasi-religious stories that are fomenting the present culture wars, I am convinced we are seeing our culture gradually become more willing to consider the value of the Christian story again.

Converts like Paul Kingsnorth make for interesting case studies. He is one of numerous examples of intelligent literary figures surprised to find themselves either returning to or starting on the path of Christian belief in their adult years. There are many more I could mention.

The influential British writer and columnist A. N. Wilson spent his midlife years as a nonbeliever, having consciously rejected his Anglican roots in his thirties. He describes his initial embrace of being a "born-again atheist" in explicitly religious terms. Delighted at being able to join the intelligentsia of friends such as Christopher Hitchens, he wrote, "I could join in the creed shared by so many (most?) of my intelligent contemporaries in the western world—that men and women are purely material beings."[15]

However, once the afterglow of this conversion experience began to fade, he realized that the materialist creed could not contain any of the things he valued most in life. "Materialist atheism says we are just a collection of chemicals. It has no answer whatsoever to the question of how we should be capable of love or heroism or poetry if we are simply animated pieces of meat."[16]

He began stealing sheepishly back into the Anglo-Catholic churches he had once frequented and found himself moved, not just by the music and ceremony but, for the first time, by the substance of what was being proclaimed. "I also realised, looking back, that I had a long, long phase—probably most of my grown-up life—of being a keen churchgoer without really believing it."[17]

Wilson says his subsequent return to Christian faith "surprised no one more than myself." Despite writing a highly skeptical book on the historical Jesus during his atheist years, he has written movingly about his new appreciation of the Resurrection. "In the past, I have questioned its veracity and suggested that it should not be taken literally. But the more I read the Easter story, the better it seems to fit and apply to the human condition. That, too, is why I now believe in it."[18]

It's worth noting that this return to faith was not prompted by the discovery of an unassailable apologetic argument for Christianity. Rather, Wilson realized that the materialist paradigm he once embraced was just as much an article of faith as Christian belief. Yet he found the beauty of the Christian story made more sense of his hopes, loves, and longings, and so he chose to step into that world-view instead.

Francis Spufford is another celebrated literary figure who found his way back to faith as an adult. In recent years he has authored critically acclaimed novels such as *Golden Hill*, but before this he was primarily known for his nonfiction, including his short book *Unapologetic*—an unashamedly polemical (and occasionally sweary) defense of the way Christianity makes "emotional" sense of life.

When I interviewed him about his journey, Spufford described being raised in a churchgoing household but says he exited it "in the usual teenage way" after categorizing it as "a piece of childhood furniture I didn't need any more."[19] He was suspicious of authority, saying he had "got God mixed up with various forms of authority that I found difficult." It was only as an adult, when he was sure the church had been emptied physically of people (and therefore also of its authority) that he was willing to consider stepping back inside.

However, his return to faith after "twenty-odd years of atheism"[20] came through encountering Christianity again in a way that spoke to the psychological and emotional aspects of his humanity, especially the experience of grace.

In a candid passage in *Unapologetic*, he describes sitting in a café the morning after an emotionally draining "scratch-your-eyes-out, scratch-each-other's-skin-off" argument with his wife. "One of those cyclical rows that reignite every time you think they've come to an exhausted close, because the thing that's wrong won't be left alone."[21]

While he "nursed [his] misery along with a cappuccino," a Mozart clarinet concerto began playing in the background, and its steady, repetitive theme seemed to speak to Spufford. "It offers a strong, absolutely calm rejoicing, but it does not pretend there is no sorrow." Suddenly, through the music, the Christian quality of mercy hit him in a new way:

I had heard it lots of times, but this time it felt to me like news. It said: everything you fear is true. And yet. And yet. Everything you have done wrong, you have really done wrong. And yet. And yet. The world is wider than you fear it is, wider than the repeating rigmaroles in your mind, and it has *this* in it, as truly as it contains your unhappiness.[22]

As an attention-grabbing alternative to the word *sin*, Spufford invented the memorable term "the human propensity to f— things up."[23] He goes on to refer to "HPtFtU" regularly throughout the book. It is the human condition, and Spufford gives a raw account of the way we are all prone to it. And yet. And yet. What if there is a God who knows all about the HPtFtU but chooses to enter the mess of our world anyway? A God who becomes immersed in it and yet mysteriously, miraculously overcomes it? "Far more can be mended than you know," says the risen Jesus in Spufford's retelling of the Resurrection.[24]

Rather than try to prove God through an objective intellectual or philosophical argument (hence the title *Unapologetic*), Spufford shows how the Christian faith speaks to our human emotions and psychology, what it feels like from the inside. Certainly, Christianity speaks to the things we value most—love, beauty, music, art—but nor does it gloss over how bad we are, meeting us in both our glory and our shame. For Spufford, it makes sense to believe because that belief makes sense of us.

In Holly Ordway's conversion there was no prior connection with church in childhood. For her, poetry and literature would themselves become the conduit to faith. As a child she had been enthralled by C. S. Lewis's Narnia and J. R. R. Tolkien's Middle Earth.

"Looking back, I can see that there had been many glimmers of transcendence as a young adult," says Ordway. "Books such as *The Lord of the Rings* had really nourished my imagination, though I didn't connect them with any Christian meaning."[25]

By the time she was studying and teaching English literature at college, Ordway says she had settled into an atheistic outlook. "I simply thought 'Christianity is all superstitious nonsense.' I had never been given any reason to think that it was true and I just dismissed it."

However, as Ordway's academic career progressed, she realized that many of the poets whose works struck the deepest chords—such as John Donne, Gerard Manley Hopkins, and T. S. Eliot—wrote squarely from their Christian convictions.

> I was explicitly thinking, "I don't believe what these guys believe, it's all complete nonsense." However, I was reading very intently in order to teach it and discovering "this is beautiful." I remember reading the opening of John Donne's sonnet "Batter my heart, three person'd God; for you / As yet but knock, breathe, shine, and seek to mend." I felt like I had touched a live wire. That was the point at which the imagination that had been a river below the surface in me started bubbling up and I thought, "There's something happening in this poetry, and I wonder what it is."

It was this encounter with the heart-stopping beauty of poetry that led Ordway to question her default atheism, a process she recounts in *Not God's Type*, the memoir of her conversion. The intensity of meaning in the poems and books she most loved seemed to point to a source beyond themselves. Alongside this imaginative journey that spoke to her soul, Ordway embarked on an intellectual quest to investigate the historical claims of the Christian faith. It was a journey which eventually led to her entering the Catholic church:

> I reread certain books and poetry with new eyes. I now see that what people like Gerard Manley Hopkins (hands down my favourite poet) gave me before I was a Christian was a little glimpse of the world that showed me that it made

sense in some way that I hadn't experienced before. I've now stepped into that world. To use CS Lewis' metaphor, I've stepped into that "beam of light" so that I can look with them, and they can show me more than they could before.

None of these conversion stories are offered as knockdown proofs of God's existence. They aren't. But they are evidence of the way, if we are willing to see it, that Christianity tells a story that makes sense of our lives, loves, and longings. These journeys were not only intellectual but involved engaging the imagination too.

THE CONVERSION OF C. S. LEWIS

The problem with the word "imagination" is that we assume it to be the equivalent of "fantasy," "fairy tale," or "fiction." But in fact imagination is where we most frequently encounter the kind of truth that really matters. The blockbuster box office superhero films and the bestselling fictional worlds of witches and wizards all involve epic battles of good versus evil. We are moved by stories of heroism. The theme of sacrifice for a greater cause runs through all our art and literature. The books we read, the songs we listen to, and the pictures we put on our walls are usually about things we can't touch, smell, or taste—beauty, justice, and love.

All of these, in my view, are echoes of the Christian story. As shocking as it may sound from somebody whose day job is in apologetics, these stories remind us that the most fruitful way we can introduce people to the Christian story is through the realm of the imagination rather than the intellect. We do that by making people *want* Christianity to be true in the first place, by showing how it meets our deepest instincts about what matters most. Only then can apologetics—the work of showing them *why* it is true—be of any use.

All the converts mentioned so far were influenced by the work of C. S. Lewis, and their journeys have, to a greater or lesser extent, mirrored his story.

Lewis's own conversion to Christianity from atheism took place between 1930 and 1931 as a young fellow in English literature at Magdalen College, Oxford University. The reason for the two dates is that his conversion took place in two stages. The first stage was an intellectual conversion to theism—he had become convinced that naturalism could not account for his belief in justice and morality and that there must be a moral lawgiver behind the universe. But the second stage—his conversion to Christianity specifically—came through the later influence of friends, including fellow fantasy writer J. R. R. Tolkien.

Lewis himself knew the power of story to bring things alive in ways that reason and logic alone cannot. In *Surprised by Joy* he writes of how his own conversion was prefaced by his experience of being an atheist whose greatest joys were found in the imaginative world of literature and poetry: "The two hemispheres of my mind were in the sharpest contrast. On the one side a many-islanded sea of poetry and myth; on the other a glib and shallow 'rationalism.' Nearly all that I loved I believed to be imaginary; nearly all that I believed to be real I thought grim and meaningless."[26]

It was his conversion to theism that allowed Lewis to begin bridging the gap between the two halves of his mind, and it was the person of Jesus who completed the union of his reason and imagination.

Lewis, an expert in ancient literature and mythology, had often encountered motifs of dying and rising gods in pagan cultures. What made the story of Jesus any different? It was Tolkien who helped clarify things. As they took a stroll along Addison's Walk, which circles the meadow behind Magdalen College, Tolkien challenged Lewis. What if all those stories, all the myths that Lewis found so enchanting, were not merely "lies breathed through silver" but were pointing to a "true myth"?[27] What if it really happened once, through one person, at one point in history?

It was this revelation that finally brought Lewis to Christian faith. He wrote to his friend Arthur Greeves, "The story of Christ is simply a true myth: a myth working on us in the same way as the others, but with this tremendous difference that *it really happened*."[28] The deep joy Lewis experienced in literature and mythology was not an illusion but had a source. The stories that seemed most meaningful to him were not lies but contained the seeds of truth that were fulfilled in the life, death, and resurrection of Jesus.

Perhaps it's no surprise that similar C. S. Lewis–like journeys to faith occur among people who are themselves storytellers, poets, and journalists. In the case of the adult converts listed earlier, the journey of realization only took place once other stories had been tried but had ultimately failed to make sense of things—the heights of human glory, the depths of human misery, the search for the meaning behind it all. Only the Christian story seemed to be able to encompass these things. Only the Christian story made sense of *their* stories.

But such experiences are not limited to writers and poets. Throughout this book I have sought to show how an eclectic mix of historians, academics, scientists, psychologists, AI researchers, philosophers, and even actors and stand-up comedians have also been surprised to find that the Christian story makes sense of their stories and the story of the world around them.

We began with the rise of New Atheism and the paucity of the story it told, which failed to unify even its own adherents and led to the implosion of the movement, leaving a generation still searching for meaning. Then we sketched the story of our present culture and how the influential psychologist Jordan Peterson seems to have become convinced that the person of Jesus connects the deepest stories of myth and meaning with our objective experience of the real world. The story of history came next, when we met the historian Tom Holland, who found himself confronted by a moral vision of the Western world that only makes sense in light of the Christian story that birthed it. We considered the story of the Bible itself and encountered Jonathan Haidt's surprise at the psychological depths of Scripture and journalist Douglas Murray's conflicted atheism over the one religious book that seems to be the key to civilization. We also encountered the story of classicist James Orr, for whom the person of Jesus stepped off the pages of the Gospels to become a living reality.

Next came the story of science, and I introduced a number of people who have come to believe that the materialist account of nature cannot explain the universe and the life it has produced. Scientists such as Francis Collins and Rosalind Picard have crossed the line to Christian faith, believing that the universe itself points to the Word that first spoke order and life into being. Then came the story of mind versus materialism, when we met psychiatrist Iain McGilchrist, who believes that only a divine mind explains the human capacity for consciousness. We also met Christian converts such as Jennifer Fulwiler, who abandoned her materialism in the search for meaning. And finally, we have explored the story of religion itself and the contention that, even in a secular age, people are no less religious; they just worship different things.

Through all of this, the story of Jesus seems to connect these different strands of culture, history, and science. *His* story makes sense of *all* stories—past, present, and future.

C. S. Lewis was at the forefront of confronting the growing meaning crisis in his generation as he saw the materialist paradigm establishing a stronghold in academia and beginning to trickle into popular culture. That trickle has become a flood in the intervening years. But what if the stories of converts like Paul Kingsnorth, A. N. Wilson, Francis Spufford, and Holly Ordway—and the many others we have met along the way—are merely the firstfruits of those making their way out of the meaning crisis in our generation? Could the tide be turning?

A WORD ABOUT CHURCH

If we are seeing things begin to change, then, as it stands, the church may seem to be the last place people would want to turn to. The abuse scandals that have rocked the Catholic church have seen many of their flock walk away for good, and much of the mainline Protestant church appears to be slipping into cultural irrelevance and terminal decline. Meanwhile, evangelical churches—especially of the "mega" variety in the United States—are facing their own crisis. The idolization of celebrity pastors, coupled with a results-driven culture that focuses on numerical rather than spiritual growth, have created an "evangelical-industrial complex" (a term coined by podcast host Skye Jethani, borrowing from US president Dwight Eisenhower).

However, an hour of reckoning seems to have befallen the evangelical world as a long list of notable ministry leaders have fallen from grace after allegations of sexual abuse or bullying behavior, leaving a trail of brokenness in their wake. Notably, in the world of Christian apologetics that I inhabit, its most senior and influential figure, Ravi Zacharias, was posthumously shown to have engaged in longstanding sexual and spiritual abuse. The revelations led to the collapse of the global ministry he founded, a reminder of how easily charisma can be mistaken for character and how quickly a lifetime's legacy can be shipwrecked.

Alongside these sad developments has emerged the growth of "exvangelicals" and many stories of deconstruction among former believers, sometimes involving the de-conversion of notable Christian musicians or church leaders. This phenomenon is partly attributable to an increasingly skeptical culture but is also the result of an evangelical subculture that has created churches that are "a mile wide but an inch deep." Narrow-minded fundamentalist churches can be a breeding ground for cognitive dissonance later on when the young people raised in them are invariably exposed to a bigger, more nuanced world.

The turnoffs are not only intellectual, however. Deconstruction can also be the result of exposure to the cynical consumerism of the evangelical subculture, or the way some Christians in the United States have conflated right-wing politics with church ministry in an effort to win back influence and power. In my experience a "crisis of faith" is more often caused by the narrow expression of church someone was raised in than by an unsolvable intellectual objection. Who can blame those who walk away from dogmatic, superficial, or toxic forms of faith if that's all they've been told the church is? Many stories of deconstruction might have been avoided if good foundations had been laid in the first place and if Christians were exposed early on to the breadth of intellectual and cultural streams that make up the global church.

Naturally, there is always a danger of focusing on the widely touted bad news stories and failing to recognize the many more positive news stories that don't make headlines—the countless faithful congregants and ministers quietly getting on with the work of enabling their churches to be good news to their communities. I am married to one such person, and I know many more who carry out their calling with great care and integrity.

Nevertheless, the recent stories of those who have fallen from grace after using their pulpit for a power trip or turning ministry into a moneymaking enterprise show that the church is an institution made up of human beings, always corruptible and always in need of reform. I don't personally spend much time wringing my hands over the latest statistics about church growth and decline or the fact that a number of people (in the West, at least) are choosing to walk away from church even as others are walking into it. 'Twas ever thus. Individual churches have come and gone, large church movements have risen and fallen. New wine has been poured into old wineskins, and they have burst. The religious revivals of previous centuries have involved the sweeping away of an old order as much as the ushering in of a new one.

In the New Testament Jesus promised, "I will build my church, and the gates of Hades will not prevail against it" (Matthew 16:18). He didn't promise to build any particular denomination or brand, nor did he give a timetable or growth chart for what his church would look like in any given age or locale. He simply promised to build *his* (not *our*) church. Building things sometimes involves demolition too. If in the early twenty-first century a certain manifestation of the evangelical church (or indeed Catholic or mainline Protestant church) finds itself unfit for its purpose, it will fall away. But happily, that will not be the end of the story. These churches are only one part of a much bigger and more glorious global body that spans many ages. Renewal and reform happen in every generation. Ours is no different.

Human institutions come and go, but for two thousand years the church of Jesus has remained. It has always been a paradox. It is often at its most beautiful when persecuted and under pressure, and often at its most ugly when allied with power and money. It is often marred by the corrupt human nature of those who run it, yet it is also capable of bringing life and transformation, thanks to the nature of the one who established it.

When I asked the former archbishop of Canterbury Rowan Williams about why people should consider joining the church with all its history of failures and abuses, he replied, "I wouldn't feel half so angry about these abuses and failures if I weren't in the church. It's the very church which fails which also gives me the perspective I need in order to see evil for what it is. It's precisely that perspective of standing in the body of Christ that should give us that resource of seeing exactly where we need to identify the works of destruction and evil."[29]

Love it or hate it, we can't live without it. And I believe God is not finished with his church. At this moment, the church stands at an important juncture in the history of the West.

People are living in a world where religion has supposedly been debunked, but atheist materialism hasn't offered a replacement. They are distracted by technology but left feeling hollow once the novelty wears off or addiction sets in. They are confused by the demands of fashioning their own identity when there is no pattern to follow and the rules keep changing. They are made anxious by a culture that demands ideological purity but extends no grace to those who fall short. They are exhausted by the search for a meaning they must invent and a purpose that seems to elude them. People can only take so much.

Perhaps we are not seeing the emptying of the churches to make way for a secular future but an emptying out that will make way for a new influx of people. Perhaps the tide of Matthew Arnold's "Sea of Faith" is approaching its furthest limit and is ready, at last, to come rushing back in.

The stories of those who have been surprised to find God already waiting for them on the deserted beaches of secularism may help us here. If they are the firstfruits of those who have come through the meaning crisis, what have they found that made the difference? And if there may yet be a tide of people coming in behind them, ready to consider religion again, what will the church be ready to offer if people come knocking at its door?

If we are seeing the telltale signs of a new great awakening, I would like to humbly propose three things that the church can do to prepare for it.

1. Embrace Both Reason and Imagination

One of the great gifts that New Atheism unwittingly imparted to the church was to remind it of its intellectual heritage. The resurgence of interest in apologetics and natural theology has seen a welcome swing of the pendulum back towards engaging popular culture with reason and evidence, not just emotional altar calls. Many churches still have a long way to go, but I've been encouraged by the proliferation of ministries and individuals willing to engage secular culture on its own terms and frequently doing a great job of it. If people are beginning to consider faith again, then apologetics will always be needed for those left-brained types, whose personality predisposes them towards an intellectual approach to matters.

However, the great danger with pendulums is that they can swing too far. As Iain McGilchrist has warned, the left brain dominance of our culture often squashes the right-brained way in which we make sense of the big picture through intuition, feeling, and emotion. Apologetics must always serve a bigger story. And stories (ones you want to read, at least) are rarely composed of pure logic and reason.

Indeed, I am convinced that most people encounter the truth of Christianity through the imaginative faculties of the right brain. In my experience, journeys to faith are never a purely intellectual exercise, even for intellectually minded people. It's why, when describing his conversion, Paul Kingsnorth said he would hesitate to use intellectual arguments to try to convince someone else of his newfound faith, because that wasn't his own route into it: "You can expound on the Christian faith in a very rational fashion. But I didn't calculate my way into it. I felt like I was pulled into it. . . . You can't argue people out of something they haven't argued themselves into. I'm happy to try and explain the things that have happened to me. But at the end of the day, it's experiential."[30]

Again, C. S. Lewis provides a pertinent example of this. After his conversion he began to use his prodigious mind to write books on the intellectual case for faith. *Mere Christianity*, *The Problem of Pain*, and *Miracles* are all classics in their genre. However, later in his life he swapped this apologetic output in favor of fiction—most famously his bestselling children's fantasy novels, The Chronicles of Narnia.

Had Lewis given up on making the case for Christianity? Far from it. Many more people have been drawn into the Christian worldview through Narnia than via the logic of the moral argument in *Mere Christianity* or his critique of materialism in *Miracles* (masterful as they are).

In fact, a careful survey of his fiction will find much of Lewis's apologetics hovering just below the surface,[31] but what Lewis did most brilliantly in those stories was to make his readers wish that Narnia really existed. How many children (and perhaps a few adults) have checked the back of a wardrobe in hopes it might just lead to a magical land of castles, fauns, and talking beasts? However, in making them hope that Narnia's tales of heroism, love, sacrifice, and redemption were true, Lewis gave readers the imaginative permission to see that maybe, just maybe, the story could be true in the real world. For of course, Lewis had transposed the story of Jesus into the world of Narnia and its Christ-character, Aslan.

Like Edmund and Lucy on their final adventure, many readers have seen the lion's words come true in their own adult journey: "But there I have another name. You must learn to know me by that name. This was the very reason why you were brought to Narnia, that by knowing me here for a little, you may know me better there."[32]

Given the circumstances of his own conversion, perhaps it's no surprise that Lewis turned to fantasy writing to reintroduce a skeptically minded age to the story of Christianity. Reflecting on the religious themes in The Chronicles of Narnia in an article for the *New York Times*, he wrote, "But supposing that by casting all these things into an imaginary world, stripping them of their stained-glass and Sunday School associations, one could make them for the first time appear in their real potency? Could one not thus steal past those watchful dragons? I thought one could."[33]

As we meet the incoming tide of refugees from the meaning crisis, the church needs both apologists in the academy and storytellers in the arts. We need people in the mold of C. S. Lewis, showing not only that the story is true but why we have wanted to believe in it all along.

2. Keep Christianity Weird

One of the oft repeated sentiments I have heard from those who have come to faith has been frustration that churches often fail to remain distinctively Christian in their efforts to look more like the culture. Even those who do not call themselves Christians are concerned about it.

In one of our conversations, Douglas Murray described himself as a "disappointed non-adherent" of the Anglican church who is dismayed that it may become yet another mouthpiece of politically correct ideology around race, gender, and sexuality. "My fear is the church is not doing what so many of us on the outside would like it to do; which is to be preaching its Gospel, to be asserting its truths and its claims. When one sees it falling into all of the latest tropes, one just thinks . . . well, that's another thing gone. It's like absolutely everything else in this boring, monotone, ill-thought out and shallow dialectic."[34]

Likewise, there is a danger when churches try to ape the values of celebrity culture and the entertainment industry in an effort to be culturally relevant. Journalist Ben Sixsmith describes himself as having an "open, curious, unsettled agnosticism"[35] and has been increasingly drawn towards the seriousness of faith and philosophy in the Catholic tradition. However, in an article for *The Spectator*, he chastised churches that water down their message in order to appear more inclusive or relevant:

> I am not religious, so it is not my place to dictate to Christians what they should and should not believe. Still, if someone has a faith worth following, I feel that their beliefs should make me feel uncomfortable for not doing so. If they share 90 percent of my lifestyle and values, then there is nothing especially inspiring about them. Instead of making me want to become more like them, it looks very much as if they want to become more like me.[36]

Similar sentiments have been expressed by Tom Holland as he navigates his way back to Christian faith. Christianity was birthed in the strange claim that the God of the universe had willingly died a slave's death and been raised to life again. Lamenting the way the church often replaces this miraculous story with a "mush" of platitudinous "thought for the day" broadcasts and politically correct public announcements, he says it's time to be bolder: "The churches need to absolutely embrace [their beliefs] rather than being slightly embarrassed about them. . . . The churches have to lay claim to everything that is weirdest, most countercultural, most peculiar. Don't duck all the stuff about angels—major on that!"[37]

This advice may seem counterintuitive. Many churches have made it their mission to appear as "normal" and unthreatening as possible in their efforts to bring people through the doors. But many who walk through the doors are looking for something completely different to their "normal," everyday life. They want to be transported into another world, a different story.

With this in mind, it's noticeable how many of those who have returned to church (including Holland and Kingsnorth) have chosen to embrace ancient forms of worship and liturgy that major on mystery and ritual.

One young convert, Harry Howard, told me why he ended up worshiping at one of London's oldest and most traditional churches, St. Bartholomew the Great, rather than a guitars-and-drums church: "You can get that outside in popular culture already, and the church tends to do a second-rate version anyway. But when I go to a service that has its roots in something really ancient, it's like a refuge from the popular culture which is now so devoid of any real meaning. I think that's why that church is so popular."[38]

Harry is not alone. The church's rector Rev. Marcus Walker says that he has seen a notable increase in millennials and younger generations attending the church's High Mass and Evensong services because they offer "beautiful language, symphonious music and an aesthetic experience that transcends normal life."[39] It's a trend that seems to be confirmed by the uptick in attendance of Anglo-Catholic services at cathedrals in the UK too,[40] in contrast to the overall picture of decline.

So should all churches embrace smells, bells, and choral music in order to embrace the meaning-seeking millennials ready to give Christianity a try? Not necessarily. The other parts of the church experiencing growth are Black Pentecostal churches and charismatic evangelical congregations. What unites them is that they each, in their own way, unashamedly embrace the "weirdness" of their expression of worship. Whether it be a passionate gospel choir or eyes-closed, hands-in-the-air worship, they are also offering something intense and otherworldly.

While there's no advantage to creating unnecessary barriers, the lesson appears to be that churches shouldn't dumb down their worship or their doctrine in order to win new converts. They should demand more, not less, of the people who come through their doors. Embrace mystery, expect the supernatural, and keep Christianity weird.

3. Create a Community That Counters Cancel Culture

Forgive the tongue-twisting title, but whatever the church of the next generation looks like, it must always be a place of grace where messy people learn to get along with other messed-up people. People are hungry for meaning, but they are also hungry for a community where they can explore that meaning with others. As the West becomes ever more consumeristic and individualistic, the opportunities to be part of a genuine community are constantly diminishing. As populations have become mobile, we have lost our rootedness in a place. We no longer know who our neighbors are. We have created structures that enable us to live independently from each other. We interact with our devices more than real people.

Technology is both a blessing and a curse in this respect. We can live entirely by ourselves as long as we have a screen for companionship. It enables connection like never before but at the cost of true relationships. The fact is, however many friends we may lay claim to on Facebook, our online encounters will always be shallow compared to those we conduct in real life.

The forced isolation of the COVID lockdowns was mitigated by the technology that allowed us to connect with friends and family over video calls and social media. Most churches met only via screens during this time and were grateful for YouTube and Zoom services that allowed participation at a distance. But I was not alone in breathing a huge sigh of relief when in-person services could resume. Zoom fatigue is a real phenomenon. We are created to look each other in the eye and connect with each other in the same physical space. Churches are among the few remaining places where people can do that regularly.

The health benefits of being part of a worshiping community have already been listed. But it's about more than just physical and mental health. We are made to be people who live and laugh together, sometimes anger and annoy each other, but who learn to love our neighbor in the process. It's part of the story of what it means to be human. The more we live independently of each other, the less we develop into fully human people.

As those emerging from the meaning crisis seek to make sense of themselves and their part in a bigger story, churches need to be places of capacious community. We need to be ready to embrace the walking wounded and make space for those at the beginning of their journey. That means being places where people can ask awkward questions without being shouted down. Places where we take seriously the experiences and stories of people who are different from each other. Places where people with different views on a whole range of social and ethical issues can hope to find something to unite them that is bigger than their differences.

This may sound like an unrealistic utopia, given the church's history of splits and fallouts. Differences over doctrines like baptism and communion now pale in comparison to the LGBT debate dividing whole denominations. Yet I remain eternally optimistic that Jesus can use even a fractured and fragile church for his glory. His power is made perfect in our weakness.

The church needs to be a place of countercultural grace in a polarized, moralistic, and unforgiving society. Grace is the antidote to cancel culture, and people are desperate for it. Perhaps the greatest witness the church can offer society is that, even when we disagree, we can still love each other. "By this everyone will know that you are my disciples, if you have love for one another," said Jesus (John 13:35). Not by your shared political views, not even by your sound theology. By your *love*.

That doesn't mean it's a free-for-all. Holiness and unity are both important, and we are often guilty of sacrificing one in favor of the other. However, the church is supposed to be a place where we work out how to bring them together. The church is meant to be the preeminent example of unity in diversity—a place where people who are fundamentally different from each other can still call each other brother and sister, because what unites us is far bigger than what separates us.

This may sound miraculous. Fortunately, Christians believe that a miracle has occurred. The forgiveness of our sins through the death and resurrection of Jesus, the Son of God. Modeling our lives and relationships after him means that we are called to be a constantly grace-filled, constantly forgiving, constantly loving community. I believe that's the kind of church that refugees from the meaning crisis can find a home in.

THE COMING TIDE

Tides go out and tides come in. Their regular movement is governed by the natural laws that operate in our world. Human life is subject to the same rhythms that nature imposes on the world—seedtime and harvest, work and rest, death and rebirth. And human history itself seems to mirror nature with its own repetitive cycles as nations rise and fall, empires come and go. The cultural influence of religion is likewise prone to ebb and flow.

Christianity has been remarkably successful until now. It flourished in the East and then swept the Western world. It has dominated art, literature, and culture and left majestic cathedrals in its wake. The revivals of Luther, Wesley, and Whitefield transformed Europe and America before Christianity swept into Africa, Asia, Latin America, and the rest of the world.

From a secular perspective it's possible to compare these high watermarks of the past with the current picture in the West and assume that Christianity, if not quite dead, is well on its way to being another relic of history. What the critics often fail to realize is that the crest of each new wave of Christianity had a trough that preceded it. History moves in cycles. Tides go out and come back in. I believe we are simply living at low tide in the Western world. Rebirth has happened before, and it can happen again.

Two thousand years ago a wandering rabbi stood on a beach and called a bunch of fishermen to put down their nets, follow him, and fish for people instead. Together they changed the world. Like them, I believe we are standing on the shores of human history, waiting for a tide that is about to rush back in. Perhaps now is the time to answer his call again.

Acknowledgments

MUCH OF THE MATERIAL IN this book is drawn from interviews conducted on "Big Conversation" editions of the *Unbelievable?* show, a series that has been generously supported by the John Templeton Foundation. There are too many individual guests to name, but my thanks to all of them for sparking the thoughts that eventually became this book. My heartfelt thanks go to my friends and colleagues who have helped to make that show (and many others, too) happen from week to week—especially Peter Byrom, Ruth Jackson, Phil Maltz, and Ben Cutting.

There are many other individuals who have been involved in the creation of this book since the seed for it was planted during the 2020 lockdown. I particularly want to thank the inimitable Keith Danby, who helped to steer the project from nascent idea to commissioned title with Tyndale. Thanks also to Jon Farrar, Jonathan Schindler, and Alyssa Clements at Tyndale who have been so helpful (and patient) during the writing, editing, and design process. Thanks also to all those who were willing to read the manuscript ahead of publication and offer endorsements.

There are many others who had a hand in reading and commenting on drafts of the manuscript along the way. My thanks go to Andy Lyon, Tom Holland, Tom Wright, Glen Scrivener, David Hutchings,

Max Baker-Hytch, Paul VanderKlay, and my dad, Crofton Brierley. My wife, Lucy, also gave invaluable advice on all the chapters as they were being written.

Writing a book in a household of four children where both parents also have full-time jobs is not without its challenges, but Lucy was the one who ensured I had the time and space needed to write and was a constant encouragement (and supplier of coffee) throughout. She is God's gift to me and the one who made this possible. Thank you.

Notes

INTRODUCTION
1. "Census 2021 Results," Office for National Statistics, accessed October 6, 2022, https://census.gov.uk/census-2021-results.
2. The quotes from Douglas Murray in this section are from "N.T. Wright and Douglas Murray: Identity, Myth, and Miracles: How Do We Live in a Post-Christian World?," *The Big Conversation*, chaired by Justin Brierley, produced by Premier in partnership with John Templeton Foundation, https://www.youtube.com/watch?v=VN8OUi9MF7w.

CHAPTER 1: THE RISE AND FALL OF NEW ATHEISM
1. "British Social Attitudes: The 36th Report," National Centre for Social Research, eds. John Curtice et al., 2019, https://www.bsa.natcen.ac.uk/media-centre/archived-press-releases/bsa36-religion-press-release.aspx.
2. "Christianity in the UK," Faith Survey, accessed October 6, 2022, https://faithsurvey.co.uk/uk-christianity.html.
3. Oscar Wilde, *The Picture of Dorian Gray*, chap. 1.
4. Nick Spencer, "Religious Think Tank Welcomes Launch of Atheist Buses," Theos, August 11, 2011, https://www.theosthinktank.co.uk/comment/2009/01/06/religious-think-tank-welcomes-launch-of-atheist-buses.
5. Sinclair McKay, "Margaret Atwood," *The Telegraph*, August 20, 2009, https://www.telegraph.co.uk/culture/books/6061404/Margaret-Atwood.html.
6. Richard Dawkins, speech at the Edinburgh International Science Festival, April 15, 1992, quoted in "EDITORIAL: A Scientist's Case against God," *The Independent* (London): 17; Paul Gomberg, *What Should I Believe?: Philosophical Essays for Critical Thinking* (Peterborough, Canada: Broadview Press, 2011), 146.
7. Aysha Khan, "A Decade after the First Reason Rally, What Happened to America's Atheist Revolution?," *Religion and Politics*, August 30, 2022, https://

religionandpolitics.org/2022/08/30/a-decade-after-the-first-reason-rally-what
-happened-to-americas-atheist-revolution/.

8. "Transcript of Richard Dawkins' Speech from Reason Rally 2012," *Ladydifadden*
   (blog), March 28, 2012, https://ladydifadden.wordpress.com/2012/03/28
   /transcript-of-richard-dawkins-speech-from-reason-rally-2012/.

9. "Hitchens vs. Blair, Roy Thomson Hall," Hitchens Debates Transcripts,
   November 26, 2010, https://hitchensdebates.blogspot.com/2010/11/hitchens
   -vs-blair-roy-thomson-hall.html.

10. Richard Dawkins, *The Greatest Show on Earth: The Evidence for Evolution*
    (New York: Free Press, 2009), 107.

11. Christopher Hitchens, *God Is Not Great: How Religion Poisons Everything*
    (New York: Hachette Book Group, 2007), 5.

12. "Francis Spufford and Philip Pullman on Why Christianity Makes Surprising
    Emotional Sense—Classic Replay," *Unbelievable?*, July 10, 2020, https://www
    .premierchristianradio.com/Shows/Saturday/Unbelievable/Episodes/Unbelievable
    -Francis-Spufford-and-Philip-Pullman-on-why-Christianity-makes-surprising
    -emotional-sense-Classic-Replay.

13. Michael Ruse, "Dawkins et al Bring Us into Disrepute," The Guardian,
    November 2, 2009, https://www.theguardian.com/commentisfree/belief
    /2009/nov/02/atheism-dawkins-ruse.

14. Tim Ross, "Richard Dawkins Accused of Cowardice for Refusing to Debate
    Existence of God," *The Telegraph*, May 14, 2011, https://www.telegraph.co
    .uk/news/religion/8511931/Richard-Dawkins-accused-of-cowardice-for
    -refusing-to-debate-existence-of-God.html.

15. Rebecca Watson, "About Mythbusters, Robot Eyes, Feminism, and Jokes,"
    Skepchick, video, June 20, 2011, https://skepchick.org/2011/06/about
    -mythbusters-robot-eyes-feminism-and-jokes/.

16. PZ Myers, "Dawkins and 'Dear Muslima,'" FreethoughtBlogs.com, June 28,
    2018, https://freethoughtblogs.com/pharyngula/2018/06/28/dawkins-and
    -dear-muslima/.

17. Peter Aldhous, Azeen Ghorayshi, and Virginia Hughes, "He Became a
    Celebrity for Putting Science before God. Now Lawrence Krauss Faces
    Allegations of Sexual Misconduct," BuzzFeed News, February 22, 2018,
    https://www.buzzfeednews.com/article/peteraldhous/lawrence-krauss
    -sexual-harassment-allegations.

18. Cormac Watson and Mairead Maguire, "The Hist Will 'Not Be Moving
    Ahead' with Richard Dawkins Address," *University Times*, September 27,
    2020, http://www.universitytimes.ie/2020/09/the-hist-will-not-be-moving
    -ahead-with-richard-dawkins-address/.

19. Sam Harris, "I'm Not the Sexist Pig You're Looking For," Sam Harris,
    September 15, 2014, https://samharris.org/blog/im-not-the-sexist-pig-youre
    -looking-for/.

20. "Safe Space: A Conversation with Jonathan Haidt," Sam Harris, podcast #137, September 9, 2008, https://samharris.org/podcasts/137-safe-space/.

21. "American Humanist Association Board Statement Withdrawing Honor from Richard Dawkins," American Humanist Association, April 19, 2021, https://americanhumanist.org/news/american-humanist-association-board-statement-withdrawing-honor-from-richard-dawkins/.

22. "Glen Scrivener and Matt Dillahunty: Morality: Can Atheism Deliver a Better World?," January 10, 2020, *The Big Conversation*, season 2, episode 6, video, https://www.youtube.com/watch?v=B3-sjyDYO2I.

23. Stephen Woodford, "I've Been Denounced by the ACA (Atheist Community of Austin)," Rationality Rules, May 11, 2019, YouTube video, https://www.youtube.com/watch?v=cX_vOpX6mt4.

24. Matt Dillahunty, "Why I Left the ACA and What's Next," October 9, 2022, video, https://www.youtube.com/watch?v=FGvlGQQlx-g.

25. PZ Myers, "The Train Wreck That Was the New Atheism," FreethoughtBlogs .com, January 25, 2019, https://freethoughtblogs.com/pharyngula/2019/01/25/the-train-wreck-that-was-the-new-atheism/.

26. The details in this and the following paragraphs are from Andy Ngo, "Chaos During Social Justice and Feminism Debate at Milwaukee Atheism Conference," *Areo*, March 10, 2017, https://areomagazine.com/2017/10/03/chaos-during-social-justice-and-feminism-debate-at-milwaukee-atheism-conference/.

27. "The Atheist Conference is Dead," *Atheism and the City* (blog), January 5, 2018, http://www.atheismandthecity.com/2018/01/the-atheist-conference-is-dead.html.

28. "Learn About Us," Sunday Assembly, accessed October 11, 2022, https://www.sundayassembly.org/about.

29. C. S. Lewis, *God in the Dock: Essays on Theology and Ethics*, ed. Walter Hooper (Grand Rapids, MI: Eerdmans, 1970), 187.

30. Jana Harmon, "Religious Conversion of Educated Atheists to Christianity in Six Contemporary Western Countries" (PhD diss., University of Birmingham, 2019), https://etheses.bham.ac.uk/id/eprint/9490/.

31. Peter Byrom, "Confessions of a Former Atheist," December 28, 2014, Unbelievable? 2012 Conference Seminar, *Reasonable Faith* podcast, https://www.reasonablefaith.org/media/reasonable-faith-podcast/confessions-of-a-former-atheist.

CHAPTER 2: THE NEW CONVERSATION ON GOD

1. Maya Oppenheim, "Jordan Peterson Suffers Year of 'Absolute Hell' and Needs Emergency Treatment for Drug Addiction That Forced Him to Withdraw from Public Life, Daughter Says," *The Independent*, February 8, 2020, https://www.independent.co.uk/news/world/europe/jordan-peterson-drug-addiction-benzo-valium-xanex-russia-mikhaila-a9324871.html.

2. David Brooks, "The Jordan Peterson Moment," editorial, *New York Times*, January 25, 2018, https://www.nytimes.com/2018/01/25/opinion/jordan -peterson-moment.html.

3. "In Full: Dr. Jordan Peterson on Masculinity, Cultural Marxism and Decline of Western Universities," Sky News Australia, July 18, 2022, video, https://www.youtube.com/watch?v=CrPIj_tf8n8.

4. "Jordan Peterson vs Susan Blackmore: Do We Need God to Make Sense of Life?," June 8, 2018, *The Big Conversation*, season 1, episode 1, video, https://youtu.be/syP-OtdCIho.

5. Jennifer Schuessler, "Hoaxers Slip Breastaurants and Dog-Park Sex into Journals," *New York Times*, October 4, 2018, https://www.nytimes.com/2018 /10/04/arts/academic-journals-hoax.html.

6. "The Grievance Studies Affair—Revealed," Mike Nayna, October 2, 2018, video, https://www.youtube.com/watch?v=kVk9a5Jcd1k&ab_channel=MikeNayna.

7. George Herbert, "The Elixir" 5.17–18.

8. John Vervaeke, quoted at Thomas Steininger, "'We Are Suffering from a Wisdom Famine in the West,'" Emerge, accessed October 17, 2022, originally published in "Auf der Suche Nach Weisheit," *evolve*, no. 28, 2020, https://www.whatisemerging.com/profiles/john-vervaeke-edba633a-50b3-4dec-920b -967d8f0f2b01.

9. Charles Taylor, *A Secular Age* (Cambridge, MA: Harvard University Press, 2007).

10. Graham Tomlin, "Why 'Being Yourself' Is Not Such a Good Idea After All," *The Times*, October 29, 2021, https://www.thetimes.co.uk/article/why -being-yourself-is-not-such-a-good-idea-after-all-0vv0cd77n.

11. "Young People's Well-Being in the UK: 2020," Office for National Statistics, October 2, 2020, https://www.ons.gov.uk/peoplepopulationandcommunity /wellbeing/bulletins/youngpeopleswellbeingintheuk/2020.

12. Gretchen Frazee and Patty Gorena Morales, "Suicide among Teens and Young Adults Reaches Highest Level Since 2000," PBS NewsHour, June 18, 2019, https://www.pbs.org/newshour/nation/suicide-among-teens-and-young-adults -reaches-highest-level-since-2000.

13. Jean M. Twenge et al., "Age, Period, and Cohort Trends in Mood Disorder Indicators and Suicide-Related Outcomes in a Nationally Representative Dataset, 2005–2017," *Journal of Abnormal Psychology* 128, no. 3 (2019): 185–199, https://www.apa.org/pubs/journals/releases/abn-abn0000410.pdf.

14. Tomlin, "Why 'Being Yourself.'"

15. "Millennial Melancholy: Nine in Ten Young Brits Believe Their Life Lacks Purpose, according to Shocking New Study," *The Sun*, August 1, 2019, https://www.thesun.co.uk/news/9637619/young-brits-life-lacks-purpose/.

16. Mike Mariani, "American Exorcism," *The Atlantic*, December 2018, https://www.theatlantic.com/magazine/archive/2018/12/catholic-exorcisms-on-the -rise/573943/.

17. David Foster Wallace, "This Is Water," commencement speech, Kenyon College, May 21, 2005, transcript and audio, Farnam Street (fs), https://fs.blog/2012/04/david-foster-wallace-this-is-water/.

18. N. T. Wright, letter to *The Times*, August 3, 2017, at Sam Hailes, "N. T. Wright Attacks 'Fashionable Fantasy' of Allowing Children to Choose Their Own Gender," *Premier Christianity*, August 3, 2017, https://www.premier christianity.com/home/nt-wright-attacks-fashionable-fantasy-of-allowing -children-to-choose-their-own-gender/543.article.

19. "Jordan Peterson vs Susan Blackmore."

20. Andrew Sutton, "Any Wonder Why Millennials Need to Be Told to Clean Their Rooms?," *Orlando Sentinel*, September 12, 2018, https://www.orlando sentinel.com/opinion/os-op-clean-your-room-jordan-peterson-20180910 -story.html; and Jordan B. Peterson, *12 Rules for Life: An Antidote to Chaos* (Toronto: Random House Canada, 2018), 351.

21. (username deleted), "Atheist Here," Reddit, July 17, 2018, https://www .reddit.com/r/Christianity/comments/8zkeu5/atheist_here_on_the_edge _of_conversion_to/.

22. "N. T. Wright and Douglas Murray: Identity, Myth, and Miracles: How Do We Live in a Post-Christian World?," May 13, 2021, *The Big Conversation*, season 3, episode 3, video, https://www.youtube.com /watch?v=VN8OUi9MF7w.

23. "N. T. Wright and Douglas Murray."

24. "Dave Rubin: I'm No Longer an Atheist (and Jordan Peterson Helped)," December 4, 2019, from *The Big Conversation*, season 2, episode 5, video, https://www.youtube.com/watch?v=7mG6YIA54jc.

25. "Dave Rubin and John Lennox: Is God Dead? Faith, Culture and the Modern World, Part 1," November 15, 2019, *The Big Conversation*, season 2, episode 4, video, https://www.youtube.com/watch?v=m0Ov4HBperc.

26. Weiss to A. G. Sulzberger, July 14, 2020, Bari Weiss (website), https://www .bariweiss.com/resignation-letter.

27. Weiss to A. G. Sulzberger.

28. "Journalist or Heretic? Bari Weiss," June 10, 2021, *The Jordan B. Peterson Podcast*, season 4, episode 29, video, https://www.youtube.com/watch ?v=tFTA9MJZ4KY.

29. Aviva Engel, "Former NYT Writer Bari Weiss: 'Jewish Values Are Bigger Than Any Fancy Title,'" Times of Israel, July 24, 2020, https://www.timesofisrael .com/former-nyt-writer-bari-weiss-jewish-values-are-bigger-than-any-fancy -title/.

30. "Ricky Gervais and Russell Brand: God vs Atheism—Full Episode," April 25, 2020, *Under the Skin* (podcast), video, https://www.youtube.com/watch?v =5Szj5jJeUec.

31. "Tom Holland Tells N. T. Wright: Why I Changed My Mind about Christianity," July 17, 2018, from *Unbelievable?*, video, https://youtu.be/AIJ9gK47Ogw.

32. Larissa Nolan, "How Nuns Schooled Today's Torch-Bearers of Feminism," *Irish Times*, October 20, 2020, https://www.irishtimes.com/news/education/how-nuns-schooled-today-s-torch-bearers-of-feminism-1.4378480.

33. "Alister McGrath and Bret Weinstein: Religion: Useful Fiction or Ultimate Truth? Part 1," September 13, 2019, *The Big Conversation*, season 2, episode 1, video, https://youtu.be/kRx2uNMJFnU.

34. Terry Eagleton, "Lunging, Flailing, Mispunching," review of *The God Delusion*, by Richard Dawkins, *London Review of Books*, October 19, 2006, https://www.lrb.co.uk/the-paper/v28/n20/terry-eagleton/lunging-flailing-mispunching.

35. "Jordan Peterson vs Susan Blackmore."

36. "Jordan Peterson vs Susan Blackmore."

37. "Jordan Peterson vs Susan Blackmore."

38. "Jordan Peterson vs Susan Blackmore."

39. Jordan B. Peterson, *12 Rules for Life*, 186.

40. "Jordan Peterson vs Susan Blackmore."

41. "#61: Dr. Jordan Peterson on Catholicism, Suffering, Evil, and the Origin of 'Bucko,'" February 6, 2018, *The Patrick Coffin Show*, podcast, audio and video, https://www.patrickcoffin.media/dr-jordan-peterson-interview/.

42. "The Perfect Mode of Being: Jonathan Pageau," March 1, 2021, *The Jordan B. Peterson Podcast*, season 4, episode 8, video, https://youtu.be/2rAqVmZwqZM.

43. "Mikhaila Peterson's Story of Finding God and Coming to Christian Faith," August 3, 2022, from *The Big Conversation*, season 4, episode 6, video, https://youtu.be/TVrYijRce8w.

CHAPTER 3: SHAPED BY THE CHRISTIAN STORY

1. Tom Holland, *Dominion: How the Christian Revolution Remade the World*, 1st US ed. (New York: Basic Books, 2019), 541.

2. A. C. Grayling, *The History of Philosophy* (New York: Penguin, 2019), 3.

3. "Tom Holland and A. C. Grayling: History: Did Christianity Give Us Our Human Values?," December 6, 2019, *The Big Conversation*, season 2, episode 5, video, https://www.youtube.com/watch?v=7eSyz3BaVK8.

4. "Tom Holland and A. C. Grayling."

5. Tim O'Neill, "'The Dark Ages'—Popery, Periodisation and Pejoratives," *History for Atheists* (blog), November 19, 2016, https://historyforatheists.com/2016/11/the-dark-ages-popery-periodisation-and-pejoratives/.

6. The quotations in this section are from "N. T. Wright and Tom Holland: How St. Paul Changed the World (Full Show)," July 20, 2018, *Unbelievable?*, video, https://www.youtube.com/watch?v=nlf_ULB26cU.

7. "Tom Holland and A. C. Grayling."

8. UN General Assembly, Universal Declaration of Human Rights, A/RES/217 (III) A, article 1 (December 10, 1948), https://www.un.org/en/about-us/universal-declaration-of-human-rights.

9. "Steven Pinker vs Nick Spencer: Have Science, Reason and Humanism Replaced Faith?," June 22, 2018, *The Big Conversation*, season 1, episode 2, video, https://www.youtube.com/watch?v=Ssf5XN5o9q4.

10. Universal Declaration of Human Rights, article 1.

11. "Steven Pinker vs Nick Spencer."

12. "Steven Pinker vs Nick Spencer."

13. Declaration of Independence (July 4, 1776), U.S. National Archives and Records Administration, https://www.archives.gov/founding-docs/declaration-transcript.

14. Yuval Noah Harari, *Sapiens: A Brief History of Humankind*, 1st US ed. (New York: Harper, 2015), 109.

15. John H. Walton, *Genesis* (Grand Rapids, MI: Zondervan Academic, 2011), e-book, "Day Six (1:24-31)."

16. Walton, "Day Six (1:24-31)."

17. Aristotle, *Politics* 1.5.

18. "Tom Holland and A. C. Grayling."

19. "Tom Holland and A. C. Grayling."

20. Joseph Henrich, *The WEIRDest People in the World: How the West Became Psychologically Peculiar and Particularly Prosperous* (New York: Farrar, Straus and Giroux, 2020).

21. Rodney Stark, *For the Glory of God: How Monotheism Led to Reformations, Science, Witch-Hunts, and the End of Slavery* (New Jersey: Princeton University Press, 2004), 345.

22. Rodney Stark, *The Rise of Christianity: A Sociologist Reconsiders History* (New Jersey: Princeton University Press, 1996), 95.

23. Stark, *Rise of Christianity*, 95.

24. Stark, *Rise of Christianity*, 97.

25. *Oxyrhynchus papyri*, document no. 744 (Egypt, 1 BC).

26. Didache, trans. and ed. J. B. Lightfoot, 2:2, University of Pennsylvania, Center for Computer Analysis of Text (CCAT), accessed October 25, 2022, http://ccat.sas.upenn.edu/gopher/text/religion/churchwriters/ApostolicFathers/Didache.

27. Rodney Stark, *The Triumph of Christianity: How the Jesus Movement Became the World's Largest Religion* (New York: HarperOne, 2011), 118.

28. Justin Brierley, "Tom Wright: How Christians Responded to Ancient Plagues," *Premier Christianity*, March 25, 2020, https://www.premierchristianity.com/home/tom-wright-how-christians-responded-to-ancient-plagues/2496.article.

29. N. T. Wright, "Anti-Racism in the Church," N. T. Wright (website), originally published in *The Spectator*, March 27, 2021, https://ntwrightpage.com/2021/03/27/anti-racism-in-the-church/.

30. The quotes in this section are from a personal interview I recorded with Tom Holland.

31. The quotes in this section, unless noted otherwise, are from a personal interview I recorded with Tom Holland.

32. Tom Holland, "Invisible Fire: Christianity in a Post-Western World," lecture for Open Doors, November 17, 2021, British Library, London, in "Tom Holland: Christianity, Persecution and the Meaning of the Cross," December 30, 2021, *Unbelievable?*, video, https://youtu.be/p6w7qw9kJ9k.

33. Tom Holland, "Invisible Fire."

34. Tom Holland, "Invisible Fire."

35. Tom Holland, personal interview recorded with author.

36. "Why the Bible Makes Sense of Modern Life: Tom Holland and Andrew Ollerton," *Unbelievable?*, April 30, 2021, video, https://www.youtube.com/watch?v=f2_W6eCijV4.

37. "Why the Bible Makes Sense."

38. "Why the Bible Makes Sense."

39. Tom Holland, personal interview recorded with author.

40. Tom Holland, *Dominion*, 17.

CHAPTER 4: REDISCOVERING THE BIBLE

1. David Suchet's quotes and details in this section are from an interview with the author in "David Suchet: Playing Poirot, Reading the Bible and Why I Love St. Paul," September 27, 2019, *The Profile*, radio show and podcast, https://theprofileinterview.podbean.com/e/david-suchet-playing-poirot-reading-the-bible-and-why-i-love-st-paul/.

2. For a helpful defense of the historicity of this contested quote and story about Voltaire, see Daniel Merritt, "Voltaire's Prediction, Home, and the Bible Society: Truth or Myth?," Bellator Christi, March 18, 2019, https://bellatorchristi.com/2019/03/18/voltaires-prediction-home-and-the-bible-society-truth-or-myth/.

3. "Sam Harris: On Interpreting Scripture," July 7, 2011, *Big Think*, video, https://www.youtube.com/watch?v=8zV3vIXZ-1Y.

4. Lawrence Krauss, in "Is There Evidence for God? The Craig-Krauss Debate," March 30, 2011, North Carolina State University, transcript, Reasonable Faith, https://www.reasonablefaith.org/media/debates/the-craig-krauss-debate-at-north-carolina-state-university; Richard Dawkins (@RichardDawkins), "Bible and Quran were the best that Bronze Age desert tribes could do," Twitter, May 17, 2015, 2:11 a.m., https://twitter.com/richarddawkins/status/599834516274978816.

5. Richard Dawkins, *The God Delusion*, 1st Mariner Books ed. (Boston: Houghton Mifflin, 2008), 51.

6. "Chief Rabbi Lord Sacks and Richard Dawkins Debate Deity," *Jewish Chronicle*, September 13, 2012, https://www.thejc.com/news/uk/chief-rabbi-lord-sacks-and-richard-dawkins-debate-deity-1.36074.

7. "Richard Dawkins: You Ask the Questions Special," *The Independent*, December 4, 2006, https://www.independent.co.uk/news/people/profiles/richard-dawkins-you-ask-the-questions-special-427003.html.

8. Pamela Choo, "The Greater Miracle: Amity Press Prints Its 200 Millionth Bible," United Bible Societies, September 16, 2020, https://www.ubscp.org/the-greater-miracle-200-millionth-bible/.

9. Christopher Hitchens, "When the King Saved God," *Vanity Fair*, April 1, 2011, https://www.vanityfair.com/culture/2011/05/hitchens-201105.

10. Richard Dawkins, "Why I Want All Our Children to Read the King James Bible," *The Guardian*, May 19, 2012, https://www.theguardian.com/science/2012/may/19/richard-dawkins-king-james-bible.

11. Marilynne Robinson, "The Book of Books: What Literature Owes the Bible," *New York Times*, December 22, 2011, https://www.nytimes.com/2011/12/25/books/review/the-book-of-books-what-literature-owes-the-bible.html.

12. "Why William Tyndale's Bible Changed the World: Melvyn Bragg and Ben Virgo," March 29, 2019, *Unbelievable?*, podcast, https://unbelievable.podbean.com/e/why-william-tyndale-s-bible-changed-the-world-melvyn-bragg-and-ben-virgo/.

13. "Why William Tyndale's Bible Changed the World."

14. Vishal Mangalwadi, *The Book That Made Your World: How the Bible Created the Soul of Western Civilization* (Nashville: Thomas Nelson, 2011), 55–56.

15. "Hugh Ross vs Peter Atkins: Debating the Origins of the Laws of Nature," August 10, 2018, *Unbelievable?*, video, https://www.youtube.com/watch?v=hVCVt-dvVOc.

16. C. S. Lewis, *Surprised by Joy: The Shape of My Early Life* (New York: Harcourt Brace, 1955).

17. Sarah Eekhoff Zylstra, "'An Unlikely Ally': What a Secular Atheist Is Teaching Christian Leaders," The Gospel Coalition (TGC), February 28, 2018, https://www.thegospelcoalition.org/article/what-a-secular-atheist-is-teaching-christian-leaders/.

18. "*Unbelievable?* Are We Raising a 'Snowflake' Generation? Jonathan Haidt and Andrew Wilson," January 11, 2019, *Unbelievable?*, podcast, https://www.premierunbelievable.com/unbelievable/unbelievable-are-we-raising-a-snowflake-generation-jonathan-haidt-and-andrew-wilson/11500.article.

19. "Jonathan Haidt and Andrew Wilson."

20. "Jonathan Haidt and Andrew Wilson."

21. "N. T. Wright and Douglas Murray: Identity, Myth, and Miracles: How Do We Live in a Post-Christian World?," May 13, 2021, *The Big Conversation*, season 3, episode 3, video, https://www.youtube.com/watch?v=VN8OUi9MF7w.

22. "N. T. Wright and Douglas Murray."

23. Allan Bloom, *The Closing of the American Mind: How Higher Education Has Failed Democracy and Impoverished the Souls of Today's Students* (New York: Simon and Schuster, 1987), 60.

24. "N. T. Wright and Douglas Murray."
25. "How Jordan Peterson Led Me to the Catholic Church w/ Daniel James," January 10, 2022, from *Pints with Aquinas*, video, https://www.youtube.com/watch?v=ZB7nP3rwPjE.
26. Jordan B. Peterson, "The Psychological Significance of the Biblical Stories," Jordan B. Peterson (website), accessed October 27, 2022, https://www.jordanbpeterson.com/bible-series/.
27. Jordan B. Peterson, "Equity: When the Left Goes Too Far," Jordan B. Peterson (website), accessed October 27, 2022, https://www.jordanbpeterson.com/political-correctness/equity-when-the-left-goes-too-far/.
28. Jordan B. Peterson, *12 Rules for Life: An Antidote to Chaos* (Toronto: Random House Canada, 2018), 177.
29. "Jordan Peterson vs Susan Blackmore: Do We Need God to Make Sense of Life?," June 8, 2018, *The Big Conversation*, season 1, episode 1, video, https://youtu.be/syP-OtdCIho.
30. Peterson, *12 Rules for Life*, 180.
31. "#1769—Jordan Peterson," January 25, 2022, *The Joe Rogan Experience*, podcast, https://open.spotify.com/episode/7IVFm4085auRaIHS7N1NQl.
32. "#1769—Jordan Peterson."
33. James Orr, personal interview with author.
34. Barna Group and ComRes, *Talking Jesus: Perceptions of Jesus, Christians and Evangelism in England* (Talking Jesus, 2018), https://talkingjesus.org/wp-content/uploads/2018/04/Talking-Jesus.pdf.
35. "N. T. Wright: Why Jesus' Crucifixion Is a Fact of History," April 13, 2017, Premier Christian Radio, video, https://youtu.be/7dQZTLcNSLs.
36. "Peter J. Williams and Bart Ehrman: The Story of Jesus: Are the Gospels Historically Reliable?" October 25, 2019, *The Big Conversation*, season 2, episode 3, video, https://www.youtube.com/watch?v=ZuZPPGvF_2I.
37. "Peter J. Williams and Bart Ehrman."
38. Lydia McGrew, introduction to *Hidden in Plain View: Undesigned Coincidences in the Gospels and Acts* (Chillicothe, OH: DeWard, 2017).
39. Mark D. Roberts, *Can We Trust the Gospels?: Investigating the Reliability of Matthew, Mark, Luke, and John* (Wheaton, IL: Crossway, 2007), 153–154.
40. The quotes throughout this section are from a personal interview with James Orr.
41. It is worth noting that the word *myth* does not necessarily mean "legendary" or "untrue" but is more often used by these thinkers to denote a truth about reality that is told through stories which are primarily symbolic or poetic in nature.
42. C. S. Lewis, *God in the Dock: Essays on Theology and Ethics*, ed. Walter Hooper (Grand Rapids, MI: Eerdmans, 1970), 67.
43. "Douglas Murray: What Would It Take for Me to Become a Christian?," January 14, 2020, from *Unbelievable?*, video, https://www.youtube.com/watch?v=_Nbi9oh3Hag.

CHAPTER 5: THE ALTERNATIVE STORY OF SCIENCE

1. Christopher Hitchens, "Unanswerable Prayers," *Vanity Fair*, September 2, 2010, https://www.vanityfair.com/culture/2010/10/hitchens-201010.

2. "Richard Dawkins and Francis Collins: Biology, Belief and Covid," May 20, 2022, *The Big Conversation*, season 4, episode 1, video, https://www.youtube.com/watch?v=SQ3EU58AzFs.

3. Thomas Nagel, *The Last Word* (New York: Oxford University Press, 1997), 130.

4. "Hugh Ross vs Peter Atkins: Debating the Origins of the Laws of Nature," August 10, 2018, *Unbelievable?*, video, https://www.youtube.com/watch?v=hVCVt-dvVOc.

5. David Masci, "Scientists and Belief," Pew Research Center, November 5, 2009, https://www.pewresearch.org/religion/2009/11/05/scientists-and-belief/.

6. Courtney Johnson, Cary Lynne Thigpen, and Cary Funk, "On the Intersection of Science and Religion," *Trend*, Pew Charitable Trusts, February 9, 2021, https://www.pewtrusts.org/en/trend/archive/winter-2021/on-the-intersection-of-science-and-religion.

7. Nick Spencer and Hanna Waite, *"Science and Religion": Moving Away from the Shallow End* (London: Theos, 2022), executive summary, https://www.theosthinktank.co.uk/cmsfiles/Science-and-religion-2-Exective-summary.pdf.

8. Galileo Galilei to the Grand Duchess Christina of Tuscany, 1615, Internet Modern History Sourcebook, Bard College at Simon's Rock, https://digitalcommons.bard.edu/sr-instruct/97/.

9. John Hedley Brooke, *Science and Religion: Some Historical Perspectives* (Cambridge, UK: Cambridge University Press, 1991), 19.

10. Rodney Stark, *The Victory of Reason: How Christianity Led to Freedom, Capitalism, and Western Success* (New York: Random House, 2005), 11–12.

11. Friedrich Nietzsche, *On the Genealogy of Morals and Ecce Homo*, trans. Walter Kaufmann (New York: Vintage Books, 1989), 151–152.

12. C. S. Lewis, *Miracles: A Preliminary Study* (New York: Macmillan, 1978), 106.

13. Baruch Aba Shalev, "Religion of Nobel Prize Winners," in *100 Years of Nobel Prizes*, 3rd ed. (Los Angeles: Americas Group, 2005).

14. For an excellent analysis of the influence of Draper and White, I recommend David Hutchings and James C. Ungureanu, *Of Popes and Unicorns: Science, Christianity, and How the Conflict Thesis Fooled the World* (New York: Oxford University Press, 2022).

15. Richard Dawkins, "Explaining the Very Improbable," in *The Blind Watchmaker: Why the Evidence of Evolution Reveals a Universe without Design*, rev. ed. (New York: W. W. Norton, 1996), 6.

16. "Paul Davies and Jeremy England: The Origins of Life: Do We Need a New Theory for How Life Began?," June 25, 2021, *The Big Conversation*, season 3, episode 5, video, https://www.youtube.com/watch?v=R9IU2ZWrkhg.

17. James Tour, "Animadversions of a Synthetic Chemist," *Inference* 2, no. 2 (May 2016), https://inference-review.com/article/animadversions-of-a-synthetic-chemist.

18. "Paul Davies and Jeremy England."

19. "Paul Davies and Jeremy England."

20. Paul Davies, "How Bio-Friendly Is the Universe?," *International Journal of Astrobiology* 2, no. 2 (April 2003): 115–120.

21. See Geraint F. Lewis and Luke A. Barnes, *A Fortunate Universe: Life in a Finely Tuned Cosmos* (Cambridge, UK: Cambridge University Press, 2016) for a much fuller exploration of the evidence for fine-tuning and responses to multiverse theory.

22. Fred Hoyle, "The Universe: Past and Present Reflections," *Engineering and Science* 45, no. 2 (November 1981): 8–12, http://calteches.library.caltech.edu/527/2/Hoyle.pdf.

23. Stephen Hawking, *A Brief History of Time: From the Big Bang to Black Holes* (New York: Bantam Books, 1988), 174.

24. The quotes in this section from Sean Carroll and Luke Barnes are from "Unbelievable? Does God or Naturalism Best Explain the Universe? Sean Carroll vs Luke Barnes," October 27, 2017, *Unbelievable?*, podcast, https://www.premierchristianradio.com/Shows/Saturday/Unbelievable/Episodes/Unbelievable-Does-God-or-Naturalism-best-explain-the-Universe-Sean-Carroll-vs-Luke-Barnes.

25. "Professor Sir Roger Penrose FRS, OM," Humanists UK, accessed November 2, 2022, https://humanists.uk/about/our-people/patrons/sir-roger-penrose/.

26. This and the following quotes from Penrose are from "Sir Roger Penrose and William Lane Craig: The Universe: How Did It Get Here and Why Are We Part of It?," October 4, 2019, *The Big Conversation*, season 2, episode 2, video, https://www.youtube.com/watch?v=9wLtCqm72-Y.

27. Eugene P. Wigner, "The Unreasonable Effectiveness of Mathematics in the Natural Sciences," *Communications on Pure and Applied Mathematics* 13, no. 1 (February 1960): 1–14.

28. Albert Einstein, "Physics and Reality," in *Ideas and Opinions*, trans. Sonja Bargmann (New York: Bonanza, 1954), 292.

29. Einstein to Maurice Solovine, March 30, 1952, in *Letters to Solovine*, trans. Wade Baskin (New York: Philosophical Library, 1987), 131.

30. "Paul Davies and Jeremy England."

31. Antony Flew, with Roy Abraham Varghese, *There Is a God: How the World's Most Notorious Atheist Changed His Mind* (New York: HarperOne, 2007), 124.

32. Steven Pinker (@sapinker), "What has gotten into Thomas Nagel?," Twitter, October 16, 2012, 6:36 p.m., https://twitter.com/sapinker/status/258350644979695616.

33. Jerry Coyne, "Philosopher Thomas Nagel Goes the Way of Alvin Plantinga, Disses Evolution," *Why Evolution Is True* (blog), October 13, 2012, https://

whyevolutionistrue.com/2012/10/13/philosopher-thomas-nagel-goes-the
-way-of-alvin-plantinga-disses-evolution/.

34. Stuart Wavell, "In the Beginning There Was Something," *The Times*,
December 19, 2004, https://www.thetimes.co.uk/article/in-the-beginning
-there-was-something-2skcb3z8nfz.

35. "Professor Rosalind Picard: 'I Used to Think Religious People Had Thrown
Their Brains out the Window,'" interview by Ruth Jackson, *Premier Christianity*,
May 25, 2021, https://www.premierchristianity.com/interviews/professor
rosalind-picard-i-used-to-think-religious-people-had-thrown-their-brains
-out-the-window/4359.article.

36. "Rosalind Picard: From Atheist Skeptic to Christian Tech Pioneer," May 24,
2021, from *The Big Conversation*, season 3, episode 2, video, https://www
.youtube.com/watch?v=MM4tzXdZ6Xk.

37. "Atheist Skeptic to Christian Tech Pioneer."

38. "Professor Rosalind Picard," interview by Ruth Jackson.

39. "Atheist Skeptic to Christian Tech Pioneer."

40. This and the following quotes from Francis Collins are from "Francis Collins:
The Christian Scientist Looking for a Covid-19 Vaccine," interview by Justin
Brierley, *Premier Christianity*, June 28, 2020, https://www.premierchristianity
.com/home/francis-collins-the-christian-scientist-looking-for-a-covid-19
-vaccine/1845.article.

41. "Profile: Alister McGrath," interview by Justin Brierley, *Premier Christianity*,
February 4, 2014, https://www.premierchristianity.com/home/profile-alister
-mcgrath/670.article.

42. Richard Dawkins, *River out of Eden: A Darwinian View of Life* (New York:
Basic Books, 1995), 133.

43. Douglas Adams, *The Hitchhiker's Guide to the Galaxy* (New York: Pocket Books,
1981; Harmony, 1979), 118. Citation refers to the Pocket Books edition.

CHAPTER 6: MIND, MEANING, AND THE MATERIALISTS

1. Nico, personal correspondence with author, used with permission.

2. Nico, personal correspondence with author, used with permission.

3. Tamara, personal correspondence with author, used with permission.

4. Jacqui, personal correspondence with author, used with permission.

5. Dean Mayes, "My 'Unbelievable' Journey," September 23, 2019, *Dean
Mayes—Author* (blog), https://deanmayesauthor.wordpress.com/2019/09/23
/my-unbelievable-journey/.

6. "Unbelievable? Suffering and God in the Intensive Care Unit: Dean Mayes
and Dan Paterson," January 7, 2022, *Unbelievable?*, podcast, https://www
.premierunbelievable.com/unbelievable/unbelievable-suffering-and-god-in
-the-intensive-care-unit-dean-mayes-and-dan-paterson/12409.article.

7. See, for instance, this CDC report showing 26 percent rise in suicide rate
among men between 1999 and 2017: Holly Hedegaard, Sally C. Curtin,

and Margaret Warner, "Suicide Mortality in the United States, 1999–2017," NCHS data brief, no. 330 (Hyattsville, MD: National Center for Health Statistics, November 2018), https://www.cdc.gov/nchs/products/databriefs /db330.htm. While the suicide rate for women rose 53% during the same time period, the suicide rate for men is considerably higher, at 22.4 per 100,000 (versus 6.1 per 100,000 for women).

8. Jonathan Haidt, "Why the Past 10 Years of American Life Have Been Uniquely Stupid: It's Not Just a Phase," *The Atlantic*, April 11, 2022, https:// www.theatlantic.com/magazine/archive/2022/05/social-media-democracy -trust-babel/629369/.

9. See studies such as Christina Sagioglou and Tobias Greitemeyer, "Facebook's Emotional Consequences: Why Facebook Causes a Decrease in Mood and Why People Still Use It," *Computers in Human Behavior* 35 (June 2014): 359–363, https://www.sciencedirect.com/science/article /abs/pii/S0747563214001241.

10. Alan Noble, *You Are Not Your Own: Belonging to God in an Inhuman World* (Downers Grove, IL: IVP, 2021), 1.

11. Noble, 4.

12. C. S. Lewis, "On Living in an Atomic Age," in *Present Concerns*, ed. Walter Hooper, 1st US ed. (San Diego: Harcourt, Brace, Jovanovich, 1987), 74.

13. Bertrand Russell, *A Free Man's Worship*, 2nd ed. (Portland, ME: Mosher, 1927), 6–7.

14. For more on this, see "Daniel Dennett vs Keith Ward: Are We More Than Matter? Mind, Consciousness and Free Will," October 5, 2018, *The Big Conversation*, season 1, episode 5, video, https://youtu.be/mongL_2KMGg.

15. Daniel C. Dennett, "Reflections on Free Will," review of *Free Will*, by Sam Harris, Sam Harris (website), January 26, 2014, https://www.samharris.org /blog/reflections-on-free-will.

16. Kant, *Critique of Practical Reason* 5:96.

17. James Hemming, *Individual Morality* (London: Nelson, 1969), 191, quoted in Andrew Copson and Alice Roberts, eds., *The Little Book of Humanism* (London: Piatkus, 2020), ebook.

18. Jane Austen, *Pride and Prejudice* (1813), chap. 8.

19. For more on this debate, see Bahar Gholipour, "A Famous Argument against Free Will Has Been Debunked," *The Atlantic*, September 10, 2019, https:// www.theatlantic.com/health/archive/2019/09/free-will-bereitschaftspotential /597736/.

20. C. S. Lewis, *The Case for Christianity* (New York: Macmillan, 1944), 32.

21. Richard Dawkins, *River out of Eden: A Darwinian View of Life* (New York: Basic Books, 1995), 133.

22. "Iain McGilchrist and Sharon Dirckx: Brain Science, Consciousness and God," July 1, 2022, *The Big Conversation*, season 4, episode 3, video, https://youtu.be/oiE2OcxZpRY.

23. "Iain McGilchrist and Sharon Dirckx."

24. McGilchrist's quotes throughout this section are from "Iain McGilchrist and Sharon Dirckx."

25. "Iain McGilchrist and Sharon Dirckx."

26. This is the basis of a famous thought experiment; see Frank Jackson, "Epiphenomenal Qualia," *Philosophical Quarterly* 32, no. 127 (1982): 127–136.

27. For further reading on panpsychism, see Philip Goff, William Seager, and Sean Allen-Hermanson, "Panpsychism," in *The Stanford Encyclopedia of Philosophy* (Summer 2022 edition), ed. Edward N. Zalta, https://plato.stanford.edu /archives/sum2022/entries/panpsychism/.

28. "Francis Spufford and Philip Pullman: Does Christianity Make Surprising Emotional Sense?," July 10, 2020, *Unbelievable?*, podcast, https://www .youtube.com/watch?v=nq2xqpspkzc.

29. Robbie [Ernest Massey, pseud.], "How Consciousness Demolished My Atheism and Saved My Faith," Premier Unbelievable? (website), November 21, 2018, https://www.premierunbelievable.com/topics/how-consciousness-demolished -my-atheism-and-saved-my-faith/12072.article.

30. "From Atheism to Catholicism: An Interview with Jennifer Fulwiler," Strange Notions, April 30, 2014, video, https://www.youtube.com/watch?v =YhCXSbTkjLQ.

31. "Jennifer Fulwiler Testimony—From Atheist to a Daughter of God," May 24, 2017, Godstrong Daily, video, https://www.youtube.com/watch?v =cWBmSG6APdw.

32. "Jennifer Fulwiler Testimony."

33. Jonathan Gottschall, "The Storytelling Animal: A Conversation with Jonathan Gottschall," interview by Maria Konnikova, *Scientific American*, April 19, 2012, https://blogs.scientificamerican.com/literally-psyched/the-storytelling -animal-a-conversation-with-jonathan-gottschall/.

34. Gottschall, "Storytelling Animal."

35. This and the following quotes from Vervaeke are from "John Vervaeke and Sohrab Ahmari—Ancient Wisdom and the Meaning Crisis," July 16, 2021, *Unbelievable?*, video, https://www.youtube.com/watch?v=-W0SaGIv3NA.

36. Ryan Avent, "Game Drain: Why Some Young Men Choose Video Games over Jobs," 1843, *The Economist*, February 27, 2017, https://www.economist .com/1843/2017/02/27/game-drain-why-some-young-men-choose-video -games-over-jobs.

37. Gottschall, "Storytelling Animal."

CHAPTER 7: THE SURPRISING REBIRTH OF BELIEF IN GOD

1. Timothy Keller, with Katherine Leary Alsdorf, *Every Good Endeavor: Connecting Your Work to God's Work* (New York: Penguin Books, 2016), 128.

2. The quotes from Kingsnorth in this section are from "Rowan Williams and Paul Kingsnorth: Conversion, Culture, and the Cross," June 3, 2022, *The Big*

Conversation, season 4, episode 2, video, https://www.youtube.com/watch?v
=iCxznkRKa1w.

3. The quotes from Kingsnorth in this section are from "Rowan Williams and
   Paul Kingsnorth."

4. Gregory A. Smith, "About Three-in-Ten U.S. Adults Are Now Religiously
   Unaffiliated," Pew Research Center, December 14, 2021, https://www
   .pewresearch.org/religion/2021/12/14/about-three-in-ten-u-s-adults-are-now
   -religiously-unaffiliated/; "In U.S., Decline of Christianity Continues at Rapid
   Pace," Pew Research Center, October 17, 2019, https://www.pewresearch.org
   /religion/2019/10/17/in-u-s-decline-of-christianity-continues-at-rapid-pace/.

5. "British Social Attitudes: The 36th Report," National Centre for Social
   Research, eds. John Curtice et al., 2019, https://www.bsa.natcen.ac.uk/media
   /39293/1_bsa36_religion.pdf.

6. Michael Lipka and David McClendon, "Why People with No Religion Are
   Projected to Decline as a Share of the World's Population," Pew Research
   Center, April 7, 2017, https://www.pewresearch.org/fact-tank/2017/04/07
   /why-people-with-no-religion-are-projected-to-decline-as-a-share-of-the
   -worlds-population/.

7. For example, see Ryan Burge, "Why It's Unlikely U.S. Mainline Protestants
   Outnumber Evangelicals," Religion Unplugged, July 12, 2021, https://religion
   unplugged.com/news/2021/7/12/why-its-unlikely-us-mainline-protestants
   -outnumber-evangelicals.

8. Michael Hout and Tom W. Smith, *Fewer Americans Affiliate with Organized
   Religions, Belief and Practice Unchanged: Key Findings from the 2014 General
   Social Survey* (Chicago: NORC at the University of Chicago, 2015), 2,
   https://www.norc.org/PDFs/GSS%20Reports/GSS_Religion_2014.pdf.

9. Stephen Bullivant, *The "No Religion" Population of Britain* (London: Benedict
   XVI Centre for Religion and Society, St. Mary's University Twickenham,
   2017), 15, https://www.stmarys.ac.uk/research/centres/benedict-xvi/docs
   /2017-may-no-religion-report.pdf.

10. Pew Research Center, "Chapter 2: Religious Practices and Experiences,"
    in *U.S. Public Becoming Less Religious* (Pew Research Center: November 3,
    2015), https://www.pewresearch.org/religion/2015/11/03/chapter-2-religious
    -practices-and-experiences/.

11. See Rachel Pfeiffer, "After 2,000 UK Church Buildings Close, New Church
    Plants Get Creative," *Christianity Today*, May 25, 2022, https://www
    .christianitytoday.com/news/2022/may/uk-england-church-close-anglican
    -buildings-restore-new.html; Peter Brierley, "Churches Outnumber Pubs in
    the UK," *Christianity Today*, May 28, 2019, https://www.christianitytoday.
    com/news/2019/may/churches-outnumber-pubs-in-uk-london-attendance
    -pentecostal.html.

12. For example, see Harold Koenig, "Religion, Spirituality, and Health: The
    Research and Clinical Implications," *ISRN Psychiatry* 2012 (December 16,

2012): 278730, https://www.ncbi.nlm.nih.gov/pmc/articles/PMC3671693/; Paul S. Mueller, David J. Plevak, and Teresa A. Rummans, "Religious Involvement, Spirituality, and Medicine: Implications for Clinical Practice," *Mayo Clinic Proceedings* 76 (2001): 1225–1235, https://www.mayoclinic proceedings.org/article/S0025-6196(11)62799-7/pdf; Desmond Busteed, "Figures Reveal Christians Donate More Blood," Premier Christian News, June 14, 2015, https://premierchristian.news/en/news/article/figures-reveal -christians-donate-more-blood.

13. "Find Your Assembly," Sunday Assembly, accessed November 15, 2022, https://www.sundayassembly.org/map.

14. Glen Scrivener, "Dominic Cummings: 10 Extraordinary Things We Can All Agree On," *Premier Christianity*, May 27, 2020, https://www.premier christianity.com/home/dominic-cummings-10-extraordinary-things-we -can-all-agree-on/2813.article.

15. A. N. Wilson, "A. N. Wilson: Why I Believe Again," *New Statesman*, April 2, 2009, https://www.newstatesman.com/long-reads/2009/04/conversion -experience-atheism.

16. A. N. Wilson, "Religion of Hatred: Why We Should No Longer Be Cowed by the Chattering Classes Ruling Britain Who Sneer at Christianity," *Daily Mail*, April 10, 2009, https://www.dailymail.co.uk/news/article-1169145/Religion -hatred-Why-longer-cowed-secular-zealots.html.

17. A. N. Wilson, "A. N. Wilson Recommends the Best Christian Books," interview by Harry Mount, Five Books, December 22, 2016, https://fivebooks.com/best -books/anwilson-christian-books/.

18. Wilson, "Religion of Hatred."

19. The quotes from Spufford in this paragraph are from "Francis Spufford and Philip Pullman: Does Christianity Make Surprising Emotional Sense?," July 10, 2020, *Unbelievable?*, podcast, https://www.youtube.com/watch?v =nq2xqpspkzc.

20. Francis Spufford, *Unapologetic: Why, Despite Everything, Christianity Can Still Make Surprising Emotional Sense* (New York: HarperOne, 2013), 75.

21. Spufford, *Unapologetic*, 14–15.

22. Spufford, *Unapologetic*, 15–16.

23. Spufford, *Unapologetic*, 27.

24. Spufford, *Unapologetic*, 127.

25. The quotes from Ordway in this section are from Holly Ordway, "Why I Am a Christian: Holly Ordway," interview by Justin Brierley, Premier Christianity, March 4, 2014, https://www.premierchristianity.com/home/why-i-am-a -christian-holly-ordway/394.article.

26. C. S. Lewis, *Surprised by Joy* (1955; London: HarperCollins, 2002), 197.

27. Footnote in Lewis to Greeves, October 18, 1931, in *They Stand Together: The Letters of C. S. Lewis to Arthur Greeves, 1914–1963*, ed. Walter Hooper, 1st American ed. (New York: Macmillan, 1979), 428.

28. Lewis to Arthur Greeves, October 18, 1931 in C. S. Lewis, *The Collected Letters of C. S. Lewis*, vol. 1, ed. Walter Hooper (New York: HarperSanFrancisco, 2004), 977.
29. "Rowan Williams and Paul Kingsnorth."
30. "Rowan Williams and Paul Kingsnorth."
31. For an excellent exposition of the apologetics of Narnia, read David Marshall, *The Case for Aslan: Evidence for Jesus in the Land of Narnia* (Tampa, FL: DeWard, 2022).
32. C. S. Lewis, *The Voyage of the Dawn Treader* (1955; London: HarperCollins, 1997), 188.
33. C. S. Lewis, "Sometimes Fairy Stories May Say Best What's to Be Said," *New York Times*, November 18, 1956, https://www.nytimes.com/1956/11/18/archives/sometimes-fairy-stories-may-say-best-whats-to-be-said.html.
34. "N. T. Wright and Douglas Murray: Identity, Myth and Miracles: How Do We Live in a Post-Christian World?," May 13, 2021, *The Big Conversation*, season 3, episode 3, video, https://www.youtube.com/watch?v=VN8OUi9MF7w.
35. Ben Sixsmith, "My Experience of Catholics Has Tested My Agnosticism," *Catholic Herald*, September 29, 2020, https://catholicherald.co.uk/my-experience-of-catholics-has-tested-my-agnosticism/.
36. Ben Sixsmith, "The Sad Irony of Celebrity Pastors," *The Spectator*, December 6, 2020, https://spectatorworld.com/life/sad-irony-celebrity-pastors-carl-lentz-hillsong/.
37. Tom Holland, "Invisible Fire: Christianity in a Post-Western World," lecture for Open Doors, November 17, 2021, British Library, London, in "Tom Holland: Christianity, Persecution and the Meaning of the Cross," December 30, 2021, *Unbelievable?*, video, https://youtu.be/p6w7qw9kJ9k.
38. Harry Howard, interview by the author.
39. Marcus Walker, "Why Anglo-Catholicism Appeals to Millennials," *Catholic Herald*, February 7, 2019, https://catholicherald.co.uk/why-anglo-catholicism-appeals-to-millennials/.
40. Cathedrals showed an increase of 13 percent attendance at services between 2009 and 2019; see Church of England Research and Statistics, *Cathedral Statistics 2019* (London: Research and Statistics, 2020), 7, https://www.churchofengland.org/sites/default/files/2020-11/Cathedral%20Statistics%202019.pdf.

About the Author

JUSTIN BRIERLEY has been working in radio, podcasting, and video for two decades.

He has presented the popular *Unbelievable?* radio show and podcast on Premier Christian Radio, which brings Christians and non-Christians together for dialogue, and has hosted a regular show with New Testament scholar Tom Wright, the *Ask NT Wright Anything* podcast. Justin has also contributed to other shows and podcasts from the London-based station.

Justin was editor of *Premier Christianity* magazine from 2014 to 2018, to which he continues to contribute articles. Justin's first book, *Unbelievable?: Why, after Ten Years of Talking with Atheists, I'm Still a Christian* (SPCK), was published in 2017.

Justin is passionate about creating conversations around faith, science, theology, and culture. Through creative use of podcast, radio, print, video, and social media, he aims to showcase an intellectually compelling case for Christianity, while taking seriously the questions and objections of skeptics.

Justin also regularly speaks at events in the UK and abroad. He is followed by over 300K people on TikTok and Instagram for his short thoughts on thinking faith.

Justin is married to Lucy, a church minister in Surrey, and they have four children: Noah, Grace, Jeremy, and Toby. When he isn't working in a professional capacity, you'll find Justin involved in youth work and worship leading at church.

For more "thinking faith" from Justin Brierley, search for "Justin Brierley author" online or find Justin on these social media sites:

Twitter: unbelievablejb
Instagram: justin.brierley
Facebook: brierley.justin
TikTok: justin.brierley
YouTube: justinbrierley

For Justin's shows from Premier Unbelievable? search for the following shows:

Unbelievable?
Ask N. T. Wright Anything
The Big Conversation